Autism
and Pervasive Developmental Disorders
Disorders
SOURCEBOOK

Third Edition

Health Reference Series

Third Edition

Autism
and Pervasive
Developmental
Disorders

SOURCEBOOK

Basic Consumer Health Information about Autism Spectrum Disorder, and Pervasive Developmental Disorders such as Asperger Syndrome and Rett Syndrome

Along with Facts about Causes, Symptoms, Assessment, Interventions, Treatments, and Education, Tips for Family Members and Teachers on the Transition to Adulthood, a Glossary of Related Terms, and a Directory of Resources for More Information

OMNIGRAPHICS

615 Griswold, Ste. 901, Detroit, MI 48226

Bibliographic Note
Because this page cannot legibly accommodate all the copyright notices, the Bibliographic
Note portion of the Preface constitutes an extension of the copyright notice.

* * *

Omnigraphics, Inc.
Editorial Services provided by Omnigraphics, Inc.,
a division of Relevant Information, Inc.

Keith Jones, *Managing Editor*

* * *

Library of Congress Cataloging-in-Publication Data

Names: Omnigraphics, Inc., issuing body.

Title: Autism and pervasive developmental disorders sourcebook: basic consumer
health information about autism spectrum disorders (ASD) including autistic
disorder, Asperger Syndrome, Rett Syndrome, childhood disintegrative disorder,
and pervasive developmental disorder not otherwise specified (PDDNOS); along
with facts about causes, symptoms, assessment, interventions, treatments, and
education, tips for family members and teachers on the transition to adulthood, a
glossary of related terms, and a directory of resources for more information.

Description: Third edition. | Detroit, MI: Omnigraphics, Inc., [2016] | Series:
Health reference series | Includes bibliographical references and index.

Identifiers: LCCN 2016000962 (print) | LCCN 2016001220 (ebook) | ISBN
9780780814646 (hardcover: alk. paper) | ISBN 9780780814639 (ebook)

Subjects: LCSH: Autism in children--Popular works. | Developmental disabilities-
-Popular works.

Classification: LCC RJ506.A9 A8929 2016 (print) | LCC RJ506.A9 (ebook) |
DDC 618.92/85882dc23

LC record available at http://lccn.loc.gov/2016000962

Table of Contents

Part III: Identifying and Diagnosing Autism Spectrum Disorders

Part V: Interventions and Treatments for Autism Spectrum Disorder

Part VI: Education and Autism Spectrum Disorder

Part VII: Living with Autism Spectrum Disorder and Transitioning to Adulthood

Part VIII: Additional Help and Information

Preface

About This Book

The Centers for Disease Control and Prevention (CDC) reports that 1 in 68 children were identified with autism spectrum disorder. The new estimate is roughly 30% higher than the estimate for 2008 (1 in 88), roughly 60% higher than the estimate for 2006 (1 in 110), and roughly 120% higher than the estimates for 2002 and 2000 (1 in 150). ASD includes autistic disorder, Asperger syndrome, Rett syndrome, childhood disintegrative disorder, and pervasive developmental disorder not otherwise specified. Studies indicate that the prevalence of these neurodevelopmental disabilities, which cause significant problems with social interaction and communication, is increasing. Researchers believe genes, brain dysfunction, and environmental factors play a role in causing ASD. Although there is no cure, early diagnosis and evidence-based interventions currently provide the best long-term outcomes.

Autism and Pervasive Developmental Disorders Sourcebook, Third Edition provides updated information about the specific types of autism spectrum disorders. It explains symptoms, assessment, and diagnosis of ASD and describes the importance of early interventions. Evidence-based behavior, communication, and biomedical interventions are presented, along with educational guidelines for teachers and parents of children with ASD. Support, safety, transition, mental health, and employment information for families and individuals affected by ASD is also provided. The book concludes with a glossary of related terms and a directory of resources offer additional help and information.

How to Use This Book

This book is divided into parts and chapters. Parts focus on broad areas of interest. Chapters are devoted to single topics within a part.

Part I: Overview of Autism Spectrum Disorder (ASD) describes autistic disorder, Asperger syndrome, Rett syndrome, and pervasive developmental disorder not otherwise specified. A separate chapter reviews the prevalence of autism spectrum disorders in the United States.

Part II: Causes and Risk Factors Associated with Autism Spectrum Disorder reviews findings on the impact of genetics and the environment on ASD. Risk factors for ASD—including diseases, vaccines, premature birth, and assistive reproductive technology—are also discussed.

Part III: Identifying and Diagnosing Autism Spectrum Disorders describes the range of symptoms and developmental milestones and delays that indicate a need for further assessment. Developmental screening, medical and genetic tests, and other diagnostic methods are explained. A separate chapter reviews options for moving forward after receiving an ASD diagnosis.

Part IV: Conditions That May Accompany Autism Spectrum Disorders provides information about communication difficulties, non-verbal learning disability, seizures, and osteoporosis. Genetic disorders that co-occur with ASD—such as fragile X syndrome, Landau-Kleffner syndrome, and Prader-Willi syndrome—are also described.

Part V: Interventions and Treatments for Autism Spectrum Disorder gives detailed information about practices that are often effective for individuals with ASD. Topics include early intervention for children with developmental delays and interventions for individuals with Asperger syndrome. Communication and behavior therapies, and medical treatments are described. Information on current ASD research and clinical studies is also provided.

Part VI: Education and Autism Spectrum Disorder describes the special education process and offers tips for teaching students with ASD, managing challenging ASD behavior, classroom management, and promoting social interaction. Separate chapters address secondary school experiences, and preparing ASD students for postsecondary education.

Part VII: Living with Autism Spectrum Disorder and Transitioning to Adulthood provides practical information about safety and support for ASD children and adults focusing on specific concerns such as anxiety and toilet training. It also provides information on transition planning, finding housing, career planning, and job accommodations for adults with autism spectrum disorder.

Part VIII: Additional Help and Information provides a glossary of terms related to autism spectrum disorders. A directory of organizations with additional information about autism spectrum disorders is also included.

Bibliographic Note

This volume contains documents and excerpts from publications issued by the following U.S. and other government agencies: Agency for Healthcare Research and Quality (AHRQ); Centers for Disease Control and Prevention (CDC); Department of Education (ED); Disability.gov; Environmental Protection Agency (EPA); National Human Genome Research Institute (NHGRI); National Insitute of Child Health and Human Development (NICHD); National Institute of Dental and Craniofacial Research (NIDCR); National Institute of Environmental Health Sciences (NIEHS); National Institute of Mental Health (NIMH); National Institute of Neurological Disorders and Stroke (NINDS); National Institute of Standards and Technology (NIST); National Institute on Deafness and Other Communication Disorders (NIDCD); National Institutes of Health (NIH); Office of Disability Employment Policy (ODEP); Office of Personnel Management (OPM); Social Security Act (SSA); U.S. Department of Health and Human Services (HHS); U.S. Food and Drug Administration (FDA); and U.S. National Library of Medicine (NLM).

In addition, this volume contains copyrighted documents from the following organization: The Nemours Foundation.

It may also contain original material produced by Omnigraphics, Inc. and reviewed by medical consultants.

About the Health Reference Series

The *Health Reference Series* is designed to provide basic medical information for patients, families, caregivers, and the general public. Each volume takes a particular topic and provides comprehensive coverage. This is especially important for people who may be dealing with a newly diagnosed disease or a chronic disorder in themselves or in a family member. People looking for preventive guidance, information about disease warning signs, medical statistics, and risk factors for health problems will also find answers to their questions in the *Health Reference Series*. The *Series*, however, is not intended to serve as a tool for diagnosing illness, in prescribing treatments, or as a substitute for the physician/patient relationship. All people concerned about medical symptoms or the possibility of disease are encouraged to seek professional care from an appropriate health care provider.

A Note about Spelling and Style

Health Reference Series editors use *Stedman's Medical Dictionary* as an authority for questions related to the spelling of medical terms and the *Chicago Manual of Style* for questions related to grammatical structures, punctuation, and other editorial concerns. Consistent adherence is not always possible, however, because the individual volumes within the *Series* include many documents from a wide variety of different producers, and the editor's primary goal is to present material from each source as accurately as is possible. This sometimes means that information in different chapters or sections may follow other guidelines and alternate spelling authorities.

Medical Review

Omnigraphics contracts with a team of qualified, senior medical professionals who serve as medical consultants for the *Health Reference Series*. As necessary, medical consultants review reprinted and originally written material for currency and accuracy. Citations including the phrase, "Reviewed (month, year)" indicate material reviewed by this team. Medical consultation services are provided to the *Health Reference Series* editors by:

Dr. Vijayalakshmi, MBBS, DGO, MD
Dr. Senthil Selvan, MBBS, DCH, MD
Dr. K. Sivanandham, MBBS, DCH, MS (Research), PhD

Our Advisory Board

We would like to thank the following board members for providing initial guidance on the development of this series:

- Dr. Lynda Baker, Associate Professor of Library and Information Science, Wayne State University, Detroit, MI

- Nancy Bulgarelli, William Beaumont Hospital Library, Royal Oak, MI

- Karen Imarisio, Bloomfield Township Public Library, Bloomfield Township, MI

- Karen Morgan, Mardigian Library, University of Michigan-Dearborn, Dearborn, MI

- Rosemary Orlando, St. Clair Shores Public Library, St. Clair Shores, MI

Health Reference Series *Update Policy*

The inaugural book in the *Health Reference Series* was the first edition of *Cancer Sourcebook* published in 1989. Since then, the *Series* has been enthusiastically received by librarians and in the medical community. In order to maintain the standard of providing high-quality health information for the layperson the editorial staff at Omnigraphics felt it was necessary to implement a policy of updating volumes when warranted.

Medical researchers have been making tremendous strides, and it is the purpose of the *Health Reference Series* to stay current with the most recent advances. Each decision to update a volume is made on an individual basis. Some of the considerations include how much new information is available and the feedback we receive from people who use the books. If there is a topic you would like to see added to the update list, or an area of medical concern you feel has not been adequately addressed, please write to:

Managing Editor
Health Reference Series
Omnigraphics, Inc.
615 Griswold, Ste. 901
Detroit, MI 48226

Part One

Overview of Autism Spectrum Disorder (ASD)

Chapter 1

What Are ASD and Autistic Disorder?

What Is Autism Spectrum Disorder?

Autism spectrum disorder (ASD) refers to a group of complex neurodevelopment disorders characterized by repetitive and characteristic patterns of behavior and difficulties with social communication and interaction. The symptoms are present from early childhood and affect daily functioning.

The term "spectrum" refers to the wide range of symptoms, skills, and levels of disability in functioning that can occur in people with ASD. Some children and adults with ASD are fully able to perform all activities of daily living while others require substantial support to perform basic activities. The *Diagnostic and Statistical Manual of Mental Disorders* (DSM-5, published in 2013) includes Asperger syndrome, childhood disintegrative disorder, and pervasive developmental disorders not otherwise specified (PDD-NOS) as part of ASD rather than as separate disorders. A diagnosis of ASD includes an assessment of intellectual disability and language impairment.

ASD occurs in every racial and ethnic group, and across all socioeconomic levels. However, boys are significantly more likely to develop

Text in this chapter is excerpted from "Autism Spectrum Disorder Fact Sheet," National Institute of Neurological Disorders and Stroke (NINDS), November 3, 2015.

ASD than girls. The latest analysis from the Centers for Disease Control and Prevention estimates that 1 in 68 children has ASD.

What Disorders Are Related to ASD?

Certain known genetic disorders are associated with an increased risk for autism, including Fragile X syndrome (which causes intellectual disability) and tuberous sclerosis (which causes benign tumors to grow in the brain and other vital organs)—each of which results from a mutation in a single, but different, gene. Recently, researchers have discovered other genetic mutations in children diagnosed with autism, including some that have not yet been designated as named syndromes. While each of these disorders is rare, in aggregate, they may account for 20 percent or more of all autism cases.

People with ASD also have a higher than average risk of having epilepsy. Children whose language skills regress early in life—before age 3—appear to have a risk of developing epilepsy or seizure-like brain activity. About 20 to 30 percent of children with ASD develop epilepsy by the time they reach adulthood. Additionally, people with both ASD and intellectual disability have the greatest risk of developing seizure disorder.

What Are Some Common Signs of ASD?

Even as infants, children with ASD may seem different, especially when compared to other children their own age. They may become overly focused on certain objects, rarely make eye contact, and fail to engage in typical babbling with their parents. In other cases, children may develop normally until the second or even third year of life, but then start to withdraw and become indifferent to social engagement.

The severity of ASD can vary greatly and is based on the degree to which social communication, insistence of sameness of activities and surroundings, and repetitive patterns of behavior affect the daily functioning of the individual.

Social impairment and communication difficulties

Many people with ASD find social interactions difficult. The mutual give-and-take nature of typical communication and interaction is often particularly challenging. Children with ASD may fail to respond to their names, avoid eye contact with other people, and only interact with others to achieve specific goals. Often children with ASD do not understand how to play or engage with other children and may prefer to be alone. People with ASD may find it difficult to understand other people's feelings or talk about their own feelings.

People with ASD may have very different verbal abilities ranging from no speech at all to speech that is fluent, but awkward and inappropriate. Some children with ASD may have delayed speech and language skills, may repeat phrases, and give unrelated answers to questions. In addition, people with ASD can have a hard time using and understanding non-verbal cues such as gestures, body language, or tone of voice. For example, young children with ASD might not understand what it means to wave goodbye. People with ASD may also speak in flat, robot-like or a sing-song voice about a narrow range of favorite topics, with little regard for the interests of the person to whom they are speaking.

Repetitive and characteristic behaviors

Many children with ASD engage in repetitive movements or unusual behaviors such as flapping their arms, rocking from side to side, or twirling. They may become preoccupied with parts of objects like the wheels on a toy truck. Children may also become obsessively interested in a particular topic such as airplanes or memorizing train schedules. Many people with ASD seem to thrive so much on routine that changes to the daily patterns of life—like an unexpected stop on the way home from school—can be very challenging. Some children may even get angry or have emotional outbursts, especially when placed in a new or overly stimulating environment.

What Causes ASD?

Scientists believe that both genetics and environment likely play a role in ASD. There is great concern that rates of autism have been increasing in recent decades without full explanation as to why. Researchers have identified a number of genes associated with the disorder. Imaging studies of people with ASD have found differences in the development of several regions of the brain. Studies suggest that ASD could be a result of disruptions in normal brain growth very early in development. These disruptions may be the result of defects in genes that control brain development and regulate how brain cells communicate with each other. Autism is more common in children born prematurely.

Environmental factors may also play a role in gene function and development, but no specific environmental causes have yet been identified. The theory that parental practices are responsible for ASD has long been disproved. Multiple studies have shown that vaccination to prevent childhood infectious diseases does not increase the risk of autism in the population.

How Is ASD Diagnosed?

ASD symptoms can vary greatly from person to person depending on the severity of the disorder. Symptoms may even go unrecognized for young children who have mild ASD or less debilitating handicaps.

Very early indicators that require evaluation by an expert include:

- no babbling or pointing by age 1
- no single words by age 16 months or two-word phrases by age 2
- no response to name
- loss of language or social skills previously acquired
- poor eye contact
- excessive lining up of toys or objects
- no smiling or social responsiveness

Later indicators include:

- impaired ability to make friends with peers
- impaired ability to initiate or sustain a conversation with others
- absence or impairment of imaginative and social play
- repetitive or unusual use of language
- abnormally intense or focused interest
- preoccupation with certain objects or subjects
- inflexible adherence to specific routines or rituals

Health care providers will often use a questionnaire or other screening instrument to gather information about a child's development and behavior. Some screening instruments rely solely on parent observations, while others rely on a combination of parent and doctor observations. If screening instruments indicate the possibility of ASD, a more comprehensive evaluation is usually indicated.

A comprehensive evaluation requires a multidisciplinary team, including a psychologist, neurologist, psychiatrist, speech therapist, and other professionals who diagnose and treat children with ASD. The team members will conduct a thorough neurological assessment and in-depth cognitive and language testing. Because hearing problems can cause behaviors that could be mistaken for ASD, children with delayed speech development should also have their hearing tested.

Do Symptoms of Autism Change over Time?

For many children, symptoms improve with age and behavioral treatment. During adolescence, some children with ASD may become depressed or experience behavioral problems, and their treatment may need some modification as they transition to adulthood. People with ASD usually continue to need services and supports as they get older, but depending on severity of the disorder, people with ASD may be able to work successfully and live independently or within a supportive environment.

How is autism treated?

There is no cure for ASD. Therapies and behavioral interventions are designed to remedy specific symptoms and can substantially improve those symptoms. The ideal treatment plan coordinates therapies and interventions that meet the specific needs of the individual. Most health care professionals agree that the earlier the intervention, the better.

Educational/Behavioral interventions

Early behavioral/educational interventions have been very successful in many children with ASD. In these interventions therapists use highly structured and intensive skill-oriented training sessions to help children develop social and language skills, such as applied behavioral analysis, which encourages positive behaviors and discourages negative ones. In addition, family counseling for the parents and siblings of children with ASD often helps families cope with the particular challenges of living with a child with ASD.

Medications

While medication can't cure ASD or even treat its main symptoms, there are some that can help with related symptoms such as anxiety, depression, and obsessive-compulsive disorder. Antipsychotic medications are used to treat severe behavioral problems. Seizures can be treated with one or more anticonvulsant drugs. Medication used to treat people with attention deficit disorder can be used effectively to help decrease impulsivity and hyperactivity in people with ASD. Parents, caregivers, and people with autism should use caution before adopting any unproven treatments.

Chapter 2

Pervasive Developmental Disorder

What Are Pervasive Developmental Disorders?

The diagnostic category of pervasive developmental disorders (PDD) refers to a group of disorders characterized by delays in the development of socialization and communication skills. Parents may note symptoms as early as infancy, although the typical age of onset is before 3 years of age. Symptoms may include problems with using and understanding language; difficulty relating to people, objects, and events; unusual play with toys and other objects; difficulty with changes in routine or familiar surroundings, and repetitive body movements or behavior patterns.

Autism (a developmental brain disorder characterized by impaired social interaction and communication skills, and a limited range of activities and interests) is the most characteristic and best studied PDD. Other types of PDD include Asperger's syndrome, childhood disintegrative disorder, and Rett syndrome. Children with PDD vary widely in abilities, intelligence, and behaviors. Some children do not speak at all, others speak in limited phrases or conversations, and some have relatively normal language development. Repetitive play skills

Text in this chapter is excerpted from "NINDS Pervasive Developmental Disorders Information Page," National Institute of Neurological Disorders and Stroke (NINDS), November 3, 2015; and text from "What Are Autism Spectrum Disorders (ASD)?" National Institute of Health (NIH), February 17, 2013.

and limited social skills are generally evident. Unusual responses to sensory information, such as loud noises and lights, are also common.

Is There Any Treatment?

There is no known cure for PDD. Medications are used to address specific behavioral problems; therapy for children with PDD should be specialized according to need. Some children with PDD benefit from specialized classrooms in which the class size is small and instruction is given on a one-to-one basis. Others function well in standard special education classes or regular classes with additional support.

What Is the Prognosis?

Early intervention including appropriate and specialized educational programs and support services plays a critical role in improving the outcome of individuals with PDD. PDD is not fatal and does not affect normal life expectancy.

What Research Is Being Done?

The NINDS conducts and supports research on developmental disabilities, including PDD. Much of this research focuses on understanding the neurological basis of PDD and on developing techniques to diagnose, treat, prevent, and ultimately cure this and similar disorders.

Pervasive Developmental Disorder Not Otherwise Specified (PDD-NOS)

People who meet some of the criteria for autistic disorder or Asperger syndrome, but not all, may be diagnosed with PDD-NOS. They may have only social and communication challenges.

Chapter 3

Asperger Syndrome (High-Functioning Autism)

What Is Asperger Syndrome?

Asperger syndrome (AS) is an autism spectrum disorder (ASD), one of a distinct group of complex neurodevelopment disorders characterized by social impairment, communication difficulties, and restrictive, repetitive, and stereotyped patterns of behavior. Other ASDs include autistic disorder, childhood disintegrative disorder, and pervasive developmental disorder not otherwise specified (usually referred to as PDD-NOS). ASDs are considered neurodevelopmental disorders and are present from infancy or early childhood. Although early diagnosis using standardized screening by age 2 is the goal, many with ASD are not detected until later because of limited social demands and support from parents and caregivers in early life.

The severity of communication and behavioral deficits, and the degree of disability, is variable in those affected by ASD. Some individuals with ASD are severely disabled and require very substantial support for basic activities of daily living. Asperger syndrome is considered by many to be the mildest form of ASD and is synonymous with the most highly functioning individuals with ASD.

Text in this chapter is excerpted from "Asperger Syndrome Fact Sheet," National Institute of Neurological Disorders and Stroke (NINDS), November 3, 2015.

11

Two core features of autism are: a) social and communication deficits and b) fixated interests and repetitive behaviors. The social communication deficits in highly functioning persons with Asperger syndrome include lack of the normal back and forth conversation; lack of typical eye contact, body language, and facial expression; and trouble maintaining relationships. Fixated interests and repetitive behaviors include repetitive use of objects or phrases, stereotyped movements, and excessive attachment to routines, objects, or interests. Persons with ASD may also respond to sensory aspects of their environment with unusual indifference or excessive interest.

The prevalence of AS is not well established. It is often not recognized before age 5 or 6 because language development is normal. Although ASD varies significantly in character and severity, it occurs in all ethnic and socioeconomic groups and affects every age group. Experts estimate that as many as 1 in 88 children age 8 will have an autism spectrum disorder No studies have yet been conducted to determine the incidence of Asperger syndrome in adult populations, but studies of children with the disorder suggest that their problems with socialization and communication continue into adulthood. Some of these children develop additional psychiatric symptoms and disorders in adolescence and adulthood. Males are four times more likely than girls to have ASD.

Studies of children with Asperger syndrome suggest that their problems with socialization and communication continue into adulthood. Some of these children develop additional psychiatric symptoms and disorders in adolescence and adulthood.

Why Is It Called Asperger Syndrome?

In 1944, an Austrian pediatrician named Hans Asperger observed four children in his practice who had difficulty integrating socially. Although their intelligence appeared normal, the children lacked nonverbal communication skills, failed to demonstrate empathy with their peers, and were physically awkward. Their speech was either disjointed or overly formal, and their all-absorbing interest in a single topic dominated their conversations. Dr. Asperger called the condition "autistic psychopathy" and described it as a personality disorder primarily marked by social isolation.

Asperger's observations, published in German, were not widely known until 1981, when an English doctor named Lorna Wing published a series of case studies of children showing similar symptoms, which she called "Asperger's" syndrome. Wing's writings were widely published and popularized. AS became a distinct disease and diagnosis in 1992, when it was included in the tenth published edition of the World Health Organization's diagnostic manual, International Classification of Diseases (ICD-10), and in 1994 it was added to the *Diagnostic and Statistical Manual of Mental Disorders* (DSM-IV), the American Psychiatric Association's diagnostic reference book. However, scientific studies have not been able to definitively differentiate Asperger syndrome from highly functioning autism. Because autism is defined by a common set of behaviors, changes that were announced in DSM-V (which took effect in mid-2013) represent the various forms under a single diagnostic category, ASD.

What Are Some Common Signs or Symptoms?

Children with Asperger syndrome may have speech marked by a lack of rhythm, an odd inflection, or a monotone pitch. They often lack the ability to modulate the volume of their voice to match their surroundings. For example, they may have to be reminded to talk softly every time they enter a library or a movie theatre.

Unlike the severe withdrawal from the rest of the world that is characteristic of autism, children with Asperger syndrome are isolated because of their poor social skills and narrow interests. Children with the disorder will gather enormous amounts of factual information about their favorite subject and will talk incessantly about it, but the conversation may seem like a random collection of facts or statistics, with no point or conclusion. They may approach other people, but make normal conversation difficult by eccentric behaviors or by wanting only to talk about their singular interest.

Many children with AS are highly active in early childhood, but some may not reach milestones as early as other children regarding motor skills such as pedaling a bike, catching a ball, or climbing outdoor play equipment. They are often awkward and poorly coordinated with a walk that can appear either stilted or bouncy.

Some children with AS may develop anxiety or depression in young adulthood. Other conditions that often co-exist with Asperger syndrome are Attention Deficit Hyperactivity Disorder (ADHD), tic disorders (such as Tourette syndrome), depression, anxiety disorders, and obsessive compulsive disorder (OCD).

What Causes Asperger Syndrome?

The cause of ASD, including Asperger syndrome, is not known. Current research points to brain abnormalities in Asperger syndrome.

Using advanced brain imaging techniques, scientists have revealed structural and functional differences in specific regions of the brains of children who have Asperger syndrome versus those who do not have the disorder. These differences may be caused by the abnormal migration of embryonic cells during fetal development that affects brain structure and "wiring" in early childhood and then goes on to affect the neural circuits that control thought and behavior.

For example, one study found a reduction of brain activity in the frontal lobe of children with Asperger syndrome when they were asked to respond to tasks that required them to use their judgment. Another study found differences in activity when children were asked to respond to facial expressions. A different study investigating brain function in adults with AS revealed abnormal levels of specific proteins that correlate with obsessive and repetitive behaviors.

Scientists have long suspected that there are genetic and environmental components to Asperger syndrome and the other ASDs because of their tendency to run in families and their high concordance in twins. Additional evidence for the link between inherited genetic mutations and AS was observed in the higher incidence of family members who have behavioral symptoms similar to AS but in a more limited form, including slight difficulties with social interaction, language, or reading.

A specific gene for Asperger syndrome, however, has never been identified. Instead, the most recent research indicates that there are most likely a common group of genes whose variations or deletions make an individual vulnerable to developing ASD. This combination of genetic variations or deletions, in combination with yet unidentified environmental insults, probably determines the severity and symptoms for each individual with Asperger syndrome.

How Is It Diagnosed?

The diagnosis of Asperger syndrome is complicated by the lack of a standardized diagnostic test. In fact, because there are several screening instruments in current use, each with different criteria, the same child could receive different diagnoses, depending on the screening tool the doctor uses.

Asperger syndrome, also sometimes called high-functioning autism (HFA), is viewed as being on the mild end of the ASD spectrum with symptoms that differ in degree from autistic disorder.

Some of the autistic behaviors may be apparent in the first few months of a child's life, or they may not become evident until later.

The diagnosis of Asperger syndrome and all other autism spectrum disorders is done as part of a two-stage process. The first stage begins with developmental screening during a "well-child" check-up with a family doctor or pediatrician. The second stage is a comprehensive team evaluation to either rule in or rule out AS. This team generally includes a psychologist, neurologist, psychiatrist, speech therapist, and additional professionals who have expertise in diagnosing children with AS.

The comprehensive evaluation includes neurologic and genetic assessment, with in-depth cognitive and language testing to establish IQ and evaluate psychomotor function, verbal and non-verbal strengths and weaknesses, style of learning, and independent living skills. An assessment of communication strengths and weaknesses includes evaluating non-verbal forms of communication (gaze and gestures); the use of non-literal language (metaphor, irony, absurdities, and humor); patterns of inflection, stress and volume modulation; pragmatics (turn-taking and sensitivity to verbal cues); and the content, clarity, and coherence of conversation. The physician will look at the testing results and combine them with the child's developmental history and current symptoms to make a diagnosis.

Are There Treatments Available?

There is no cure for Asperger syndrome and the autism spectrum disorders. The ideal treatment plan coordinates therapies and interventions that meet the specific needs of individual children. There is no single best treatment package for all children with AS, but most health care professionals agree that early intervention is best.

An effective treatment program builds on the child's interests, offers a predictable schedule, teaches tasks as a series of simple steps, actively engages the child's attention in highly structured activities, and provides regular reinforcement of behavior. This kind of program generally includes:

Social skills training, a form of group therapy that teaches children with AS the skills they need to interact more successfully with other children cognitive behavioral therapy, a type of "talk" therapy that can help the more explosive or anxious children to manage their emotions better and cut back on obsessive interests and repetitive routines medication, if necessary, for co-existing conditions such as depression and anxiety occupational or physical therapy, for children with sensory integration problems or poor motor coordination specialized speech/language therapy, to help children who have trouble with the pragmatics of speech—the give and take of normal conversation, and parent training and support, to teach parents behavioral techniques to use at home

Do Children with Asperger Syndrome Get Better?

With effective treatment, children with AS can learn to overcome their disabilities, but they may still find social situations and personal relationships challenging. Many adults with Asperger syndrome work successfully in mainstream jobs, although they may continue to need encouragement and moral support to maintain an independent life.

Chapter 4

Rett Syndrome

What Is Rett Syndrome?

Rett syndrome is a neurodevelopmenal disorder that affects girls almost exclusively. It is characterized by normal early growth and development followed by a slowing of development, loss of purposeful use of the hands, distinctive hand movements, slowed brain and head growth, problems with walking, seizures, and intellectual disability.

The disorder was identified by Dr. Andreas Rett, an Austrian physician who first described it in a journal article in 1966. It was not until after a second article about the disorder, published in 1983 by Swedish researcher Dr. Bengt Hagberg, that the disorder was generally recognized.

The course of Rett syndrome, including the age of onset and the severity of symptoms, varies from child to child. Before the symptoms begin, however, the child generally appears to grow and develop normally, although there are often subtle abnormalities even in early infancy, such as loss of muscle tone (hypotonia), difficulty feeding, and jerkiness in limb movements. Then, gradually, mental and physical symptoms appear. As the syndrome progresses, the child loses purposeful use of her hands and the ability to speak. Other early symptoms may include problems crawling or walking and diminished eye contact. The loss of functional use of the hands is followed by compulsive hand

Text in this chapter is excerpted from "Rett Syndrome Fact Sheet," National Institute of Neurological Disorders and Stroke (NINDS), July 27, 2015.

movements such as wringing and washing. The onset of this period of regression is sometimes sudden.

Apraxia—the inability to perform motor functions—is perhaps the most severely disabling feature of Rett syndrome, interfering with every body movement, including eye gaze and speech.

Children with Rett syndrome often exhibit autistic-like behaviors in the early stages. Other symptoms may include walking on the toes, sleep problems, a wide-based gait, teeth grinding and difficulty chewing, slowed growth, seizures, cognitive disabilities, and breathing difficulties while awake such as hyperventilation, apnea (breath holding), and air swallowing.

What Are the Stages of the Disorder?

Scientists generally describe four stages of Rett syndrome. Stage I, called early onset, typically begins between 6 and 18 months of age. This stage is often overlooked because symptoms of the disorder may be somewhat vague, and parents and doctors may not notice the subtle slowing of development at first. The infant may begin to show less eye contact and have reduced interest in toys. There may be delays in gross motor skills such as sitting or crawling. Hand-wringing and decreasing head growth may occur, but not enough to draw attention. This stage usually lasts for a few months but can continue for more than a year.

Stage II, or the rapid destructive stage, usually begins between ages 1 and 4 and may last for weeks or months. Its onset may be rapid or gradual as the child loses purposeful hand skills and spoken language. Characteristic hand movements such as wringing, washing, clapping, or tapping, as well as repeatedly moving the hands to the mouth often begin during this stage. The child may hold the hands clasped behind the back or held at the sides, with random touching, grasping, and releasing. The movements continue while the child is awake but disappear during sleep. Breathing irregularities such as episodes of apnea and hyperventilation may occur, although breathing usually improves during sleep. Some girls also display autistic-like symptoms such as loss of social interaction and communication. Walking may be unsteady and initiating motor movements can be difficult. Slowed head growth is usually noticed during this stage.

Stage III, or the plateau or pseudo-stationary stage, usually begins between ages 2 and 10 and can last for years. Apraxia, motor problems, and seizures are prominent during this stage. However, there may be improvement in behavior, with less irritability, crying, and autistic-like features. A girl in stage III may show more interest in her surroundings and her alertness, attention span, and communication skills may improve. Many girls remain in this stage for most of their lives.

Stage IV, or the late motor deterioration stage, can last for years or decades. Prominent features include reduced mobility, curvature of the spine (scoliosis) and muscle weakness, rigidity, spasticity, and increased muscle tone with abnormal posturing of an arm, leg, or top part of the body. Girls who were previously able to walk may stop walking. Cognition, communication, or hand skills generally do not decline in stage IV. Repetitive hand movements may decrease and eye gaze usually improves.

What Causes Rett Syndrome?

Nearly all cases of Rett syndrome are caused by a mutation in the methyl CpG binding protein 2, or MECP2 gene. Scientists identified the gene—which is believed to control the functions of many other genes—in 1999. The MECP2 gene contains instructions for the synthesis of a protein called methyl cytosine binding protein 2 (MeCP2), which is needed for brain development and acts as one of the many biochemical switches that can either increase gene expression or tell other genes when to turn off and stop producing their own unique proteins. Because the MECP2 gene does not function properly in individuals with Rett syndrome, insufficient amounts or structurally abnormal forms of the protein are produced and can cause other genes to be abnormally expressed.

Not everyone who has an MECP2 mutation has Rett syndrome. Scientists have identified mutations in the CDKL5 and FOXG1 genes in individuals who have atypical or congenital Rett syndrome, but they are still learning how those mutations cause the disorder. Scientists believe the remaining cases may be caused by partial gene deletions, mutations in other parts of the MECP2 gene, or additional genes that have not yet been identified, and they continue to look for other causes.

Is Rett Syndrome Inherited?

Although Rett syndrome is a genetic disorder, less than 1 percent of recorded cases are inherited or passed from one generation to the next. Most cases are spontaneous, which means the mutation occurs randomly. However, in some families of individuals affected by Rett syndrome, there are other female family members who have a mutation of their MECP2 gene but do not show clinical symptoms. These females are known as "asymptomatic female carriers."

Who Gets Rett Syndrome?

Rett syndrome is estimated to affect one in every 10,000 to 15,000 live female births and in all racial and ethnic groups worldwide. Prenatal testing is available for families with an affected daughter who has an identified MECP2 mutation. Since the disorder occurs spontaneously in most affected individuals, however, the risk of a family having a second child with the disorder is less than 1 percent.

Genetic testing is also available for sisters of girls with Rett syndrome who have an identified MECP2 mutation to determine if they are asymptomatic carriers of the disorder, which is an extremely rare possibility.

The MECP2 gene is found on a person's X chromosome, one of the two sex chromosomes. Girls have two X chromosomes, but only one is active in any given cell. This means that in a girl with Rett syndrome only a portion of the cells in the nervous system will use the defective gene. Some of the child's brain cells use the healthy gene and express normal amounts of the protein.

The severity of Rett syndrome in girls is in part a function of the percentage of their cells that express a normal copy of the MECP2 gene. If the active X chromosome that is carrying the defective gene is turned off in a large proportion of cells, the symptoms will be mild, but if a larger percentage of cells have the X chromosome with the normal MECP2 gene turned off, onset of the disorder may occur earlier and the symptoms may be more severe.

The story is different for boys who have a MECP2 mutation known to cause Rett syndrome in girls. Because boys have only one X chromosome (and one Y chromosome) they lack a back-up copy that could compensate for the defective one, and they have no protection from the harmful effects of the disorder. Boys with such a defect frequently do not show clinical features of Rett syndrome but experience severe problems when they are first born and die shortly after birth. A very small number of boys may have a different mutation in the MECP2 gene or a sporadic mutation after conception that can cause some degree of intellectual disability and developmental problems.

How Is Rett Syndrome Diagnosed?

Doctors clinically diagnose Rett syndrome by observing signs and symptoms during the child's early growth and development, and conducting ongoing evaluations of the child's physical and neurological status. Scientists have developed a genetic test to complement the clinical diagnosis, which involves searching for the MECP2 mutation on the child's X chromosome.

A pediatric neurologist, clinical geneticist, or developmental pediatrician should be consulted to confirm the clinical diagnosis of Rett syndrome. The physician will use a highly specific set of guidelines that are divided into three types of clinical criteria: main, supportive, and exclusion. The presence of any of the exclusion criteria negates a diagnosis of classic Rett syndrome.

Examples of main diagnostic criteria or symptoms include partial or complete loss of acquired purposeful hand skills, partial or complete loss of acquired spoken language, repetitive hand movements (such has hand wringing or squeezing, clapping or rubbing), and gait abnormalities, including toe-walking or an unsteady, wide-based, stiff-legged walk.

Supportive criteria are not required for a diagnosis of Rett syndrome but may occur in some individuals. In addition, these symptoms—which vary in severity from child to child—may not be observed in very young girls but may develop with age. A child with supportive criteria but none of the essential criteria does not have Rett syndrome. Supportive criteria include scoliosis. teeth-grinding, small cold hands and feet in relation to height, abnormal sleep patterns, abnormal muscle tone, inappropriate laughing or screaming, intense eye communication, and diminished response to pain.

In addition to the main diagnostic criteria, a number of specific conditions enable physicians to rule out a diagnosis of Rett syndrome. These are referred to as exclusion criteria. Children with any one of the following criteria do not have Rett syndrome: brain injury secondary to trauma, neurometabolic disease, severe infection that causes neurological problems; and grossly abnormal psychomotor development in the first 6 months of life.

Is treatment available?

There is no cure for Rett syndrome. Treatment for the disorder is symptomatic—focusing on the management of symptoms—and supportive, requiring a multidisciplinary approach. Medication may be needed for breathing irregularities and motor difficulties, and anticonvulsant drugs may be used to control seizures. There should be regular monitoring for scoliosis and possible heart abnormalities. Occupational therapy can help children develop skills needed for performing self-directed activities (such as dressing, feeding, and practicing arts and crafts), while physical therapy and hydrotherapy may prolong mobility. Some children may require special equipment and aids such as braces to arrest scoliosis, splints to modify hand movements, and nutritional programs to help them maintain adequate weight. Special academic, social, vocational, and support services may be required in some cases.

What Is the Outlook for Those with Rett Syndrome?

Despite the difficulties with symptoms, many individuals with Rett syndrome continue to live well into middle age and beyond. Because the disorder is rare, very little is known about long-term prognosis and life expectancy. While there are women in their 40s and 50s with the disorder, currently it is not possible to make reliable estimates about life expectancy beyond age 40.

Chapter 5

Statistics on ASD in the United States

Chapter Contents

Section 5.1

Prevalence, Risk Factors, and Economic Costs of ASD

Text in this section is excerpted from "Data & Statistics,"
Centers for Disease Control and Prevention (CDC), August 12, 2015.

Prevalence of ASD

- About 1 in 68 children has been identified with autism spectrum disorder (ASD) according to estimates from CDC's Autism and Developmental Disabilities Monitoring (ADDM) Network.

- ASD is reported to occur in all racial, ethnic, and socioeconomic groups.

- ASD is almost 5 times more common among boys (1 in 42) than among girls (1 in 189).

- Studies in Asia, Europe, and North America have identified individuals with ASD with an average prevalence of about 1%. A study in South Korea reported a prevalence of 2.6%.

- About 1 in 6 children in the United States had a developmental disability in 2006-2008, ranging from mild disabilities such as speech and language impairments to serious developmental disabilities, such as intellectual disabilities, cerebral palsy, and autism.

Risk Factors and Characteristics of ASD

- Studies have shown that among identical twins, if one child has ASD, then the other will be affected about 36–95% of the time. In non-identical twins, if one child has ASD, then the other is affected about 0–31% of the time.

- Parents who have a child with ASD have a 2%–18% chance of having a second child who is also affected.

- ASD tends to occur more often in people who have certain genetic or chromosomal conditions. About 10% of children with

24

Identified Prevalence of Autism Spectrum Disorder ADDM Network 2000-2010 Combining Data from All Sites				
Surveillance Year	Birth Year	Number of ADDM Sites Reporting	Prevalence per 1,000 Children (Range)	This is about 1 in X children...
2000	1992	6	6.7 (4.5 – 9.9)	1 in 150
2002	1994	14	6.6 (3.3 – 10.6)	1 in 150
2004	1996	8	8.0 (4.6 – 9.8)	1 in 125
2006	1998	11	9.0 (4.2 – 12.1)	1 in 110
2008	2000	14	11.3 (4.8 – 21.2)	1 in 88
2010	2002	11	14.7 (5.7 – 21.9)	1 in 68

Figure 5.1. *Identified prevalence of ASD*

autism are also identified as having Down syndrome, fragile X syndrome, tuberous sclerosis, or other genetic and chromosomal disorders.

- Almost half (46%) of children identified with ASD has average to above average intellectual ability.

- Children born to older parents are at a higher risk for having ASD.

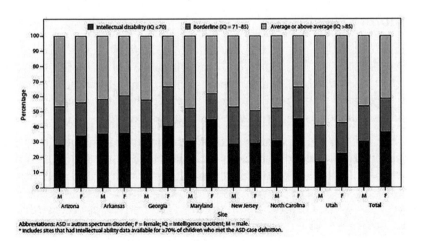

Abbreviations: ASD = autism spectrum disorder; F = female; IQ = intelligence quotient; M = male.
* Includes sites that had intellectual ability data available for ≥70% of children who met the ASD case definition.

Figure 5.2. *Most recent intelligence quotient (IQ)*

- A small percentage of children who are born prematurely or with low birth weight are at greater risk for having ASD.

- ASD commonly co-occurs with other developmental, psychiatric, neurologic, chromosomal, and genetic diagnoses. The co-occurrence of one or more non-ASD developmental diagnoses is 83%. The co-occurrence of one or more psychiatric diagnoses is 10%.

Diagnosis

- Research has shown that a diagnosis of autism at age 2 can be reliable, valid, and stable.

- On average, children identified with ASD were not diagnosed until after age 4, even though children can be diagnosed as early as age 2. When looking at age of first diagnosis by subtype, on average, those children were diagnosed with Autistic Disorder at age 4, Pervasive Developmental Disorder-Not Otherwise Specified at age 4 years and 2 months, and Asperger Disorder at age 6 years and 2 months.

- Studies have shown that parents of children with ASD notice a developmental problem before their child's first birthday. Concerns about vision and hearing were more often reported in the first year, and differences in social, communication, and fine motor skills were evident from 6 months of age.

Economic Costs

- The total costs per year for children with ASD in the United States were estimated to be between $11.5 billion – $60.9 billion (2011 U.S. dollars). This significant economic burden represents a variety of direct and in-direct costs, from medical care to special education to lost parental productivity.

- Children and adolescents with ASD had average medical expenditures that exceeded those without ASD by $4,110–$6,200 per year. On average, medical expenditures for children and adolescents with ASD were 4.1–6.2 times greater than for those without ASD. Differences in median expenditures ranged from $2,240 to $3,360 per year with median expenditures 8.4–9.5 times greater.

- In 2005, the average annual medical costs for Medicaid-enrolled children with ASD were $10,709 per child, which was about six times higher than costs for children without ASD ($1,812).

- In addition to medical costs, intensive behavioral interventions for children with ASD cost $40,000 to $60,000 per child per year.

Section 5.2

Diagnosis of ASD Made at Earlier Ages

Text in this section is excerpted from "Learn the Signs.
Act Early," Centers for Disease Control and Prevention (CDC),
December 10, 2015.

The Importance of Early Identification of Developmental Delay and Disability

- CDC estimates that 1 in 68 children has been identified with an autism spectrum disorder and about 1 in 6 children aged 3–17 has a developmental disability.

- Many children with a developmental disability are not identified until after entering school.

- Early intervention (before school age) can have a significant impact on a child's ability to learn new skills as well as reduce the need for costly interventions over time.

Improving Early Identification of Developmental Delay and Disability

The Centers for Disease Control and Prevention's (CDC) "Learn the Signs. Act Early." program aims to improve early identification of children with autism and other developmental disabilities so children and families can get the services and support they need as early as possible.

The program is made up of three components:

- Health education campaign promotes awareness of
  - healthy developmental milestones in early childhood
  - the importance of tracking each child's development
  - the importance of acting early if there are concerns
- Act Early Initiative works with state, territorial, and national partners to improve early childhood systems by
  - enhancing collaborative efforts to improve screening and referral to early intervention services
  - supporting the work of Act Early Ambassadors to promote "Learn the Signs. Act Early." messages and tools and improve early identification efforts in their state
- Research and evaluation improves campaign materials and implementation activities and increases our understanding of the factors that influence early identification and referral

CDC works with the Health Resources and Services Administration, the Association of University Centers on Disabilities, the Association of Maternal and Child Health Programs and other partners in the delivery of this program.

Chapter 6

FAQs on ASD

How Many Children in the United States Have ASD?

There is not a full count of all individuals with ASD living in the United States. However, based on the ADDM Network reports to date, we can estimate that over 1% of children from birth to 21 years of age have ASD.

Does This Mean That the Prevalence of ASD Is 1 in 68 Children in All U.S. Communities?

It is important to remember that this estimate is based on children living in 11 communities across the United States. The number of children with ASD varied widely by community, from 1 in 175 in part of Alabama to 1 in 45 in part of New Jersey.

What Do You Think Is Causing the Variation by Geographic Area, Sex, Race / Ethnicity, and Level of Intellectual Ability?

Currently, research does not show that living in certain communities, being a boy, being of white race or having a certain intellectual ability puts children at greater risk for developing ASD. Although true differences in risk have not been ruled out, the variation in the estimated number of children identified with ASD by geographic area,

---

Text in this chapter is excerpted from "Community Report on Autism," Centers for Disease Control and Prevention (CDC), 2014.

by sex, by race and ethnicity, and level of intellectual may be due to other factors. For example, it may be that providers diagnose ASD and document ASD symptoms in different ways. Or, it may be that families have unequal access to services based on where they live, how much money they make, how educated they are, or what language they speak. More work is needed to understand if and how variation in the number of children identified with ASD is due to these and other factors. There are many opportunities for public health professionals to collaborate with parents, providers, and educators to reduce potential disparities in the identification of children with ASD.

How Can I Tell If a Child's Development Is on Track?

You can follow a child's development by looking for developmental milestones—that is, how he or she plays, learns, speaks, moves, and acts. Developmental milestones are things most children can do by a certain age. The American Academy of Pediatrics recommends that children be screened for general development using standardized, validated tools at 9, 18, and 24 or 30 months and for ASD at 18 and 24 months or whenever a parent or provider has a concern. Parents should talk with their child's doctor at every visit about the milestones the child has reached and what to expect next.

Do Schools Help and What Is IDEA?

This ADDM Network report highlights the important role public school systems play in providing ASD evaluations and services to children. The Individuals with Disabilities Education Act (IDEA) is a law that ensures that all children with disabilities, from birth through 21 years of age, can get free, appropriate public education that emphasizes special education and related services designed to meet their unique needs and prepare them for employment and independent living. IDEA also provides for evaluation of children who might have or be at risk for developmental disabilities.

What Kinds of Treatments or Educational Interventions Can Help People with ASD?

There are many different types of treatments available for people with ASD, and there is no single best treatment. Each person with ASD has unique strengths. Promoting these strengths while supporting new skills is important. Early intervention is also important, but intervention at any age can be life changing.

Can Medication Help Children with ASD?

There are no medications that can cure ASD or treat the core symptoms; however, there are medications that can help some people with ASD function better.

What Do We Know about Adolescents and Adults Living with ASD?

The number, characteristics, and needs of adolescents and adults living with ASD in the United States are understudied. By parent report, almost 2% of adolescents have ASD. They may face unique challenges during adolescence and as they transition to adulthood. Adolescents with ASD seem to be at greater risk for certain health conditions. For example, adolescents with ASD are more likely to be obese than adolescents without developmental disabilities. Adolescents also encounter significant issues with accessing appropriate services and gaining employment.

Over time, the number of young adults with ASD seeking vocational rehabilitation services has increased, but the percent of adults with ASD who are employed, the number of hours they work, and the wages they earn have not improved.

Part Two

Causes and Risk Factors Associated with Autism Spectrum Disorder

Chapter 7

Causes of Autism Spectrum Disorder

What Causes Autism Spectrum Disorder (ASD)?

Scientists believe that both genetics and environment likely play a role in ASD. There is great concern that rates of autism have been increasing in recent decades without full explanation as to why. Researchers have identified a number of genes associated with the disorder. Imaging studies of people with ASD have found differences in the development of several regions of the brain. Studies suggest that ASD could be a result of disruptions in normal brain growth very early in development. These disruptions may be the result of defects in genes that control brain development and regulate how brain cells communicate with each other.

Autism is more common in children born prematurely. Environmental factors may also play a role in gene function and development, but no specific environmental causes have yet been identified. The theory that parental practices are responsible for ASD has long been disproved. Multiple studies have shown that vaccination to prevent childhood infectious diseases does not increase the risk of autism in the population.

Text in this chapter is excerpted from "Autism Spectrum Disorder Fact Sheet," National Institute of Neurological Disorders and Stroke (NINDS), February 1, 2016; and text from "What Causes Autism Spectrum Disorder (ASD)?" National Institute of Child Health and Human Development (NICHD), December 18, 2013.

Genes and ASD

> **Genes**: Bits of DNA that carry information about making the proteins that form your body.
> **Chromosomes**: Packages of DNA in each cell in your body.

A great deal of evidence supports the idea that genes are one of the main causes of ASD. More than 100 genes on different chromosomes may be involved in causing ASD, to different degrees.

People with autism have slight changes, called **mutations** in many of these genes. However, the link between genetic mutations and autism is complex:

- Most people with autism have different mutations and combinations of mutations. Not everyone with autism has changes in every gene that scientists have linked to ASD

- Many people without autism or autism symptoms also have some of these genetic mutations that scientists have linked to autism

This evidence means that different genetic mutations probably play different roles in ASD. For example, certain mutations or combinations of mutations might:

- Cause specific symptoms of ASD

- Control how mild or severe those symptoms are

- Increase susceptibility to autism. This means someone with one of these gene mutations is at greater risk for autism than someone without the mutation

Interactions between Genes and the Environment

If someone is susceptible to ASD because of genetic mutations, then certain situations might cause autism in that person. For instance, an infection or contact with chemicals in the environment could cause autism in someone who is susceptible because of genetic mutations. However, someone who is genetically susceptible might not get an ASD even if he or she has the same experiences.

Other Biological Causes

Researchers are also looking into biological factors other than genes that might be involved in ASD. Some of these include:

- Problems with brain connections

- Problems with growth or overgrowth in certain areas of the brain

- Problems with metabolism (the body's energy production system)

- Problems in the body's immune system, which protects against infections

Chapter 8

Autism and the Environment

Research has shown that environmental factors likely play a role in autism. Studies also indicate that genetics contribute to the disorder. The National Institute of Environmental Health Sciences (NIEHS) supports research to discover how the environment may influence autism. This important environmental research offers real promise for prevention—because you can't change your genes, but you can change your environment.

What Is Autism?

Autism is a group of developmental brain disorders, known as autism spectrum disorders, that begin early in life and affect how a person acts and interacts with others, communicates, and learns.

What Are the Symptoms?

Although people with autism have a variety of symptoms that vary in severity, they all have difficulties communicating and interacting with others, and show restricted and repetitive patterns of behavior and interests. Most symptoms are noticeable by the time a child is 2–3 years old, but many children are not diagnosed until later. Early intensive behavioral intervention can improve communication, learning, and social skills in children with autism.

Text in this chapter is excerpted from "Autism and the Environment," National Institute of Environmental Health Sciences (NIEHS), July 2014; and text from "Prenatal Inflammation Linked to Autism Risk," National Institute of Environmental Health Sciences (NIEHS), January 24, 2013.

Autism affects people for their entire lives, and often comes with other conditions, such as epilepsy, sleep disturbances, and gastrointestinal problems. At present, no drugs have proven effective for treating core autism symptoms.

The Impact of Autism

- Autism affects about one in 68 children.

- The number of children with autism more than doubled from 2000 to 2010.

- Autism is nearly five times more common in boys, one in 42, than girls, one in 189.

- People with autism had average medical expenses of $4,110 to $6,200 more per year than people without autism.

- Nearly half of children with autism, 46 percent, have average or above average intellectual ability.

Environmental Factors Play a Role in Autism

Air Pollution

Work supported by NIEHS indicates that early-life exposure to air pollution is a risk factor for autism.

- A 2011 study reported that children living within 1,014 feet, or a little less than 3.5 football fields, of a freeway, at birth, were twice as likely to develop autism.

- Building on those findings, in 2013, researchers reported an association between exposure to traffic-related air pollution, as well as components of regional air pollution, and an increased risk of autism.

- A 2014 study pointed to a likely gene-environment interaction. Children whose genetic makeup causes them to be more susceptible to the health effects of high levels of air pollution showed the highest risk for autism.

Prenatal Conditions

Researchers funded by NIEHS discovered that problems with the immune system, as well as maternal conditions during pregnancy, are linked with higher autism risk.

- Research showed that some children are born to mothers with antibodies that interfere with fetal brain development in ways that could lead to autism.

- Maternal diabetes and obesity, which are associated with inflammation, both have strong links to the likelihood of having a child with autism or another developmental disability.

- During pregnancy, elevated levels of inflammation, which can come from an infection, were linked with an increased risk of having a child with autism. This finding may help to identify preventive strategies.

Nutrition

According to NIEHS-funded research, prenatal vitamins may help lower autism risk.

- Women who took a daily prenatal vitamin during the three months before and during the first month of pregnancy, were less likely to have a child with autism than women not taking the supplements. This was more evident in genetically susceptible women or children, suggesting that a gene-environment interaction could be responsible.

- A later study identified folic acid as the source of the protective effects of prenatal vitamins. Women who consumed the daily recommended dosage during the first month of pregnancy had a reduced risk of having a child with autism.

Mercury and Other Contaminants

There continues to be concern about autism and mercury exposure. NIEHS funds research examining this and exposures to other contaminants.

- Eating fish is the primary way that we are exposed to organic mercury. A 2013 study examined people in the Republic of Seychelles, where fish consumption is high. The study found no association between prenatal organic mercury exposure and autism behaviors.

- Scientists can test for recent exposure to organic mercury with blood tests. Researchers found that after adjusting for dietary and other mercury sources, children with autism had blood mercury levels that were similar to those found in children without autism.

41

- Researchers are also studying other contaminants, such as bisphenol A (BPA), phthalates, heavy metals, flame retardants, polychlorinated biphenyls (PCBs), and pesticides, to see if they affect early brain development and play a role in autism.

Collaborations

Much of the research funded by NIEHS addresses priorities identified by the Inter agency Autism Coordinating Committee, which coordinates all autism efforts within the U.S. Department of Health and Human Services. NIEHS also collaborates with the U.S. Environmental Protection Agency, other NIH institutes, and various autism research and advocacy groups.

Prenatal Inflammation and Autism Risk

Maternal inflammation during early pregnancy may be related to an increased risk of autism in children, according to new findings supported by the National Institute of Environmental Health Sciences (NIEHS), part of the National Institutes of Health. Researchers found this in children of mothers with elevated C-reactive protein (CRP), a well-established marker of systemic inflammation.

The risk of autism among children in the study was increased by 43 percent among mothers with CRP levels in the top 20th percentile, and by 80 percent for maternal CRP in the top 10th percentile. The findings appear in the journal Molecular Psychiatry and add to mounting evidence that an overactive immune response can alter the development of the central nervous system in the fetus.

"Elevated CRP is a signal that the body is undergoing a response to inflammation from, for example, a viral or bacterial infection," said lead scientist on the study, Alan Brown, M.D., professor of clinical psychiatry and epidemiology at Columbia University College of Physicians and Surgeons, New York State Psychiatric Institute, and Mailman School of Public Health. "The higher the level of CRP in the mother, the greater the risk of autism in the child."

Brown cautioned that the results should be viewed in perspective since the prevalence of inflammation during pregnancy is substantially higher than the prevalence of autism.

"The vast majority of mothers with increased CRP levels will not give birth to children with autism," Brown said. "We don't know enough yet to suggest routine testing of pregnant mothers for CRP for this reason alone; however, exercising precautionary measures to prevent infections during pregnancy may be of considerable value."

"The brain develops rapidly throughout pregnancy," said Linda Birnbaum, Ph.D., director of NIEHS, which funds a broad portfolio of autism and neurodevelopmental-related research. "This has important implications for understanding how the environment and our genes interact to cause autism and other neurodevelopmental disorders."

The study capitalized on a unique national birth cohort known as the Finnish Maternity Cohort (FMC), which contains an archive of samples collected from pregnant women in Finland, where a component of whole blood, referred to as serum, is systematically collected during the early part of pregnancy. The FMC consists of 1.6 million specimens from about 810,000 women, archived in a single, centralized biorepository. Finland also maintains diagnoses of virtually all childhood autism cases from national registries of both hospital admissions and outpatient treatment.

From this large national sample, the researchers analyzed CRP in archived maternal serum corresponding to 677 childhood autism cases and an equal number of matched controls. The findings were not explained by maternal age, paternal age, gender, previous births, socioeconomic status, preterm birth, or birth weight. The work was conducted in collaboration with investigators in Finland, including the University of Turku and the National Institute for Health and Welfare in Oulu and Helsinki.

"Studying autism can be challenging, because symptoms may not be apparent in children until certain brain functions, such as language, come on line," said Cindy Lawler, Ph.D., head of the NIEHS Cellular, Organ, and Systems Pathobiology Branch and program lead for the Institute's extramural portfolio of autism research. "This study is remarkable, because it uses biomarker data to give us a glimpse back to a critical time in early pregnancy."

This work is expected to stimulate further research on autism, which is complex and challenging to identify causes. Future studies may help define how infections, other inflammatory insults, and the body's immune response interact with genes to elevate the risk for autism and other neurodevelopmental disorders. Preventative approaches addressing environmental causes of autism may also benefit from additional research.

43

Chapter 9

Genetics Impact ASD

Chapter Contents

Section 9.1

Is Autism Inherited?

Text in this section is excerpted from "Learning about Autism,"
National Human Genome Research Institute (NHGRI),
October 22, 2012. Reviewed February 2016.

Scientists are not certain what causes autism, but it's likely that both genetics and environment play a role.

The causes of autism may be divided into 'idiopathic'; (of unknown cause) which is the majority of cases, and 'secondary,' in which a chromosome abnormality, single-gene disorder or environmental agent can be identified. Approximately 15 percent of individuals with autism can be diagnosed with secondary autism; the remaining 85 percent have idiopathic autism.

Exposure during pregnancy to rubella (German measles), valproic acid, and thalidomide, are recognized causes of secondary autism; however, it remains unclear whether those who develop autism after such an exposure are also genetically predisposed.

The search for new environmental causes of secondary autism has centered primarily on childhood immunizations given around the time that regressive-onset autism is recognized. Both childhood immunizations and mercury in thimerosal, which was used as a preservative in some routine immunizations until 2001, have both been under scrutiny; however, no scientific evidence for a relationship between vaccines and autism has been identified.

Researchers have identified a number of genes associated with autism. Studies of people with autism have found irregularities in several regions of the brain. Other studies suggest that people with autism have abnormal levels of serotonin or other neurotransmitters in the brain. These abnormalities indicate that autism usually results from the disruption of normal brain development early in fetal development caused by defects in genes that control brain growth and that regulate how neurons communicate with each other. These are preliminary findings and require further study.

The risk that a brother or sister of an individual who has idiopathic autism will also develop autism is around 4 percent, plus an additional 4 to 6 percent risk for a milder condition that includes language, social or behavioral symptoms. Brothers have a higher risk (about 7 percent) of developing autism, plus the additional 7 percent risk of milder autism spectrum symptoms, over sisters whose risk is only about 1 to 2 percent.

When the cause of autism is a chromosome abnormality or a single-gene alteration, the risk that other brothers and sisters will also have autism depends on the specific genetic cause.

Section 9.2

Oxytocin and Facial Recognition in ASD

Text in this section is excerpted from
"Oxytocin Affects Facial Recognition,"
National Institutes of Health (NIH), January 13, 2014.

A genetic variation in the receptor for oxytocin, a hormone involved in social bonding, affects the ability to remember faces in families with a child who has autism. The finding points the way to a better understanding of oxytocin's role in social behavior.

Animals that live in social groups need to be able to recognize individuals from their own species. Rodents and many others rely on smells or pheromones to identify each other. Humans and other primates rely more on sights and sounds. Evidence has been building that the hormones oxytocin and vasopressin are involved in social recognition. Studies in mice, for example, show that oxytocin receptors are essential for recognizing individuals.

The ability to remember faces varies among people, and these differences are partly heritable. Researchers from Emory University, University College London, and the University of Tampere in Finland explored whether variations in the genes for oxytocin and vasopressin receptors play a role. Their study was supported primarily by NIH's National Institute of Mental Health (NIMH).

The scientists analyzed 198 families from the United Kingdom and Finland in which a single child had been diagnosed with autism spectrum disorder (ASD). Included in the study were 153 nonautistic siblings and 311 parents (178 mothers and 133 fathers), none of whom had significant autistic traits. The scientists chose such families because of their wide variation in face recognition memory and other social skills.

The researchers first created unique standardized "growth charts" from general population data for 3 social characteristics that are often impaired in people with ASD: face recognition memory, gaze fixation, and facial emotion recognition. These charts allowed the team to derive and assign standardized scores for these skills to all the participants, regardless of age or gender.

The children with ASD scored lower on each skill than did either of their parents or siblings. The scientists next searched for associations between test performance and variations in the vasopressin receptor (AVPR1a) and oxytocin receptor (OXTR) genes. The analysis revealed a single genetic variation in the oxytocin receptor that was strongly associated with facial recognition memory. The researchers estimate that this variation accounted for 2% to 10% of the test performance variance in both groups studied.

"It's definitely not fully predictive of face recognition memory," says study co-author Dr. Larry Young of Emory. "But the important thing is that it suggests that the oxytocin receptor and oxytocin itself plays some role in face recognition memory."

Although rodents and primates rely on different sensory cues to recognize each other, the same gene appears to be involved in processing that social information. The researchers are now working to manipulate the oxytocin system to further explore how it affects social cue processing. This information may be useful for developing approaches to improve social cognition in people with autism.

Section 9.3

Mental Disorder and Their Genetic Roots

Text in this section is excerpted from "Five Major
Mental Disorders Share Genetic Roots," National
Institute of Mental Health (NIMH), March 1, 2013.

Five major mental disorders share some of the same genetic risk factors, the largest genome-wide study of its kind has found. Evidence for such genetic overlap had previously been limited to pairs of disorders.

National Institutes of Health-funded researchers discovered that people with disorders traditionally thought to be distinct – autism, ADHD, bipolar disorder, major depression and schizophrenia – were more likely to have suspect genetic variation at the same four chromosomal sites. These included risk versions of two genes that regulate the flow of calcium into cells.

"These results will help us move toward diagnostic classification informed by disease cause," said Jordan Smoller, M.D., of Massachusetts General Hospital, Boston, a coordinator of the study, which was supported by NIH's National Institute of Mental Health. "Although statistically significant, each of these genetic associations individually can account for only a small amount of risk for mental illness, making them insufficient for predictive or diagnostic usefulness by themselves."

Smoller, Kenneth Kendler, M.D., Virginia Commonwealth University, Richmond; Nicholas Craddock, PhD., Cardiff University, England; Stephan Ripke, M.D., Massachusetts General, Patrick Sullivan, M.D., University of North Carolina at Chapel Hill, and colleagues in the Cross-Disorder Group of the Psychiatric Genomics Consortium, report on their findings February 28, 2013 in The Lancet.

Prior to the study, researchers had turned up evidence of shared genetic risk factors for pairs of disorders, such as schizophenia and bipolar disorder, autism and schizophrenia and depression and bipolar disorder. Such evidence of overlap at the genetic level has blurred the boundaries of traditional diagnostic categories and given rise to research domain criteria, or RDoC, an NIMH initiative to develop new

49

ways of classifying psychopathology for research based on neuroscience and genetics as well as observed behavior.

To learn more, the consortium researchers analyzed the five key disorders as if they were the same illness. They screened for evidence of illness-associated genetic variation across the genomes of 33,332 patients with all five disorders and 27,888 controls, drawing on samples from previous consortium mega-analyses.

For the first time, specific variations significantly associated with all five disorders were among several suspect genomic sites that turned up. These included variation in two genes that code for the cellular machinery for regulating the flow of calcium into neurons. Variation in one of these, called CACNA1C, which had previously been implicated in susceptibility to bipolar disorder, schizophrenia and major depression, is known to impact brain circuitry involved in emotion, thinking, attention and memory – functions disrupted in mental illnesses. Variation in another calcium channel gene, called CACNB2, was also linked to the disorders.

Alterations in calcium-channel signaling could represent a fundamental mechanism contributing to a broad vulnerability to psychopathology, suggest the researchers.

They also discovered illness-linked variation for all five disorders in certain regions of chromosomes 3 and 10. Each of these sites spans several genes, and the specific causal factors within them remain elusive. However, one region, called 3p21, which produced the strongest signal of illness association, harbors suspect variations identified in previous genome-wide studies of bipolar disorder and schizophrenia.

Section 9.4

Gene Disruptions Associated with Autism Risk

Text in this section is excerpted from "Gene Disruptions
Associated with Autism Risk," National Institutes
of Health (NIH), November 24, 2014.

At a Glance

- Researchers identified mutations in 107 genes that may contribute to the risk for autism spectrum disorder.

- The findings provide a better understanding of pathways thought to be involved in the disorder, and may help lead to potential therapies.

Illustration of puzzle pieces in a human head. Many genes that are important for normal development may have a modest impact on the risk for autism spectrum disorder.

Autism is a complex brain disorder characterized by difficulties with social interactions and communication. The symptoms and levels of disability can range from mild to severe. The wide range of disorders is collectively referred to as autism spectrum disorder (ASD). ASD affects about 1 in 68 American children.

Researchers previously linked less than a dozen genes to ASD. To further uncover genes that might be associated with the disorder, a large international team led by Dr. Joseph D. Buxbaum at the Icahn School of Medicine at Mount Sinai, Dr. Mark J. Daly at Broad Institute of Harvard and MIT, and the Autism Sequencing Consortium analyzed more than 14,000 DNA samples. More than 3,800 were from children with autism. The others were from parents and control samples of unrelated people. The study was funded in part by NIH's National Human Genome Research Institute (NHGRI) and National Institute of Mental Health (NIMH). Results were published on November 13, in Nature.

The scientists looked for genetic lesions that were either inherited or de novo—spontaneous variations found in a child's DNA but not in either parent's. The team sequenced the exome regions of DNA, which comprise the 1% of the human genome that codes for proteins. This is in contrast to whole-genome sequencing, which analyzes the entire 3 billion DNA base pairs of the human genome.

The researchers identified changes in 107 genes that are likely to contribute to the risk for ASD. More than 5% of the people with ASD had de novo loss-of-function mutations, which prevent production of a normal protein. The researchers predicted that more than 1,000 genes may be involved in the risk for ASD, many of which will only have a modest impact on risk.

Among the genes found to be associated with a risk for ASD, many coded for proteins involved in 3 pathways important for normal development. One involves the structure of synapses, the connections between nerve cells across which brain signals travel. A second involves the remodeling of chromatin—the way DNA is packaged in cells, which can affect whether genes are turned on or off. A third pathway involves transcription, the process by which instructions in genes are read to build proteins.

Together, the findings provide a better understanding of some of the genetic and cellular changes in the pathways and processes thought to be involved in ASD. Eventually, this knowledge may help lead to potential therapies.

"The steps we added to our analysis over past studies provide the most complete theoretical picture to date of how many genetic changes pile up to affect the brains of children with autism," Buxbaum says. "While we have very strong findings in these genetic analyses, new-found genetic discoveries must next be moved into molecular, cell, and animal studies to realize future benefits for families."

Chapter 10

Vaccines and ASD

Chapter Contents

Section 10.1

Facts on Vaccines and ASD

This chapter includes excerpts from "Autism Spectrum Disorder (ASD): Frequently Asked Questions," Centers for Disease Control and Prevention (CDC), August 12, 2015; text from "Understanding Thimerosal, Mercury, and Vaccine Safety," Centers for Disease Control and Prevention (CDC), February 2013; text from "Vaccines Do Not Cause Autism," Centers for Disease Control and Prevention (CDC), November 23, 2015; and text from "Is There a Connection between Vaccines and Autism?" © 1995–2016. The Nemours Foundation/KidsHealth®. Reprinted with permission.

Is There a Connection between Vaccines and Autism

No. Autism is a condition that affects the brain and makes communicating and interacting with other people more difficult. The cause(s) of autism—also known as autism spectrum disorder (ASD) or pervasive developmental disorder (PDD)—is unknown. However, genetics, differences in brain anatomy, and toxic substances in the environment are thought to contribute to children developing the condition.

So how did the idea that vaccines play a role get started? Much of the blame lies with a study published in 1998 that suggested that the MMR (measles-mumps-rubella) vaccine, or infection with the naturally occurring measles virus itself, might cause autism. Since then, numerous scientific studies have shown that there is no link between vaccines—or any of their ingredients—and autism. And the research used in that study was found to be false, the doctor who wrote it lost his medical license, and the medical journal that published it retracted the paper (this means that they believe it never should have been published).

Even with the overwhelming evidence that vaccines are safe and effective, some parents still decide not to have their children vaccinated or to delay vaccinations. But this is extremely risky because vaccine-preventable diseases like measles are still very much around. So if an unvaccinated child gets one of these preventable diseases, other people around that child could get very sick.

Sometimes, kids can have a reaction to a vaccine like a mild fever or rash. But it's clear that the risk of serious reactions to the MMR and other recommended vaccines is small compared with the health risks associated with the often-serious diseases they prevent.

If you have concerns about any vaccine recommended for your child, talk to your doctor. Ask about the benefits and risks of each vaccine and why they're so important for safeguarding your child's health.

Some people have had concerns that ASD might be linked to the vaccines children receive, but studies have shown that there is no link between receiving vaccines and developing ASD. In 2011, an Institute of Medicine (IOM) report on eight vaccines given to children and adults found that with rare exceptions, these vaccines are very safe.

A 2013 CDC study added to the research showing that vaccines do not cause ASD. The study looked at the number of antigens (substances in vaccines that cause the body's immune system to produce disease-fighting antibodies) from vaccines during the first two years of life. The results showed that the total amount of antigen from vaccines received was the same between children with ASD and those that did not have ASD.

Vaccine Ingredients Do Not Cause Autism

One vaccine ingredient that has been studied specifically is thimerosal, a mercury-based preservative used to prevent contamination of multidose vials of vaccines. Research shows that thimerosal does not cause ASD. In fact, a 2004 scientific review by the IOM concluded that "the evidence favors rejection of a causal relationship between thimerosal–containing vaccines and autism." Since 2003, there have been nine CDC-funded or conducted studies that have found no link between thimerosal-containing vaccines and ASD, as well as no link between the measles, mumps, and rubella (MMR) vaccine and ASD in children.

Between 1999 and 2001, thimerosal was removed or reduced to trace amounts in all childhood vaccines except for some flu vaccines. This was done as part of a broader national effort to reduce all types of mercury exposure in children before studies were conducted that determined that thimerosal was not harmful. It was done as a precaution. Currently, the only childhood vaccines that contain thimerosal are flu vaccines packaged in multidose vials. Thimerosal-free alternatives are also available for flu vaccine.

Besides thimerosal, some people have had concerns about other vaccine ingredients in relation to ASD as well. However, no links have been found between any vaccine ingredients and ASD.

Section 10.2

The Facts on Thimerosal, Mercury, and Vaccine Safety

Text in this section is excerpted from "Understanding Thimerosal, Mercury, and Vaccine Safety," Centers for Disease Control and Prevention (CDC), February 2013.

What Is Thimerosal? Is It the Same as Mercury?

Thimerosal is a compound that contains mercury. Mercury is a metal found naturally in the environment.

Why Is Thimerosal Used in Some Vaccines?

Because it prevents the growth of dangerous microbes, thimerosal is used as a preservative in multi-dose vials of flu vaccines, and in two other childhood vaccines, it is used in the manufacturing process. When each new needle is inserted into the multi-dose vial, it is possible for microbes to get into the vial. The preservative, thimerosal, prevents contamination in the multi-dose vial when individual doses are drawn from it. Receiving a vaccine contaminated with bacteria can be deadly.

For two childhood vaccines, thimerosal is used to prevent the growth of microbes during the manufacturing process. When thimerosal is used this way, it is removed later in the process. Only trace (very tiny) amounts remain. The only childhood vaccines today that have trace amounts of thimerosal are one DTaP and one DTaP-Hib combination vaccine.

Why Was Thimerosal Removed from Vaccines Given to Children?

In 1999, the U.S. Food and Drug Administration (FDA) was required by law to assess the amount of mercury in all the products the agency oversees, not just vaccines. The U.S. Public Health Service decided that as much mercury as possible should be removed from vaccines, and thimerosal was the only source of mercury in vaccines. Even though there was no evidence that thimerosal in vaccines was dangerous, the decision to remove it was a made as a precautionary measure to decrease overall exposure to mercury among young infants. This decision was possible because childhood vaccines could be reformulated to leave out thimerosal without threatening their safety, effectiveness, and purity.

Today, no childhood vaccine used in the United States—except some formulations of flu vaccine in multi-dose vials—use thimerosal as a preservative.

Why Is Thimerosal Still in Some Flu Vaccines That Children May Receive?

To produce enough flu vaccine for the entire country, some of it must be put into multi-dose vials. When each individual vaccine dose is drawn from the vial with a fresh needle, it is possible for microbes to get into the vial. So, this preservative is needed to prevent contamination of the vial when individual doses are drawn from it. Children can safely receive flu vaccine that contains thimerosal. Flu vaccine in single-dose vials that does not contain thimerosal also is available.

Was Thimerosal in Vaccines a Cause of Autism?

Reputable scientific studies have shown that mercury in vaccines given to young children is not a cause of autism.

The studies used different methods. Some examined rates of autism in a state or a country, comparing autism rates before and after thimerosal was removed as a preservative from vaccines. In the United States and other countries, the number of children diagnosed with autism has not gone down since thimerosal was removed from vaccines.

What Keeps Childhood Vaccines from Becoming Contaminated If They Do Not Contain Thimerosal as a Preservative?

The childhood vaccines that used to contain thimerosal as a preservative are now put into single-dose vials, so no preservative is needed. In the past, the vaccines were put into multi-dose vials, which could become contaminated when new needles were used to get vaccine out of the vial for each dose.

Was Thimerosal Used in All Childhood Vaccines?

No. A few vaccines contained other preservatives, and they still do. Some other vaccines, including the measles, mumps, and rubella vaccine (MMR) never contained any preservative or any mercury.

Chapter 11

Premature Birth and Autism

Preterm Birth – a Growing Global Healthcare Crisis

Preterm Birth (PB) is the leading cause of death in the first month of life and a contributing factor in more than a third of all infant deaths. Moreover, infants who survive an early birth face the risk of serious lifelong health problems. Even late preterm infants have a greater risk of respiratory problems, feeding difficulties, temperature instability, delayed brain development and an increased risk of autism, cerebral palsy and mental retardation. In fact, according to a very recent analysis of nearly 7 million U.S. live births, preterm infants are more than twice as likely to have major birth defects as full term infants.

The high rate of premature births in the United States alone constitutes a public health concern that costs society at least $26 billion a year. The heartbreaking toll in terms of human and family suffering cannot be calculated. For the underprivileged and those in underdeveloped and developing countries, additional tens of millions are even more devastated—as the families and children struggling with this condition and suffering these outcomes are unable to obtain medical assistance and are also often outcast by their societies.

The increasing prevalence of PB, related mortality, and lifelong disability is a complex public health issue that requires multifaceted

---

Text in this chapter is excerpted from "Preterm Birth: A Growing Human Healthcare Crisis," National Institute of Standards and Technology (NIST), May 23, 2011. Reviewed February 2016.

solutions. Currently, the subject of PB is described by a confused cluster of datum, with a complex set of overlapping factors of influence. Its causes may include individual-level behavioral and psychosocial factors, socio-demographic and neighborhood characteristics, environmental exposure, medical conditions, infertility treatments, and biological factors. Many of these factors co-occur, particularly in those who are socioeconomically disadvantaged or who are members of racial and ethnic minority groups, further complicating the equation.

While advances in perinatal and neonatal care have improved survival for preterm infants, those infants who do survive have a greater risk than infants born at full term for developmental disabilities, health problems, and poor growth. The birth of a preterm infant can also bring considerable emotional and economic costs to families and have implications for public sector services, such as health insurance, educational, and other social support systems.

Autism – Directly Related to Preterm Birth

Autism is a brain development disorder characterized by impaired social interaction and communication, and by restricted and repetitive behavior. According to the most recent fact-finding, compiled from sources including the National Institutes of Health, the Centers for Disease Control and Prevention, the U.S. Department of Education, and the Autism Society of America, autism is the fastest growing developmental disease (which correlates with the growing incidence of PB birth due specifically to IC).

While research in this critical area is limited at this time, a study in U.S. focused on children born more than three months prematurely provided fresh evidence supporting the thesis of this paper – including the link between PB birth and autism. Those children were found to be two to three times more likely to show signs of autism at age 2 (as measured in a standard screening tool compared to other children).

Autism refers to a group of developmental problems known as autism spectrum disorders that appear in early childhood and impair the ability to communicate and interact with others. Early research suggesting a link between PB and Autism followed 988 U.S. children born very prematurely, at least three months before their due date. At age 2, the children were evaluated using a screening method in which they are rated on a checklist of 23 behaviors for signs of autism. This tool flags children who may have autism but is not considered a definitive diagnosis. While more typically, a formal diagnosis of autism does not occur until around age 3, in this study, less than 6 percent of infants born full term screened positive for possible autism, while 21 percent of infants born preterm scored positive.

Even with this dramatic evidence, researchers remain confused, partially because preterm infants may also demonstrate certain developmental problems unrelated to autism that could trigger a positive score. For example, researchers typically excluded children with motor, vision and hearing impairments. Even after doing that, 16 percent of the preterm infants scored positive for possible autism. Moreover, after also excluding infants with cognitive impairment on the premise that it may not be autism related, about 10 percent of the preterm children still had a positive screening score. What researchers are likely missing is the fact that multiple disorders are possible as a result of PB (just as multiple injuries to an individual are possible as a result of a single automobile accident).

Confused research or not, it is very clear that PB is associated with a long list of health risks for infants. About 1 in 150 U.S. children has an autism spectrum disorder, according to U.S. government figures. The socioeconomic consequences of autism, all told exceed $90 billion annually (U.S. only).

Chapter 12

Early Development Risk Factors for ASD

Understanding Autism Spectrum Disorders and Other Developmental Disabilities

- CDC estimates that 1 in 88 children has been identified with an autism spectrum disorder (ASD).

- ASDs occur among all racial, ethnic, and socioeconomic groups.

- ASDs are almost five times more common among boys than among girls.

- Medical costs for children with ASDs are estimated to be six times higher than for children without ASDs.

- In addition to medical costs, intensive behavioral interventions for children with ASDs can cost $40,000 to $60,000 per child per year.

Text in this chapter is excerpted from "Study to Explore Early Development (SEED)," Centers for Disease Control and Prevention (CDC), August 12, 2015; and text from "SEED Frequently Asked Questions," Centers for Disease Control and Prevention (CDC), September 14, 2015.

Identifying Risk Factors for Autism Spectrum Disorders and Other Developmental Disabilities

There is still a lot to learn about ASDs. Research on ASDs has increased a great deal in recent years and the Centers for Disease Control and Prevention (CDC) is part of the larger group of public and private organizations working to better understand ASDs through research. CDC is undertaking efforts to find out how many children have ASDs, discover the risk factors for and causes of ASDs, and raise awareness of the signs and symptoms of ASDs.

Study to Explore Early Development (SEED)

The Study to Explore Early Development (SEED) is a multi-year study funded by CDC. It is currently the largest study in the United States to help identify factors that may put children at risk for autism spectrum disorder (ASD) and other developmental disabilities. Understanding the risk factors that make a person more likely to develop an ASD will help us learn more about the causes.

So far, over 3,700 children and their parents are enrolled across all the study sites. We plan to enroll an additional 2,500 children and parents before SEED is complete.

SEED is looking at three main areas:

- Physical and behavioral characteristics of children with ASDs, children with other developmental disabilities, and children without a developmental delay or disability:

ASDs are complex disorders. CDC expects to learn more about why people with ASD are the way they are—how they behave, grow, think, and interact with the world around them.

- Health conditions among children with and without ASDs:

CDC is interested in learning more about the health conditions and disorders that might affect children with and without ASDs. Some smaller studies have shown that certain medical conditions seem to be found more often among children with ASDs and their families. SEED provides an opportunity to compare health conditions and health-related issues such as sleeping and eating patterns in children with ASDs, in children with other developmental disabilities, and in children without a developmental delay or disability.

- Factors associated with a child's risk for developing ASDs:

It is expected that SEED will give us a better idea which of the many possible risk factors that we will be evaluating seem to be associated with or related to ASDs. The risk factors may be related to genes, health conditions, experiences of the mother during pregnancy, and the health and development of the child during infancy and the first few years of life.

Chapter 13

Assisted Reproductive Technology and Autism Spectrum Disorder

What Is Assisted Reproductive Technology?

Although various definitions have been used for ART, the definition used by CDC is based on the 1992 Fertility Clinic Success Rate and Certification Act that requires CDC to publish the annual ART Success Rates Report. According to this definition, ART includes all fertility treatments in which both eggs and sperm are handled. In general, ART procedures involve surgically removing eggs from a woman's ovaries, combining them with sperm in the laboratory, and returning them to the woman's body or donating them to another woman. They do NOT include treatments in which only sperm are handled (i.e., intrauterine—or artificial—insemination) or procedures in which a woman takes medicine only to stimulate egg production without the intention of having eggs retrieved.

This chapter includes excerpts from "Assisted Reproductive Technology (ART)," Centers for Disease Control and Prevention (CDC), November 14, 2014; and text from "Key Findings: The Association between Assisted Reproductive Technology and Autism Spectrum Disorder," Centers for Disease Control and Prevention (CDC), March 20, 2015.

20 Years of ART Surveillance

ART can alleviate the burden of infertility on individuals and families, but it can also present challenges to public health as evidenced by the high rates of multiple delivery, preterm delivery, and low birthweight delivery experienced with ART. Monitoring the outcomes of technologies that affect reproduction, such as contraception and ART, has become an important public health activity.

CDC's Division of Reproductive Health has a long history of surveillance and research in women's health and fertility, adolescent reproductive health, and safe motherhood. In response to congressional mandate, CDC began work to strengthen existing data collection efforts initiated by the American Society for Reproductive Medicine (ASRM) and the Society for Assisted Reproductive Technology (SART) and to develop a national system for monitoring ART use and outcomes.

In 1997, CDC submitted to Congress the first annual report, titled Assisted Reproductive Technology Success Rates: National Summary and Fertility Clinic Reports. This report gained a wide audience, including potential ART patients and their families, policy makers, researchers and health care providers. Maternal and child health professionals, as well as state and local public health departments, also began requesting data on birth outcomes among infants born using ART technologies in their localities. In 2002, CDC prepared the first ART surveillance report on ART use and outcomes by state.

Expanding the Scope of ART Outcomes Research

The National ART Surveillance System (NASS) does not contain information on long-term outcomes of ART. This information can be obtained by linking ART surveillance data with other surveillance systems and registries, while paying close attention to confidentiality protection. Since 2001, CDC has collaborated with health departments of three states (Massachusetts, and later Michigan and Florida), to link NASS with vital records, hospital discharge data, birth defects registries, cancer registries, and other surveillance systems of these states. This project, called States Monitoring ART (SMART) Collaborative, provides a unique opportunity for federal and state public health agencies to work together on establishing state-based public health surveillance of ART, infertility and related issues.

Does Assisted Reproductive Technology Increase the Risk for Autism Spectrum Disorder?

- Overall, children conceived using ART were about two times more likely to be diagnosed with ASD compared to children conceived without using ART.

- Evidence suggests that for pregnancies conceived with ART, the increased risk for ASD is, in large part, due to the higher likelihood of adverse pregnancy and delivery outcomes. In other words, using ART may lead to factors that are known to put children at risk for ASD, such as being born a twin or multiple (triplets, quadruplets, etc.), being born too early, or being born too small.

- More research is needed to explore what exactly underlies the observed relationship between ART and ASD.

- However, these findings suggest that single embryo transfer, where appropriate, may reduce the risk of ASD among children conceived using ART

Does Type of ART Procedure Impact the Relationship between Assisted Reproductive Technology and Autism Spectrum Disorder?

- Among children conceived using ART, about 0.8% of those born as singletons (only one baby carried during the pregnancy) and about 1.2% of those born as a twin or multiple were diagnosed with ASD.

- Children conceived using ART were more likely to be diagnosed with ASD if intracytoplasmic sperm injection (ICSI) was used compared to conventional in vitro fertilization. ICSI and in vitro fertilization are procedures in which fertilization (a sperm entering an egg) occurs outside of the body; ICSI occurs by injecting a sperm directly into an egg while in vitro fertilization involves mixing sperm with eggs in a laboratory dish and allowing fertilization to occur.

- More research is needed to explore what exactly underlies the observed relationship between ICSI and ASD.

Part Three

Identifying and Diagnosing Autism Spectrum Disorders

Chapter 14

Symptoms of ASD

Chapter Contents

Section 14.1

Range of Symptoms

Text in this section is excerpted from "Signs and Symptoms," Centers for Disease Control and Prevention (CDC), February 26, 2015.

Signs and Symptoms

Autism spectrum disorder (ASD) is a developmental disability caused by differences in the brain. Scientists do not know yet exactly what causes these differences for most people with ASD. However, some people with ASD have a known difference, such as a genetic condition. There are multiple causes of ASD, although most are not yet known.

There is often nothing about how people with ASD look that sets them apart from other people, but they may communicate, interact, behave, and learn in ways that are different from most other people. The learning, thinking, and problem-solving abilities of people with ASD can range from gifted to severely challenged. Some people with ASD need a lot of help in their daily lives; others need less.

A diagnosis of ASD now includes several conditions that used to be diagnosed separately: autistic disorder, pervasive developmental disorder not otherwise specified (PDD-NOS), and Asperger syndrome. These conditions are now all called autism spectrum disorder.

ASD begins before the age of 3 and last throughout a person's life, although symptoms may improve over time. Some children with ASD show hints of future problems within the first few months of life. In others, symptoms may not show up until 24 months or later. Some children with an ASD seem to develop normally until around 18 to 24 months of age and then they stop gaining new skills, or they lose the skills they once had. Studies have shown that one third to half of parents of children with an ASD noticed a problem before their child's first birthday, and nearly 80%–90% saw problems by 24 months of age.

It is important to note that some people without ASD might also have some of these symptoms. But for people with ASD, the impairments make life very challenging.

Possible "Red Flags"

A person with ASD might:

- Not respond to their name by 12 months of age
- Not point at objects to show interest (point at an airplane flying over) by 14 months
- Not play "pretend" games (pretend to "feed" a doll) by 18 months
- Avoid eye contact and want to be alone
- Have trouble understanding other people's feelings or talking about their own feelings
- Have delayed speech and language skills
- Repeat words or phrases over and over (echolalia)
- Give unrelated answers to questions
- Get upset by minor changes
- Have obsessive interests
- Flap their hands, rock their body, or spin in circles
- Have unusual reactions to the way things sound, smell, taste, look, or feel

Social Skills

Social issues are one of the most common symptoms in all of the types of ASD. People with an ASD do not have just social "difficulties" like shyness. The social issues they have cause serious problems in everyday life.

Examples of social issues related to ASD:

- Does not respond to name by 12 months of age
- Avoids eye-contact
- Prefers to play alone
- Does not share interests with others
- Only interacts to achieve a desired goal
- Has flat or inappropriate facial expressions
- Does not understand personal space boundaries

- Avoids or resists physical contact

- Is not comforted by others during distress

- Has trouble understanding other people's feelings or talking about own feelings

Typical infants are very interested in the world and people around them. By the first birthday, a typical toddler interacts with others by looking people in the eye, copying words and actions, and using simple gestures such as clapping and waving "bye bye". Typical toddlers also show interests in social games like peek-a-boo and pat-a-cake. But a young child with an ASD might have a very hard time learning to interact with other people.

Some people with an ASD might not be interested in other people at all. Others might want friends, but not understand how to develop friendships. Many children with an ASD have a very hard time learning to take turns and share—much more so than other children. This can make other children not want to play with them.

People with an ASD might have problems with showing or talking about their feelings. They might also have trouble understanding other people's feelings. Many people with an ASD are very sensitive to being touched and might not want to be held or cuddled. Self-stimulatory behaviors (e.g., flapping arms over and over) are common among people with an ASD. Anxiety and depression also affect some people with an ASD. All of these symptoms can make other social problems even harder to manage.

Communication

Each person with ASD has different communication skills. Some people can speak well. Others can't speak at all or only very little. About 40% of children with an ASD do not talk at all. About 25%–30% of children with ASD have some words at 12 to 18 months of age and then lose them. Others might speak, but not until later in childhood.

Examples of communication issues related to ASD:

- Delayed speech and language skills

- Repeats words or phrases over and over (echolalia)

- Reverses pronouns (e.g., says "you" instead of "I")

- Gives unrelated answers to questions

- Does not point or respond to pointing

- Uses few or no gestures (e.g., does not wave goodbye)
- Talks in a flat, robot-like, or sing-song voice
- Does not pretend in play (e.g., does not pretend to "feed" a doll)
- Does not understand jokes, sarcasm, or teasing

People with ASD who do speak might use language in unusual ways. They might not be able to put words into real sentences. Some people with ASD say only one word at a time. Others repeat the same words or phrases over and over. Some children repeat what others say, a condition called echolalia. The repeated words might be said right away or at a later time. For example, if you ask someone with ASD, "Do you want some juice?" he or she might repeat "Do you want some juice?" instead of answering your question. Although many children without an ASD go through a stage where they repeat what they hear, it normally passes by three years of age. Some people with an ASD can speak well but might have a hard time listening to what other people say.

People with ASD might have a hard time using and understanding gestures, body language, or tone of voice. For example, people with ASD might not understand what it means to wave goodbye. Facial expressions, movements, and gestures may not match what they are saying. For instance, people with an ASD might smile while saying something sad.

People with ASD might say "I" when they mean "you," or vice versa. Their voices might sound flat, robot-like, or high-pitched. People with an ASD might stand too close to the person they are talking to, or might stick with one topic of conversation for too long. They might talk a lot about something they really like, rather than have a back-and-forth conversation with someone. Some children with fairly good language skills speak like little adults, failing to pick up on the "kid-speak" that is common with other children.

Unusual Interests and Behaviors

Many people with ASD have unusual interest or behaviors.

Examples of unusual interests and behaviors related to ASD:

- Lines up toys or other objects
- Plays with toys the same way every time
- Likes parts of objects (e.g., wheels)
- Is very organized

- Gets upset by minor changes
- Has obsessive interests
- Has to follow certain routines
- Flaps hands, rocks body, or spins self in circles

Repetitive motions are actions repeated over and over again. They can involve one part of the body or the entire body or even an object or toy. For instance, people with an ASD might spend a lot of time repeatedly flapping their arms or rocking from side to side. They might repeatedly turn a light on and off or spin the wheels of a toy car. These types of activities are known as self-stimulation or "stimming."

People with ASD often thrive on routine. A change in the normal pattern of the day—like a stop on the way home from school—can be very upsetting to people with ASD. They might "lose control" and have a "melt down" or tantrum, especially if in a strange place.

Some people with ASD also may develop routines that might seem unusual or unnecessary. For example, a person might try to look in every window he or she walks by a building or might always want to watch a video from beginning to end, including the previews and the credits. Not being allowed to do these types of routines might cause severe frustration and tantrums.

Other Symptoms

Some people with ASD have other symptoms. These might include:

- Hyperactivity (very active)
- Impulsivity (acting without thinking)
- Short attention span
- Aggression
- Causing self injury
- Temper tantrums
- Unusual eating and sleeping habits
- Unusual mood or emotional reactions
- Lack of fear or more fear than expected
- Unusual reactions to the way things sound, smell, taste, look, or feel

People with ASD might have unusual responses to touch, smell, sounds, sights, and taste, and feel. For example, they might over- or under-react to pain or to a loud noise. They might have abnormal eating habits. For instance, some people with an ASD limit their diet to only a few foods. Others might eat nonfood items like dirt or rocks (this is called pica). They might also have issues like chronic constipation or diarrhea.

People with ASD might have odd sleeping habits. They also might have abnormal moods or emotional reactions. For instance, they might laugh or cry at unusual times or show no emotional response at times you would expect one. In addition, they might not be afraid of dangerous things, and they could be fearful of harmless objects or events.

Development

Children with ASD develop at different rates in different areas. They may have delays in language, social, and learning skills, while their ability to walk and move around are about the same as other children their age. They might be very good at putting puzzles together or solving computer problems, but they might have trouble with social activities like talking or making friends. Children with an ASD might also learn a hard skill before they learn an easy one. For example, a child might be able to read long words but not be able to tell you what sound a "b" makes.

Children develop at their own pace, so it can be difficult to tell exactly when a child will learn a particular skill. But, there are age-specific developmental milestones used to measure a child's social and emotional progress in the first few years of life. To learn more about developmental milestones, visit "Learn the Signs. Act Early," a campaign designed by CDC and a coalition of partners to teach parents, health care professionals, and child care providers about early childhood development, including possible "red flags" for autism spectrum disorders.

Section 14.2

Autism Symptoms Emerge in Infancy

This section includes excerpts from "When Do Children
Usually Show Symptoms of Autism Spectrum Disorder (ASD)?"
National Institute of Child Health and Human Development
(NICHD), December 18, 2013; text from "Autism," © 1995–2016.
The Nemours Foundation/KidsHealth®. Reprinted with permission;
and text from "What Causes Autism Spectrum Disorder (ASD)?"
National Institute of Child Health and Human Development
(NICHD), December 18, 2013.

When Do Children Usually Show Symptoms of Autism Spectrum Disorder (ASD)?

The symptoms of autism always appear early in development. Many children show symptoms of autism by 12 months to 18 months of age, for example:

- Problems with eye contact

- No response to his or her name

- Problems following another person's gaze or pointed finger to an object (or "joint attention")

- Poor skills in pretend play and imitation

- Problems with nonverbal communication

Many parents are not aware of these "early" signs of autism and don't start thinking about autism until their children do not start speaking at a typical age.

Most children with autism are not diagnosed until after age 3, even though health care providers can often see developmental problems before that age.

Research shows that early detection and early intervention greatly improve outcomes, so it's important to look for these symptoms when a child is as young as possible.

Regression

Some children with autism **regress**, meaning they stop using language, play, or social skills that they've already learned. This regression usually happens between ages 1 and 2 years. It might happen earlier for some social behaviors, such as looking at faces and sharing a smile. Researchers don't know why some children regress into autism or which children are likely to regress.

Other Early Signs

There also may be early biological signs of ASD. Recent studies have shown that:

- People with autism have unique brain activity, structures, and connections.

- There are differences in brain growth in ASD as early as 6 months of age.

What Causes Autism Spectrum Disorder (ASD)?

Scientists don't know exactly what causes autism. Autism was first described in the 1940s, but very little was known about it until the last few decades. Even today, there is a great deal that we don't know about autism. Because the disorder is so complex and no two people with autism are exactly alike, there are probably many causes for autism.

Genes and ASD

Causes of autism are not yet fully understood, but scientists believe that genes and environmental factors are involved. In fact, new research has found that genes play a major role; there's a 30% chance of a child developing autism if a sibling has it.

But this doesn't necessarily mean that autism is passed down from parent to child. Some studies suggest that kids with a genetic risk or predisposition to autism might develop it when they are exposed to something (yet unknown) in the environment.

Other studies have suggested that autism could be caused by viruses, allergies, or vaccines. But none of these theories have been scientifically proven. In fact, the vast majority of scientific studies on vaccines have found no link between vaccines—or any of their ingredients—and autism. The fraudulent 1998 study that suggested such a link was later retracted by the medical journal that originally published it and the study's author was stripped of his medical license.

It's also important to remember that autism is not caused by parenting or bad experiences. Earlier theories that suggested this have been disproved.

Interactions between Genes and the Environment

If someone is susceptible to ASD because of genetic mutations, then certain situations might cause autism in that person.

For instance, an infection or contact with chemicals in the environment could cause autism in someone who is susceptible because of genetic mutations. However, someone who is genetically susceptible might not get an ASD even if he or she has the same experiences.

Other Biological Causes

Researchers are also looking into biological factors other than genes that might be involved in ASD. Some of these include:

- Problems with brain connections
- Problems with growth or overgrowth in certain areas of the brain
- Problems with metabolism (the body's energy production system)
- Problems in the body's immune system, which protects against infections

Section 14.3

Eye Response to Light a Possible Autism Biomarker

Text in this section is excerpted from "Earliest Marker
for Autism Found in Young Infants," National Institute
of Mental Health (NIMH), November 6, 2013.

Eye contact during early infancy may be a key to early identification
of autism, according to a study funded by the National Institute of
Mental Health (NIMH), part of the National Institutes of Health. Published this week in the journal Nature, the study reveals the earliest
sign of developing autism ever observed—a steady decline in attention
to others' eyes within the first two to six months of life.

"Autism isn't usually diagnosed until after age 2, when delays in a
child's social behavior and language skills become apparent. This study
shows that children exhibit clear signs of autism at a much younger
age," said Thomas R. Insel, M.D., director of NIMH. "The sooner we
are able to identify early markers for autism, the more effective our
treatment interventions can be."

Typically developing children begin to focus on human faces within
the first few hours of life, and they learn to pick up social cues by
paying special attention to other people's eyes. Children with autism,
however, do not exhibit this sort of interest in eye-looking. In fact, a
lack of eye contact is one of the diagnostic features of the disorder.

To find out how this deficit in eye-looking emerges in children with
autism, Warren Jones, Ph.D., and Ami Klin, Ph.D., of the Marcus
Autism Center, Children's Healthcare of Atlanta, and Emory University
School of Medicine followed infants from birth to age 3. The infants were
divided into two groups, based on their risk for developing an autism
spectrum disorder. Those in the high risk group had an older sibling
already diagnosed with autism; those in the low risk group did not.

Jones and Klin used eye-tracking equipment to measure each
child's eye movements as they watched video scenes of a caregiver.
The researchers calculated the percentage of time each child fixated on
the caregiver's eyes, mouth, and body, as well as the non-human spaces

83

in the images. Children were tested at 10 different times between 2 and 24 months of age.

By age 3, some of the children—nearly all from the high risk group— had received a clinical diagnosis of an autism spectrum disorder. The researchers then reviewed the eye-tracking data to determine what factors differed between those children who received an autism diagnosis and those who did not.

"In infants later diagnosed with autism, we see a steady decline in how much they look at mom's eyes," said Jones. This drop in eye-looking began between two and six months and continued throughout the course of the study. By 24 months, the children later diagnosed with autism focused on the caregiver's eyes only about half as long as did their typically developing counterparts.

This decline in attention to others' eyes was somewhat surprising to the researchers. In opposition to a long-standing theory in the field— that social behaviors are entirely absent in children with autism— these results suggest that social engagement skills are intact shortly after birth in children with autism. If clinicians can identify this sort of marker for autism in a young infant, interventions may be better able to keep the child's social development on track.

"This insight, the preservation of some early eye-looking, is important," explained Jones. "In the future, if we were able to use similar technologies to identify early signs of social disability, we could then consider interventions to build on that early eye-looking and help reduce some of the associated disabilities that often accompany autism."

Chapter 15

How Is ASD Diagnosed?

Chapter Contents

Section 15.1

Diagnosis of Autism Spectrum Disorder

This chapter includes excerpts from "Screening and Diagnosis," Centers for Disease Control and Prevention (CDC), February 26, 2015; and text from "A Parent's Guide to Autism Spectrum Disorder," National Institute of Mental Health (NIMH), Revised 2011. Reviewed February 2016.

ASD diagnosis is often a two-stage process. The first stage involves general developmental screening during well-child checkups with a pediatrician or an early childhood health care provider. Children who show some developmental problems are referred for additional evaluation. The second stage involves a thorough evaluation by a team of doctors and other health professionals with a wide range of specialities. At this stage, a child may be diagnosed as having autism or another developmental disorder.

Children with autism spectrum disorder (ASD) can usually be reliably diagnosed by age 2, though research suggests that some screening tests can be helpful at 18 months or even younger.

Many people—including pediatricians, family doctors, teachers, and parents—may minimize signs of ASD at first, believing that children will "catch up" with their peers. While you may be concerned about labeling your young child with ASD, the earlier the disorder is diagnosed, the sooner specific interventions may begin. Early intervention can reduce or prevent the more severe disabilities associated with ASD. Early intervention may also improve your child's IQ, language, and everyday functional skills, also called adaptive behavior.

Developmental Screening

Developmental screening is a short test to tell if children are learning basic skills when they should, or if they might have delays. During developmental screening the doctor might ask the parent some questions or talk and play with the child during an exam to see how she learns, speaks, behaves, and moves. A delay in any of these areas could be a sign of a problem.

All children should be screened for developmental delays and disabilities during regular well-child doctor visits at:

- 9 months
- 18 months
- 24 or 30 months

Additional screening might be needed if a child is at high risk for developmental problems due to preterm birth, low birth weight or other reasons.

In addition, all children should be screened specifically for ASD during regular well-child doctor visits at:

- 18 months
- 24 months

Additional screening might be needed if a child is at high risk for ASD (e.g., having a sister, brother or other family member with an ASD) or if behaviors sometimes associated with ASD are present.

It is important for doctors to screen all children for developmental delays, but especially to monitor those who are at a higher risk for developmental problems due to preterm birth, low birth weight, or having a brother or sister with an ASD. If your child's doctor does not routinely check your child with this type of developmental screening test, ask that it be done. If the doctor sees any signs of a problem, a comprehensive diagnostic evaluation is needed.

For parents, your own experiences and concerns about your child's development will be very important in the screening process. Keep your own notes about your child's development and look through family videos, photos, and baby albums to help you remember when you first noticed each behavior and when your child reached certain developmental milestones.

Types of ASD Screening Instruments

Sometimes the doctor will ask parents questions about the child's symptoms to screen for ASD. Other screening instruments combine information from parents with the doctor's own observations of the child. Examples of screening instruments for toddlers and preschoolers include:

- Checklist of Autism in Toddlers (CHAT)
- Modified Checklist for Autism in Toddlers (M-CHAT)
- Screening Tool for Autism in Two-Year-Olds (STAT)

- Social Communication Questionnaire (SCQ)
- Communication and Symbolic Behavior Scales (CSBS)

To screen for mild ASD or Asperger syndrome in older children, the doctor may rely on different screening instruments, such as:

- Autism Spectrum Screening Questionnaire (ASSQ)
- Australian Scale for Asperger's Syndrome (ASAS)
- Childhood Asperger Syndrome Test (CAST)

Some helpful resources on ASD screening include the Center for Disease Control and Prevention's General Developmental Screening tools and ASD Specific Screening tools.

Comprehensive Diagnostic Evaluation

The second stage of diagnosis must be thorough in order to find whether other conditions may be causing your child's symptoms.

A team that includes a psychologist, a neurologist, a psychiatrist, a speech therapist, or other professionals experienced in diagnosing ASD may do this evaluation. The evaluation may assess the child's cognitive level (thinking skills), language level, and adaptive behavior (age-appropriate skills needed to complete daily activities independently, for example eating, dressing, and toileting).

Because ASD is a complex disorder that sometimes occurs along with other illnesses or learning disorders, the comprehensive evaluation may include brain imaging and gene tests, along with in-depth memory, problem-solving, and language testing. Children with any delayed development should also get a hearing test and be screened for lead poisoning as part of the comprehensive evaluation.

Although children can lose their hearing along with developing ASD, common ASD symptoms (such as not turning to face a person calling their name) can also make it seem that children cannot hear when in fact they can. If a child is not responding to speech, especially to his or her name, it's important for the doctor to test whether a child has hearing loss.

The evaluation process is a good time for parents and caregivers to ask questions and get advice from the whole evaluation team. The outcome of the evaluation will help plan for treatment and interventions to help your child. Be sure to ask who you can contact with follow-up questions.

In some cases, the primary care doctor might choose to refer the child and family to a specialist for further assessment and diagnosis. Specialists who can do this type of evaluation include:

- Developmental Pediatricians (doctors who have special training in child development and children with special needs)

- Child Neurologists (doctors who work on the brain, spine, and nerves)

- Child Psychologists or Psychiatrists (doctors who know about the human mind)

Section 15.2

Diagnostic Criteria for Autism Spectrum Disorder

Text in this section is excerpted from "Diagnostic Criteria," Centers for Disease Control and Prevention (CDC), February 26, 2015.

1. Persistent deficits in social communication and social interaction across multiple contexts, as manifested by the following, currently or by history:

- Deficits in social-emotional reciprocity, ranging, for example, from abnormal social approach and failure of normal back-and-forth conversation; to reduced sharing of interests, emotions, or affect; to failure to initiate or respond to social interactions.

- Deficits in nonverbal communicative behaviors used for social interaction, ranging, for example, from poorly integrated verbal and nonverbal communication; to abnormalities in eye contact and body language or deficits in understanding and use of gestures; to a total lack of facial expressions and nonverbal communication.

- Deficits in developing, maintaining, and understand relationships, ranging, for example, from difficulties adjusting behavior to suit various social contexts; to difficulties in sharing imaginative play or in making friends; to absence of interest in peers.

Severity is based on social communication impairments and restricted, repetitive patterns of behavior.

2. Restricted, repetitive patterns of behavior, interests, or activities, as manifested by at least two of the following, currently or by history:

- Stereotyped or repetitive motor movements, use of objects, or speech (e.g., simple motor stereotypes, lining up toys or flipping objects, echolalia, idiosyncratic phrases).

- Insistence on sameness, inflexible adherence to routines, or ritualized patterns of verbal or nonverbal behavior (e.g., extreme distress at small changes, difficulties with transitions, rigid thinking patterns, greeting rituals, need to take same route or eat same food every day).

- Highly restricted, fixated interests that are abnormal in intensity or focus (e.g., strong attachment to or preoccupation with unusual objects, excessively circumscribed or perseverative interests).

- Hyper- or hyporeactivity to sensory input or unusual interest in sensory aspects of the environment (e.g., apparent indifference to pain/temperature, adverse response to specific sounds or textures, excessive smelling or touching of objects, visual fascination with lights or movement).

Severity is based on social communication impairments and restricted, repetitive patterns of behavior.

3. Symptoms must be present in the early developmental period (but may not become fully manifest until social demands exceed limited capacities, or may be masked by learned strategies in later life).

4. Symptoms cause clinically significant impairment in social, occupational, or other important areas of current functioning.

5. These disturbances are not better explained by intellectual disability (intellectual developmental disorder) or global developmental delay. Intellectual disability and autism spectrum disorder frequently co-occur; to make comorbid diagnoses of autism spectrum disorder and intellectual disability, social communication should be below that expected for general developmental level.

Section 15.3

IACC Statement Regarding Diagnostic Criteria for Autism Spectrum Disorder

Text in this section is excerpted from "IACC Statement Regarding
Scientific, Practice and Policy Implications of Changes in the
Diagnostic Criteria for Autism Spectrum Disorder," U.S. Department
of Health and Human Services (HHS), April 2, 2014.

The Interagency Autism Coordinating Committee (IACC) is a Federal advisory committee, composed of Federal and public members, that coordinates all efforts within the Department of Health and Human Services (HHS) concerning autism spectrum disorder (ASD). The committee recognizes the need for diagnostic criteria for ASD that reflect current scientific knowledge and progress and define the wide range of symptom expression associated with this disorder. It was the goal of the Neurodevelopmental (ND) Workgroup for the Fifth Edition of the *Diagnostic and Statistical Manual of Mental Disorders* (DSM-5) to meet these standards.

The DSM-5 criteria were published in May 2013. Although the DSM-5 diagnostic criteria are intended primarily for use by clinicians and researchers in their diagnostic assessments, the IACC is aware that it is important to also remember that these the criteria also have a direct impact on people who have the disorders and their families, and their ability to assess symptoms and obtain services that can help them optimize their health, well-being and quality of life. Any revision of the diagnostic criteria must be made with great care so as to not have the unintended consequence of reducing critical services aimed at improving the ability of persons with autism. In this statement, the IACC describes a range of research, practice, and policy implications that arise as a result of the changes in the DSM criteria which deserve consideration as the DSM-5 is implemented in research, clinical, and educational settings.

91

Changes in the DSM Criteria

Starting with the DSM-III in 1980, autism was categorized as a Pervasive Developmental Disorders (PDD). In an effort to reflect what has been learned through research and practice since that time, the DSM-5 released in 2013 removed the PDD category and the accompanying sub types (Autistic Disorder, Asperger Disorder, Childhood Disintegrative Disorder and Pervasive Developmental Disorder – Not Otherwise Specified) with a single disorder, Autism Spectrum Disorder (ASD). The DSM-5 criteria place greater emphasis on the two core symptom domains of ASD (social communication and restrictive, repetitive behaviors), and no longer consider verbal abilities as a diagnostic feature. Other changes included adding ratings of the severity of the two symptom domains and several clinical specifiers. These specifiers provide information about etiology, co-morbidities (e.g., intellectual disability, language delay, and medical conditions such as seizures), and pattern of onset.

Since ASD continues to be defined by a pattern of developmental and behavioral symptoms, changes to the diagnostic criteria come with potential trade-offs. One goal of the recent revisions was to improve specificity of the ASD diagnosis, reducing the number of false positive cases. However, concerns exist that this increased specificity may have gone too far in reducing the sensitivity of the ASD diagnosis, increasing the number of false negative cases. For example, removing a specific age cut-off for diagnosis was intended to improve the sensitivity of the DSM-IV criteria (which had required symptom onset by 3 years of age). By DSM-5's more inclusive criterion, "Symptoms must be present in the early developmental period but may not become fully manifest until social demands exceed limited capacities, or may be masked by learned strategies in later life" may reduce diagnostic specificity by expanding the list of differential diagnoses that must be considered. The inclusion of historical information also may have unintended consequences on sensitivity and specificity.

Another major change in DSM-5 was the addition of a new diagnosis category, Social Communication Disorder (SCD) which applies to individuals who exhibit persistent difficulty with the social use of verbal and nonverbal communication that cannot be explained by low cognitive ability. The symptoms of SCD have significant overlap with those of the ASD social communication domain, but the two disorders are considered to be unique and separate from each other. The distinction is clarified in the DSM-5 criteria, which note that ASD must be ruled out before a diagnosis of SCD can be considered. However, there is limited published information on SCD with a research basis primarily in the condition previously studied as Pragmatic Language Disorder (PLD). While SCD includes PLD, there is much to learn about the definition, measurement, scope, reliability, and validity of SCD as a diagnosed condition.

Implications for Research

As we move forward with the DSM-5 diagnostic changes, research is essential to understand the impact of the new classification system on individuals who were diagnosed with a sub type of PDD in the past or with ASD in the current system. In addition, research on autism etiology and intervention is dependent on the classification system used to define the individuals included in studies and any impact of changing this system needs to be understood. It will be critically important to conduct research to understand whether the new criteria are making a difference in how, when and which people are being diagnosed with ASD, and on our understanding of the etiology of autism; on the reliability of diagnoses using the new criteria and specifiers; and the impact of the new criteria on prevalence estimates. Efforts are needed to develop or modify diagnostics instruments and tools to conform to the new criteria, and to assess the impacts of the new criteria on service provision for those with ASD. Along these lines, the IACC has identified several pressing research questions related to the implementation of the DSM-5 ASD diagnostic criteria.

Who is being identified?

- What is the reliability and validity of DSM-5 ASD diagnoses compared to experienced clinician judgment?

- Do the DSM-5 criteria identify the same individuals who were diagnosed with a DSM-IV-TR Autistic Disorder, Asperger Disorder, or PDD-NOS (particularly those individuals who had sub-threshold symptoms)?

- What is the symptom profile of individuals who meet one set of diagnostic criteria but not the other?

- What are the cognitive, demographic, and co-occurring condition profiles of persons who meet one set of diagnostic criteria but not the other?

What is the reliability and validity of the severity ratings for the two domains:

Social Communication and Interaction, and

Restricted and Repetitive Behaviors and Interests?

Do the severity ratings improve assessment of impairments in adaptive functioning and thus, help distinguish individuals with an ASD from those individuals with subthreshold symptoms or other disorders and conditions (e.g., attention deficit hyperactivity disorder (ADHD), social phobia, intellectual disability, and others)?

Does the removal of the requirement for symptom onset to be prior to 3 years of age have an impact on diagnostic applications? For example, are more adolescents eligible for a DSM-5 diagnosis? Does the phrase "early developmental period" (Criterion D) provide sufficient coverage for toddlers and facilitate early identification of young children with ASD? How will the DSM-5 criteria impact ASD prevalence estimates? How will trends be evaluated given that current ASD prevalence estimates are based on the combined DSM-IV-TR diagnoses of autistic disorder, Asperger's disorder, and PDD-NOS?

What is the reliability and validity of the SCD diagnostic criteria? What are the key features that distinguish SCD distinct from ASD?

How are people identified with an ASD?

How will existing screening and diagnostic instruments need to be modified to conform to the DSM-5 criteria (including the existing use of checklists specific to Asperger's)? What new measures are required for screening and diagnostic assessment?

How will historical and current symptoms be captured, including assessment of the individual's lifetime history of symptoms?

How will assessment tools be adapted to capture the range of symptoms and developmental stages (toddlers, preschool, school-aged, adolescents, young and older adults)? What tools are needed to address differences in clinical presentation related to gender or cultural backgrounds?

What tools are needed to provide "individualized" diagnoses that specify no only the severity of the core symptom domains, but also an individual's strengths and weaknesses, co-occurring conditions and challenges?

How will severity ratings and specifiers be assessed and documented reliably?

How do the DSM-5 criteria change the way clinicians, other health and education professionals, community members, and researchers conceptualize and identify ASD? How are the DSM-5 criteria being applied in educational and other service systems? Although special education eligibility is based on educational need, how are state and local education authorities' procedures affected by the DSM-5 changes and addition of new conditions like SCD?

What tools are to be used to assess SCD and how are these assessments related to first ruling out ASD?

What does it mean to be identified with ASD?

How does the removal of specific ASD-related diagnoses (particularly, Asperger's disorder) affect the culture of individuals with ASD and how they identify, connect, and support one another?

What are the ways that the severity levels will be used to describe the social communication and restricted and repetitive behavior domains? Do the severity levels have an impact on service eligibility or provision?

How does the addition of specifiers for severity levels, age and pattern or onset, etiologic factors, and co-occurring symptoms conditions (e.g., intellectual disability, language disorder, medical disorders) help inform the clinical management of ASD? Do the specifiers have an impact on our clinical and etiologic understanding of ASD? Are research findings published on individuals identified with DSM-IV criteria comparable to those using DSM-5 criteria? How will existing research datasets be integrated with DSM-5-based datasets?

What is the impact of the DSM-5 diagnostic changes on service provision to individuals with isolated social communication deficits who may have met PDD-NOS criteria by DSM-IV-TR standards, but meet SCD criteria by DSM-5 standards? Is eligibility for ASD services increased, decreased, or unchanged? Are therapeutic interventions designed for ASD effective for addressing symptoms of SCD, or are new interventions required?

Implications for Practice and Policy

The DSM-5 criteria are likely to have a tremendous impact on assessment and diagnosis of ASD in a variety of settings. At this early stage, it is not possible to know how the DSM-5 criteria will compare against the previous standards set by the DSM-IV. Researchers have begun to address these questions, as well as to assess the diagnostic utility, reliability and validity of the DSM-5 criteria. While we wait for those studies to produce results, clinicians will be using the DSM-5 criteria to diagnose individuals of different ages, developmental stages and cultural backgrounds. In addition to gaining familiarity with the new diagnostic criteria, professionals will need to learn how to use the diagnostic specifiers, including the severity ratings for the two core domains.

The IACC identified the following key issues that will be important to consider as DSM-5 is implemented in real-world settings:

There is concern that the new severity ratings might be inappropriately used to prescribe services. Although reliable and valid tools for rating symptom severity that could meaningfully guide decisions regarding service need may become available in the future, at this time, use of the severity ratings to determine type and level of services would not be appropriate.

Very little prospective data on the reliability and validity of the new criteria exist for children who are young, individuals from diverse ethnic backgrounds, and adults. Thus, in general, caution is needed when using the DSM-5 criteria to make a diagnosis with these populations until more research is conducted. In particular, clinicians should pay special attention to individuals with obvious ASD symptoms who narrowly missed criteria for ASD based on DSM-5, to ensure that they are not inadvertently denied needed ASD-specific services. Services should be based on need rather than diagnosis; it would not be appropriate for a child to be denied ASD-specific services because he or she does not meet full DSM-5 criteria if a qualified clinician or educator determines that the child could benefit from those services.

Clinical observation and some research suggest that some children who have ASD may not manifest the full range of ASD symptoms before 3 years of age. For example, a toddler who eventually will qualify for an ASD diagnosis based on DSM-5 criteria may exhibit a significant impairment in social communication and only exhibits one repetitive behavior and no sensory sensitivities. This toddler will not meet a diagnosis of ASD but would likely benefit from early intensive behavioral intervention. It would be appropriate for a child who is less than three years of age who shows clear autism symptoms (e.g., significant impairments in social communication or restricted, repetitive behaviors) but does not meet full criteria for ASD to be given a provisional diagnosis of ASD and an opportunity to benefit from ASD-specific early intervention services. A diagnosis of ASD or a provisional diagnosis of ASD should be considered a disability that qualifies a child for early intervention services.

If the initial diagnosis is being made with DSM-5 criteria, clinicians are encouraged to consider the full range of symptom severity described in the text for ASD. Although the criteria include a few symptom examples, these are not exhaustive and the sections on "Diagnostic Features" and "Development and Course" include a more complete description of the clinical features at various ages and developmental stages. The comprehensive listing is provided to ensure that less common presentations are considered, and to ensure that all individuals who might benefit from ASD-specific services will receive them. In particular, clinicians should pay special attention to individuals with obvious ASD symptoms who don't meet DSM-5 criteria for an ASD diagnosis. In those cases, obtaining a more complete lifetime symptom history may reveal sensory sensitivities were present in early childhood, or that the individual had difficulties with transitions (bedtimes, leaving for school, etc.) and an inflexible adherence to bedtime or bath routines. As mentioned above, in young children, the evolving nature of ASD may make it difficult for them to receive an ASD diagnosis because symptoms aren't yet present in both core domains. Clinicians should consider the larger context of the child's presentation, keeping in mind that therapeutic interventions and provision of services should be based on need rather than diagnosis.

It is important for families, individuals on the spectrum, and practitioners to know that individuals who currently have a diagnosis of ASD based on the DSM-IV system will retain an ASD diagnosis for the purposes of qualifying for clinical and educational services. Individuals who currently have a diagnosis of ASD are not required to be "re-diagnosed" with the new system in order to qualify for ASD services. The DSM-5 criteria contain the following note: "Individuals with a well-established DSM-IV diagnosis of autistic disorder, Asperger's disorder, or pervasive developmental disorder not otherwise specified (PDD-NOS) should be given the diagnosis of ASD." As the note makes clear, DSM-IV diagnoses should be retained even after DSM-5 has replaced DSM-IV as the diagnostic standard. The manual explicitly states that there is no need to "rediagnose" patients unless there is a clinical need (e.g., changes in clinical presentation), and that the new criteria should not be used as a means of excluding individuals from necessary services.

In DSM-IV, there were very broad domain diagnostic criteria for PDD-NOS and it included a wide variety of clinical presentations, including autistic symptoms that didn't fully meet criteria for one of the defined disorders, "subthreshold" symptoms, and "atypical autism" which was defined by the presence of only deficits in reciprocal social interactions, or restrictive, repetitive behaviors (e.g., stereotypes associated with intellectual disability could meet this criterion). Although it was appropriate to include these atypical cases in the broad umbrella of a DSM-IV pervasive developmental disorder (PDD), the divergent cases do not fit within the autism spectrum and are unlikely to meet DSM-5 criteria for ASD. However, as stipulated in DSM-5, it is expected that all individuals with a "well-established DSM-IV diagnosis of PDD-NOS" will retain the diagnosis.

The SCD diagnosis is new. Compared to a diagnosis of ASD, relatively little is known about the validity and reliability of a SCD diagnosis, nor is it known what interventions will be most effective for children with this diagnosis. Although the SCD diagnosis is new, there is a large literature on "pragmatic language disorder," which shares many features with SCD. Pragmatic language disorder is defined by deficits in the social use of verbal communication; in SCD, the addition of nonverbal communication deficits provides a more comprehensive picture of the impairments in social communication. SCD also overlaps with the social communication deficit of ASD. It is very likely that many children with a diagnosis of SCD will benefit from interventions and other services that are useful in addressing the social communication/reciprocity deficits of currently designed for children with ASD. Until specific treatment guidelines are developed for SCD, it will be important to evaluate the needs of each individual child and to match those needs to available services and therapeutic interventions.

While the symptoms of SCD overlap with some symptoms of ASD, the two disorders are meant to describe separate conditions. SCD is categorized as a communication disorder, and is not considered to be part of the autism spectrum. It is important for clinicians to note that the symptoms that constitute SCD criteria capture symptoms typically not present until 4 to 5 years of age (or later). As noted in the DSM-5 manual, it would be rare to diagnose SCD in children under 4 years of age. Therefore, SCD is not likely to be useful as a diagnostic justification for early intervention. However, under DSM-5 it remains possible to identify social, language, or autism spectrum disorders in children under 3 years of age but not SCD.

For billing purposes, International Classification of Diseases (ICD) codes rather than DSM diagnoses are used. The DSM manual provides information regarding how the new DSM-5 diagnoses should be mapped onto the ICD codes. Although Asperger syndrome will no longer be considered a formal DSM diagnosis, people who wish to continue to use the Asperger label are encouraged to do so. This will allow them to retain their identity as persons with Asperger syndrome. In DSM-5, the verbal and intellectual abilities which distinguished Asperger syndrome from autistic disorder in DSM-IV are indicated by use of specifiers. Thus, the DSM-5 equivalent to Asperger disorder is: ASD without intellectual or language impairments. It should be noted that some states limit access to certain services by people with an Asperger syndrome diagnosis, but will provide them to people with an ASD diagnosis.

The IACC recognizes the need for more information for clinicians and educators on use of the diagnostic specifiers and the severity ratings. The clinical specifiers have enormous potential to be used to individualize diagnoses, and to describe specific sub-types of ASD, including those with limited language function, and severe intellectual disability, known etiologies, late onset age or history of developmental regression, and medical co-morbidities, such as seizures and gastrointestinal (GI) disorders. For the first time, etiologic relationships can be indicated as part of a DSM-5 diagnosis, by utilizing the specifier, "Associated with known medical or genetic condition or environmental factor." The severity specifiers are another aid to individualizing the ASD diagnoses, but provide only a general guide to rating symptom severity. The IACC encourages the development of valid and reliable measures that can aid in the clinical assessment of symptom severity across the lifespan and various cultural backgrounds.

Chapter 16

Medical Tests and Evaluations Used to Diagnose ASD

The first signs of an autism spectrum disorder (ASD) often appear before a child reaches the age of two. These signs usually take the form of developmental delays in early language skills and social interactions. If a baby does not point or use other intentional gestures by 12 months, for instance, or use two-word spontaneous phrases by 24 months, he or she should be evaluated for an ASD. Identifying these signs as soon as possible is key to early diagnosis and treatment, which can improve skill and language development and help the child reach his or her full potential.

Under recommendations issued by the American Academy of Pediatrics, pediatricians and other health care providers are trained to screen children for ASDs during regular well-child visits. If they notice signs of developmental delays or symptoms of an ASD, they will usually refer the child to a specialist—such as a developmental pediatrician, child psychologist, pediatric neurologist, psychiatrist, or speech pathologist—for a complete evaluation.

Since autism is a spectrum disorder with varying degrees of severity, it can be difficult to diagnose. No single medical test can determine whether a child has an ASD. Instead, specialists typically conduct a series of assessments to figure out whether the developmental delays they have identified in a child are caused by an ASD or another condition that may present similar symptoms, such as a personality disorder, hearing problems, lead poisoning, or fragile X syndrome.

Medical Tests to Diagnose ASD

Specialists use various types of behavioral evaluations and physical assessments to gather the information needed to make a diagnosis of ASD. Some of the common types of behavioral evaluations include:

- Application of the American Association of Childhood and Adolescent Psychiatry (AACAP) guidelines for assessing whether a child's behavior indicates an ASD.

- Compilation of a complete medical and developmental history through interviews or questionnaires with parents or other caregivers.

- Observations of the child's behavior, social interactions, and communication skills in different situations over time.

- Administration of structured tests covering developmental level, intelligence, communication, behavior, and social interaction to determine whether the child's developmental delays affect his or her thinking, problem solving, and decision making abilities.

Specialists may also perform physical examinations and laboratory tests to help determine whether a child's symptoms indicate ASD or may be related to a physical problem. Some of these assessments include:

- A complete physical examination—including height, weight, and head measurements—to see whether the child's growth is following a normal pattern.

- An ear examination and hearing tests to see whether speech and language delays or issues with social skills and behavior may be caused by a hearing problem.

- Blood tests for lead poisoning, which can cause developmental delays.

- Chromosomal analysis to determine whether signs of intellectual disability may be related to a genetic disorder, such as fragile X syndrome.

- Brain scans, such as an electroencephalograph (EEG) or magnetic resonance imaging (MRI), to see whether differences in brain structure may be causing regression in the child's development or behavior.

All of these medical tests and evaluations are intended to rule out other conditions and pinpoint ASD as the cause of the child's developmental delays. Once the diagnosis has been made, ASD specialists can design a program of treatments and interventions to help address any deficits and enable the child to reach his or her full potential.

Reference

"Autism: Exams and Tests." WebMD, November 14, 2014.

Chapter 17

Developmental Screening

Chapter Contents

Section 17.1

Developmental Milestones

Text in this section is excerpted from "Developmental Milestones," Centers for Disease Control and Prevention (CDC), April 21, 2015.

Your Baby at Two Months

How your child plays, learns, speaks, and acts offers important clues about your child's development. Developmental milestones are things most children can do by a certain age.

Check the milestones your child has reached by the end of 2 months. Take this with you and talk with your child's doctor at every visit about the milestones your child has reached and what to expect next.

What Most babies Do at This Age:

Social and Emotional

- Begins to smile at people
- Can briefly calm himself (may bring hands to mouth and suck on hand)
- Tries to look at parent

Language/Communication

- Coos, makes gurgling sounds
- Turns head toward sounds

Cognitive (learning, thinking, problem-solving)

- Pays attention to faces
- Begins to follow things with eyes and recognize people at a distance
- Begins to act bored (cries, fussy) if activity doesn't change

Movement/Physical Development

- Can hold head up and begins to push up when lying on tummy
- Makes smoother movements with arms and legs

Act early by talking to your child's doctor if your child:

- Doesn't respond to loud sounds
- Doesn't watch things as they move
- Doesn't smile at people
- Doesn't bring hands to mouth
- Can't hold head up when pushing up when on tummy

Your Baby at Four Months

How your child plays, learns, speaks, and acts offers important clues about your child's development. Developmental milestones are things most children can do by a certain age.

Check the milestones your child has reached by the end of 4 months. Take this with you and talk with your child's doctor at every visit about the milestones your child has reached and what to expect next.

What Most Babies Do at This Age:

Social and Emotional

- Smiles spontaneously, especially at people
- Likes to play with people and might cry when playing stops
- Copies some movements and facial expressions, like smiling or frowning

Language/Communication

- Begins to babble
- Babbles with expression and copies sounds he hears
- Cries in different ways to show hunger, pain, or being tired

Cognitive (learning, thinking, problem-solving)

- Lets you know if she is happy or sad

- Responds to affection
- Reaches for toy with one hand
- Uses hands and eyes together, such as seeing a toy and reaching for it
- Follows moving things with eyes from side to side
- Watches faces closely
- Recognizes familiar people and things at a distance

Movement/Physical Development

- Holds head steady, unsupported
- Pushes down on legs when feet are on a hard surface
- May be able to roll over from tummy to back
- Can hold a toy and shake it and swing at dangling toys
- Brings hands to mouth
- When lying on stomach, pushes up to elbows

Act early by talking to your child's doctor if your child:

- Doesn't watch things as they move
- Doesn't smile at people
- Can't hold head steady
- Doesn't coo or make sounds
- Doesn't bring things to mouth
- Doesn't push down with legs when feet are placed on a hard surface
- Has trouble moving one or both eyes in all directions

Your Baby at Six Months

How your child plays, learns, speaks, and acts offers important clues about your child's development. Developmental milestones are things most children can do by a certain age.

Check the milestones your child has reached by the end of 6 months. Take this with you and talk with your child's doctor at every visit about the milestones your child has reached and what to expect next.

What Most Babies Do at This Age:

Social and Emotional

- Knows familiar faces and begins to know if someone is a stranger
- Likes to play with others, especially parents
- Responds to other people's emotions and often seems happy
- Likes to look at self in a mirror

Language/Communication

- Responds to sounds by making sounds
- Strings vowels together when babbling ("ah," "eh," "oh") and likes taking turns with parent while making sounds
- Responds to own name
- Makes sounds to show joy and displeasure
- Begins to say consonant sounds (jabbering with "m," "b")

Cognitive (learning, thinking, problem-solving)

- Looks around at things nearby
- Brings things to mouth
- Shows curiosity about things and tries to get things that are out of reach
- Begins to pass things from one hand to the other

Movement/Physical Development

- Rolls over in both directions (front to back, back to front)
- Begins to sit without support
- When standing, supports weight on legs and might bounce
- Rocks back and forth, sometimes crawling backward before moving forward

Act early by talking to your child's doctor if your child:

- Doesn't try to get things that are in reach
- Shows no affection for caregivers

- Doesn't respond to sounds around him
- Has difficulty getting things to mouth
- Doesn't make vowel sounds ("ah", "eh", "oh")
- Doesn't roll over in either direction
- Doesn't laugh or make squealing sounds
- Seems very stiff, with tight muscles
- Seems very floppy, like a rag doll

Your Baby at Nine Months

How your child plays, learns, speaks, and acts offers important clues about your child's development. Developmental milestones are things most children can do by a certain age.

Check the milestones your child has reached by the end of 9 months. Take this with you and talk with your child's doctor at every visit about the milestones your child has reached and what to expect next.

What Most Babies Do at This Age:

Social and Emotional

- May be afraid of strangers
- May be clingy with familiar adults
- Has favorite toys

Language/Communication

- Understands "no"
- Makes a lot of different sounds like "mamamama" and "babababa"
- Copies sounds and gestures of others
- Uses fingers to point at things

Cognitive (learning, thinking, problem-solving)

- Watches the path of something as it falls
- Looks for things he sees you hide
- Plays peek-a-boo

- Puts things in her mouth
- Moves things smoothly from one hand to the other
- Picks up things like cereal o's between thumb and index finger

Movement/Physical Development

- Stands, holding on
- Can get into sitting position
- Sits without support
- Pulls to stand
- Crawls

Act early by talking to your child's doctor if your child:

- Doesn't bear weight on legs with support
- Doesn't sit with help
- Doesn't babble ("mama," "baba," "dada")
- Doesn't play any games involving back-and-forth play
- Doesn't respond to own name
- Doesn't seem to recognize familiar people
- Doesn't look where you point
- Doesn't transfer toys from one hand to the other

Your Child at One Year

How your child plays, learns, speaks, and acts offers important clues about your child's development. Developmental milestones are things most children can do by a certain age. Check the milestones your child has reached by his or her 1st birthday. Take this with you and talk with your child's doctor at every visit about the milestones your child has reached and what to expect next.

What Most Children Do at This Age:

Social and Emotional

- Is shy or nervous with strangers
- Cries when mom or dad leaves

- Has favorite things and people
- Shows fear in some situations
- Hands you a book when he wants to hear a story
- Repeats sounds or actions to get attention
- Puts out arm or leg to help with dressing
- Plays games such as "peek-a-boo" and "pat-a-cake"

Language/Communication

- Responds to simple spoken requests
- Uses simple gestures, like shaking head "no" or waving "bye-bye"
- Makes sounds with changes in tone (sounds more like speech)
- Says "mama" and "dada" and exclamations like "uh-oh!"
- Tries to say words you say

Cognitive (learning, thinking, problem-solving)

- Explores things in different ways, like shaking, banging, throwing
- Finds hidden things easily
- Looks at the right picture or thing when it's named
- Copies gestures
- Starts to use things correctly; for example, drinks from a cup, brushes hair
- Bangs two things together
- Puts things in a container, takes things out of a container
- Lets things go without help
- Pokes with index (pointer) finger
- Follows simple directions like "pick up the toy"

Movement/Physical Development

- Gets to a sitting position without help
- Pulls up to stand, walks holding on to furniture ("cruising")

- May take a few steps without holding on
- May stand alone

Act early by talking to your child's doctor if your child:

- Doesn't crawl
- Can't stand when supported
- Doesn't search for things that she sees you hide
- Doesn't say single words like "mama" or "dada"
- Doesn't learn gestures like waving or shaking head
- Doesn't point to things
- Loses skills he once had

Your Child at 18 Months

How your child plays, learns, speaks, and acts offers important clues about your child's development. Developmental milestones are things most children can do by a certain age. Check the milestones your child has reached by the end of 18 months. Take this with you and talk with your child's doctor at every visit about the milestones your child has reached and what to expect next.

What Most Babies Do at This Age:

Social and Emotional

- Likes to hand things to others as play
- May have temper tantrums
- May be afraid of strangers
- Shows affection to familiar people
- Plays simple pretend, such as feeding a doll
- May cling to caregivers in new situations
- Points to show others something interesting
- Explores alone but with parent close by

Language/Communication

- Says several single words

- Says and shakes head "no"
- Points to show someone what he wants

Cognitive (learning, thinking, problem-solving)

- Knows what ordinary things are for; for example, telephone, brush, spoon
- Points to get the attention of others
- Shows interest in a doll or stuffed animal by pretending to feed
- Points to one body part
- Scribbles on his own
- Can follow 1-step verbal commands without any gestures; for example, sits when you say "sit down"

Movement/Physical Development

- Walks alone
- May walk up steps and run
- Pulls toys while walking
- Can help undress herself
- Drinks from a cup
- Eats with a spoon

Act early by talking to your child's doctor if your child:

- Doesn't point to show things to others
- Can't walk
- Doesn't know what familiar things are for
- Doesn't copy others
- Doesn't gain new words
- Doesn't have at least 6 words
- Doesn't notice or mind when a caregiver leaves or returns
- Loses skills he once had

Your Child at 2 Years

How your child plays, learns, speaks, and acts offers important clues about your child's development. Developmental milestones are things most children can do by a certain age. Check the milestones your child has reached by his or her 2nd birthday. Take this with you and talk with your child's doctor at every visit about the milestones your child has reached and what to expect next.

What Most Babies Do at This Age:

Social and Emotional

- Copies others, especially adults and older children
- Gets excited when with other children
- Shows more and more independence
- Shows defiant behavior (doing what he has been told not to)
- Plays mainly beside other children, but is beginning to include other children, such as in chase games

Language/Communication

- Points to things or pictures when they are named
- Knows names of familiar people and body parts
- Says sentences with 2 to 4 words
- Follows simple instructions
- Repeats words overheard in conversation
- Points to things in a book

Cognitive (learning, thinking, problem-solving)

- Finds things even when hidden under two or three covers
- Begins to sort shapes and colors
- Completes sentences and rhymes in familiar books
- Plays simple make-believe games
- Builds towers of 4 or more blocks
- Might use one hand more than the other

115

- Follows two-step instructions such as "Pick up your shoes and put them in the closet."

- Names items in a picture book such as a cat, bird, or dog

Movement/Physical Development

- Stands on tiptoe

- Kicks a ball

- Begins to run

- Climbs onto and down from furniture without help

- Walks up and down stairs holding on

- Throws ball overhand

- Makes or copies straight lines and circles

Act early by talking to your child's doctor if your child:

- Doesn't use 2-word phrases (for example, "drink milk")

- Doesn't know what to do with common things, like a brush, phone, fork, spoon

- Doesn't copy actions and words

- Doesn't follow simple instructions

- Doesn't walk steadily

- Loses skills she once had

Your Child at 3 Years

How your child plays, learns, speaks, and acts offers important clues about your child's development. Developmental milestones are things most children can do by a certain age. Check the milestones your child has reached by his or her 3rd birthday. Take this with you and talk with your child's doctor at every visit about the milestones your child has reached and what to expect next.

What Most Babies Do at This Age:

Social and Emotional

- Copies adults and friends

- Shows affection for friends without prompting

- Takes turns in games
- Shows concern for crying friend
- Understands the idea of "mine" and "his" or "hers"
- Shows a wide range of emotions
- Separates easily from mom and dad
- May get upset with major changes in routine
- Dresses and undresses self

Language/Communication

- Follows instructions with 2 or 3 steps
- Can name most familiar things
- Understands words like "in," "on," and "under"
- Says first name, age, and sex
- Names a friend
- Says words like "I," "me," "we," and "you" and some plurals (cars, dogs, cats)
- Talks well enough for strangers to understand most of the time
- Carries on a conversation using 2 to 3 sentences

Cognitive (learning, thinking, problem-solving)

- Can work toys with buttons, levers, and moving parts
- Plays make-believe with dolls, animals, and people
- Does puzzles with 3 or 4 pieces
- Understands what "two" means
- Copies a circle with pencil or crayon
- Turns book pages one at a time
- Builds towers of more than 6 blocks
- Screws and unscrews jar lids or turns door handle

Movement/Physical Development

- Climbs well
- Runs easily

- Pedals a tricycle (3-wheel bike)
- Walks up and down stairs, one foot on each step

Act Early by Talking to Your Child's Doctor If Your Child

- Falls down a lot or has trouble with stairs
- Drools or has very unclear speech
- Can't work simple toys (such as peg boards, simple puzzles, turning handle)
- Doesn't speak in sentences
- Doesn't understand simple instructions
- Doesn't play pretend or make-believe
- Doesn't want to play with other children or with toys
- Doesn't make eye contact
- Loses skills he once had

Your Child at 4 Years

How your child plays, learns, speaks, and acts offers important clues about your child's development. Developmental milestones are things most children can do by a certain age. Check the milestones your child has reached by his or her 4th birthday. Take this with you and talk with your child's doctor at every visit about the milestones your child has reached and what to expect next.

What Most Babies Do at This Age:

Social and Emotional

- Enjoys doing new things
- Plays "Mom" and "Dad"
- Is more and more creative with make-believe play
- Would rather play with other children than by himself
- Cooperates with other children
- Often can't tell what's real and what's make-believe
- Talks about what she likes and what she is interested in

Language/Communication

- Knows some basic rules of grammar, such as correctly using "he" and "she"
- Sings a song or says a poem from memory such as the "Itsy Bitsy Spider" or the "Wheels on the Bus"
- Tells stories
- Can say first and last name

Cognitive (learning, thinking, problem-solving)

- Names some colors and some numbers
- Understands the idea of counting
- Starts to understand time
- Remembers parts of a story
- Understands the idea of "same" and "different"
- Draws a person with 2 to 4 body parts
- Uses scissors
- Starts to copy some capital letters
- Plays board or card games
- Tells you what he thinks is going to happen next in a book

Movement/Physical Development

- Hops and stands on one foot up to 2 seconds
- Catches a bounced ball most of the time
- Pours, cuts with supervision, and mashes own food

Act early by talking to your child's doctor if your child:

- Can't jump in place
- Has trouble scribbling
- Shows no interest in interactive games or make-believe
- Ignores other children or doesn't respond to people outside the family
- Resists dressing, sleeping, and using the toilet

- Can't retell a favorite story
- Doesn't follow 3-part commands
- Doesn't understand "same" and "different"
- Doesn't use "me" and "you" correctly
- Speaks unclearly
- Loses skills he once had

Your Child at 5 Years

How your child plays, learns, speaks, and acts offers important clues about your child's development. Developmental milestones are things most children can do by a certain age. Check the milestones your child has reached by his or her 5th birthday. Take this with you and talk with your child's doctor at every visit about the milestones your child has reached and what to expect next.

What Most Babies Do At This Age:

Social and Emotional

- Wants to please friends
- Wants to be like friends
- More likely to agree with rules
- Likes to sing, dance, and act
- Shows concern and sympathy for others
- Is aware of gender
- Can tell what's real and what's make-believe
- Shows more independence (for example, may visit a next-door neighbor by himself [adult supervision is still needed])
- Is sometimes demanding and sometimes very cooperative

Language/Communication

- Speaks very clearly
- Tells a simple story using full sentences
- Uses future tense; for example, "Grandma will be here."
- Says name and address

Cognitive (learning, thinking, problem-solving)

- Counts 10 or more things
- Can draw a person with at least 6 body parts
- Can print some letters or numbers
- Copies a triangle and other geometric shapes
- Knows about things used every day, like money and food

Movement/Physical Development

- Stands on one foot for 10 seconds or longer
- Hops; may be able to skip
- Can do a somersault
- Uses a fork and spoon and sometimes a table knife
- Can use the toilet on her own
- Swings and climbs

Act early by talking to your child's doctor if your child:

- Doesn't show a wide range of emotions
- Shows extreme behavior (unusually fearful, aggressive, shy or sad)
- Unusually withdrawn and not active
- Is easily distracted, has trouble focusing on one activity for more than 5 minutes
- Doesn't respond to people, or responds only superficially
- Can't tell what's real and what's make-believe
- Doesn't play a variety of games and activities
- Can't give first and last name
- Doesn't use plurals or past tense properly
- Doesn't talk about daily activities or experiences
- Doesn't draw pictures
- Can't brush teeth, wash and dry hands, or get undressed without help
- Loses skills he once had

Section 17.2

Observing Child's Development through Play

Text in this section is excerpted from "Go Out and Play! Kit," Centers for Disease Control and Prevention (CDC), February 12, 2015.

Activities for You and Your Child

Play isn't just healthy and fun. It's also how your child learns! Time spent playing can be a chance to observe your child's development—how he or she plays, learns, speaks, and acts. You can even look for milestones during playtime. Milestones are the things your child should be doing at different ages (see some examples in the box below). Keeping track of milestones is really important. It helps you to see if your child is developing typically for his or her age or if your child could be at risk for a developmental delay. Noticing a delay and getting help for your child as early as possible can help ensure that your child reaches his or her full potential. If you are concerned about your child's development, don't wait. Talk with your child's doctor about your concerns

Following are a few activities that you can do with your child to observe his or her development. Remember to have fun and "go out and play!"

People to People—This game is fun for kids learning body parts. Call out, or have your child call out, a body part in the following manner: "toes to toes," "arm to arm," "knee to knee," etc. Then stand in front of your child with the called body parts touching his or hers (your toes touching his or her toes, etc). Take turns being the caller.

Scavenger Hunt—A traditional scavenger hunt easily can be adapted according to your child's age. It also can be adapted for tracking different milestones.

- *Sort objects by shape and color:* Tell your child to collect something green, something blue, and something red. When he or she bring the objects to you, have him or her make piles of the items according to color. You also can substitute shapes for colors.

- *Understands concept of "2":* Tell your child to find two of one thing and two of another. While he or she is looking for the objects, start a pile for each object. When your child returns, have him or her place the objects in the correct pile.

- *Recognizes common objects or pictures*: Show children pictures of items to collect, but do not tell them what the item is. For example, hold up a picture of a flower and say, "Find one of these" instead of saying, "Find a flower."

- *Follows 2- to 3-step command*: Before the children begin their search, tell them what items to find and where to put the items once they've been found. When the children begin to return, do not repeat where they are supposed to place their items.

- *Cooperates with other children*: Pair the children or place them in small groups before sending them on their search. If you have pictures of the items they are looking for, give all the pictures to one child in each group and tell these children to give pictures to their team members.

People to People—This is a game for kids who are learning their body parts. Divide the children into pairs. Call out, or have a child call out, a body part in the following manner: "toes to toes," "arm to arm," "knee to knee," etc. Children then stand with their partner with these body parts touching. At any time, the caller can call out "people to people," when that happens, the children should all run together into a group. Divide the children into new teams, and start over.

Three Little Pigs—You can engage children's skills in imitation, pretend play, and storytelling with this role-playing game. Divide the class into roles from the story "The Three Little Pigs". Several children might need to perform the same role. While the teacher or another student tells the story, the children act it out, using areas designated by the teacher as the three houses (e.g., an area behind a bench could be the house of straw, behind a tree could be the house of sticks, and so on). Each time the wolf "blows down" the "house," all the little pigs run to the next house with the wolf chasing them. Each child caught by the wolf becomes another wolf. At the end of the story, the pigs can chase the wolves away.

Follow the Leader—This classic game builds on a child's ability to imitate and the development of the concepts of "same" and "different". Put a new spin on this familiar game by instructing the children to do something different than the child in front of them.

123

Crazy Ball—This game helps children demonstrate and develop skills such as direction following, imitating, turn taking, and being able to differentiate between concepts. Have the children form a line, leaving a few feet between each child. Using one playground-sized ball, have each child do something silly with the ball while passing it down the line. You can change the direction to alter whether the child with the ball does the same thing or something different than the child before him or her.

Duck, Duck, Goose—In this classic childhood game, you can build on a child's ability to follow directions, awareness of being a boy or girl, and ability to take turns. Making slight changes to this old favorite can help you keep an eye out for some specific milestones. Tell the children that "it" can pick another child of the same (or opposite) sex only. Instead of running, instruct the children to hop, skip, or march when chasing the "goose". Have the children make up and agree to some new facet of the game.

Playground Equipment—The playground provides many opportunities to see children engaging in imitating, taking turns, engaging in fantasy play, wanting to please and be like friends, and cooperating with friends.

A great time to encourage children to use their imagination is when they are playing on playground equipment. Children on swings can fly to the moon, children on slides can sled down a hill, and children on a jungle gym can be monkeys in trees. Pull out your milestones lists, put on your thinking cap, and give children some hints that will start games that allow you to see if they are meeting their milestones.

Hide and Seek—This is a favorite game of many children. It is a great game that demonstrates a child's ability to understand placement in space, follow directions, and cooperate with others. Hide and Seek is a wonderful way to observe how children change their manner of play over time. Younger children often hide in obvious places? Sometimes in plain view? and often hide in the same place a friend was just hiding. They also tend to give away their hiding place by saying things like, "You can't find me" or giggling while they are being looked for. As children get older, their hiding skills become more advanced, and they begin to develop strategies to reach home base without being caught.

You can track milestones by adding a little more structure to the game. For example, tell children to hide under or behind something, or have the seeker call out where they see their friends (e.g., "Joe is behind the tree."). Place children in pairs or small groups and have them decide where the group will hide before the counting begins.

Have the children choose and pretend to be characters who might look for each other (e.g., a knight searching for dragons or a mother duck looking for her ducklings).

Animal Tag—A few changes can turn this traditional game of tag into an easy way to monitor milestones. During this game, children will show their ability to follow directions and recognize common objects or pictures, and their awareness of which sex they are.

Separate the children into small teams. Assign a different animal to each small team and instruct the children to act and make sounds like the animal throughout the game. When a child is tagged, they are "frozen" (must stand completely still). Only another child of the same "species" can unfreeze a frozen child. Children can identify their teammates by the noises they are making.

Check on object or picture recognition by giving each child a picture of an animal instead of telling the child what animal to be. Tag also can be altered to include identifying which sex a child is by allowing only a child of the same (or opposite) sex to be the "unfreezer" (e.g., only boys can unfreeze girls, or only boys can unfreeze other boys, depending on how you establish the rules).

Dance Party—Grab a music player and head outside for a dance party! Dance Party will showcase your child's ability to imitate and cooperate with others and dress themselves. This game also gets your child to participate in fantasy role playing, singing, dancing, and acting.

Play music and dance with your child. Take turns imitating each other's dance moves. Watch your child imitate dance moves and cooperate by taking turns with you. If possible, have your child "dress up" before going outside, but make sure that the costume is safe for moving around (e.g., clothes do not drag the ground and shoes fit properly and are safe for outside play). This game is also great for a group of children. Have each child take turn being the leader while the other children imitate his or her movements.

Section 17.3

Recommendations for Routine Health Care Developmental Screening

Text in this section is excerpted from "Recommendations and Guidelines," Centers for Disease Control and Prevention (CDC), February 26, 2015.

Developmental Surveillance and Screening

Early identification of developmental disorders is critical to the well-being of children and their families. It is an integral function of the primary-care medical home and an appropriate responsibility of all pediatric health care professionals.

AAP recommends that developmental surveillance be incorporated at every well-child preventive care visit. Any concerns raised during surveillance should be addressed promptly with standardized developmental screening tests. In addition, screening tests should be administered regularly at the 9-, 18-, and 24- or 30-month visits.

The early identification of developmental problems should lead to further developmental and medical evaluation, diagnosis, and treatment, including early developmental intervention. Children diagnosed with developmental disorders should be identified as children with special health care needs, and chronic-condition management should be initiated. Identification of a developmental disorder and its underlying etiology may also drive a range of treatment planning, from medical treatment of the child to genetic counseling for his or her parents.

Developmental Surveillance and Screening for Autism Spectrum Disorder

American Academy of Neurology and the Child Neurology Society Clinical Practice Recommendations:

1. Developmental surveillance should be performed at all well-child visits from infancy through school age, and at any age

thereafter if concerns are raised about social acceptance, learning, or behavior.

2. Recommended developmental screening tools include the Ages and Stages Questionnaire, the BRIGANCE® Screens, the Child Development Inventories, and the Parents' Evaluations of Developmental Status.

3. Because of the lack of sensitivity and specificity, the Denver-II (DDST-II) and the Revised Denver Pre-Screening Developmental Questionnaire (R-DPDQ) are not recommended for appropriate primary-care developmental surveillance.

4. Further developmental evaluation is required whenever a child fails to meet any of the following milestones: babbling by 12 months; gesturing (e.g., pointing, waving bye-bye) by 12 months; single words by 16 months; two-word spontaneous (not just echolalic) phrases by 24 months; loss of any language or social skills at any age.

5. Siblings of children with autism should be monitored carefully for acquisition of social, communication, and play skills, and the occurrence of maladaptive behaviors. Screening should be performed not only for autism-related symptoms but also for language delays, learning difficulties, social problems, and anxiety or depressive symptoms.

6. For all children failing routine developmental surveillance procedures, screening specifically for autism should be performed using one of the validated instruments.

7. Laboratory investigations, including audiologic assessment and lead screening, are recommended for any child with developmental delay and/or autism. Early referral for a formal audiologic assessment should include behavioral audiometric measures, assessment of middle ear function, and electrophysiologic procedures using experienced pediatric audiologists with current audiologic testing methods and technologies. Lead screening should be performed in any child with developmental delay and pica. Additional periodic screening should be considered if the pica persists.

Diagnosis and Evaluation for Autism Spectrum Disorder

American Academy of Neurology and the Child Neurology Society Clinical Practice Recommendations:

1. Genetic testing in children with autism, specifically high-res-
    olution chromosome studies (karyotype) and DNA analysis for
    Fragile X, should be performed in the presence of intellectual
    disability (or if intellectual disability cannot be excluded), if
    there is a family history of Fragile X or undiagnosed intellec-
    tual disability, or if dysmorphic features are present. However,
    there is little likelihood of positive karyotype or Fragile X test-
    ing in the presence of high-functioning autism.

2. Selective metabolic testing should be initiated by the presence
    of suggestive clinical and physical findings such as the follow-
    ing: evidence of lethargy, cyclic vomiting, or early seizures;
    presence of dysmorphic or coarse features; evidence of intel-
    lectual disability cannot be ruled out; or if occurrence or ade-
    quacy of newborn screening is questionable.

3. There is inadequate evidence to recommend an electroenceph-
    alogram study in all individuals with autism. Indications for
    an adequate sleep-deprived electroencephalogram with appro-
    priate sampling of slow wave sleep include clinical seizures
    or suspicion of subclinical seizures and a history of regression
    (clinically significant loss of social and communicative func-
    tion) at any age, but especially in toddlers and preschoolers.

4. Recording of event-related potentials and magnetoencephalog-
    raphy are research tools at the present time, without evidence
    of routine clinical utility.

5. There is no clinical evidence to support the role of routine clin-
    ical neuroimaging in the diagnostic evaluation of autism, even
    in the presence of megalencephaly.

6. There is inadequate supporting evidence for hair analysis,
    celiac antibodies, allergy testing (particularly food allergies
    for gluten, casein, Candida, and other molds), immunologic or
    neurochemical abnormalities, micronutrients such as vitamin
    levels, intestinal permeability studies, stool analysis, urinary
    peptides, mitochondrial disorders (including lactate and pyru-
    vate), thyroid function tests, or erythrocyte glutathione peroxi-
    dase studies.

Section 17.4

Screening Tools for Early Identification of Children with ASD

Text in this section is excerpted from "Screening and Diagnosis for Healthcare Providers," Centers for Disease Control and Prevention (CDC), July 13, 2015.

Developmental screening can be done by a number of professionals in health care, community, and school settings. However, primary health care providers are in a unique position to promote children's developmental health.

Primary care providers have regular contact with children before they reach school age and are able to provide family-centered, comprehensive, coordinated care, including a more complete medical assessment when a screening indicates a child is at risk for a developmental problem.

Screening Recommendations

Research has found that ASD can sometimes be detected at 18 months or younger. By age 2, a diagnosis by an experienced professional can be considered very reliable. However, many children do not receive a final diagnosis until they are much older. This delay means that children with an ASD might not get the help they need. The earlier an ASD is diagnosed, the sooner treatment services can begin.

The American Academy of Pediatrics (AAP) recommends that all children be screened for developmental delays and disabilities during regular well-child doctor visits at:

- 9 months

- 18 months

- 24 or 30 months

Additional screening might be needed if a child is at high risk for developmental problems because of preterm birth or low birth weight.

In addition, all children should be screened specifically for ASD during regular well-child doctor visits at:

- 18 months

- 24 months

Additional screening might be needed if a child is at high risk for ASD (e.g., having a sibling with an ASD) or if symptoms are present.

It is important for doctors to screen all children for developmental delays, but especially to monitor those who are at a higher risk for developmental problems due to preterm birth, low birth weight, or having a sibling or parent with an ASD.

Developmental Screening in Pediatric and Primary Care Practice

Integrating routine developmental screening into the practice setting can seem daunting. Following are suggestions for integrating screening services into primary care efficiently and at low cost, while ensuring thorough coordination of care.

Involving Families in Screening

Research indicates that parents are reliable sources of information about their children's development. Evidence-based screening tools that incorporate parent reports (e.g., Ages and Stages Questionnaire, the Parents' Evaluation of Developmental Status, and Child Development Inventories) can facilitate structured communication between parents and providers to discover parent concerns, increase parent and provider observations of the child's development, and increase parent awareness. Such tools can also be time- and cost-efficient in clinical practice settings. A 1998 analysis found that, depending on the instrument, the time for administering a screening tool ranged from about 2 to 15 minutes, and the cost of materials and administration (using an average salary of $50/hour) ranged from $1.19 to $4.60 per visit.

Screening children and providing parents with anticipatory guidance? that is, educating families about what to expect in their child's development, how they can promote development, and the benefits of monitoring development? can also improve the relationship between the provider and parent. By establishing relationship-based practices, providers promote positive parent-child relationships, while building the strongest possible relationship between the parent and provider. Such practices are fundamental to quality services.

Developmental Screening Tools

Screening tools are designed to help identify children who might have developmental delays. Screening tools can be specific to a disorder (for example, autism) or an area (for example, cognitive development, language, or gross motor skills), or they may be general, encompassing multiple areas of concern. Some screening tools are used primarily in pediatric practices, while others are used by school systems or in other community settings.

Screening tools do not provide conclusive evidence of developmental delays and do not result in diagnoses. A positive screening result should be followed by a thorough assessment. Screening tools do not provide in-depth information about an area of development.

Selecting a Screening Tool

When selecting a developmental screening tool, take the following into consideration:

- Domain(s) the Screening Tool Covers

  - What are the questions that need to be answered?

  - What types of delays or conditions do you want to detect?

- Psychometric Properties

  These affect the overall ability of the test to do what it is meant to do.

- The sensitivity of a screening tool is the probability that it will correctly identify children who exhibit developmental delays or disorders.

- The specificity of a screening tool is the probability that it will correctly identify children who are developing normally.

- Characteristics of the Child

  For example, age and presence of risk factors.

- Setting in which the Screening Tool will be Administered

Will the tool be used in a physician's office, daycare setting, or community setting? Screening can be performed by professionals, such as nurses or teachers, or by trained paraprofessionals.

Types of Screening Tools

There are many different developmental screening tools. CDC does not approve or endorse any specific tools for screening purposes. This list is not exhaustive, and other tests may be available.

Selected examples of screening tools for general development and ASD:

Ages and Stages Questionnaires (ASQ)

This is a general developmental screening tool. Parent-completed questionnaire; series of 19 age-specific questionnaires screening communication, gross motor, fine motor, problem-solving, and personal adaptive skills; results in a pass/fail score for domains.

Communication and Symbolic Behavior Scales (CSBS)

Standardized tool for screening of communication and symbolic abilities up to the 24-month level; the Infant Toddler Checklist is a 1-page, parent-completed screening tool.

Parents' Evaluation of Developmental Status (PEDS)

This is a general developmental screening tool. Parent-interview form; screens for developmental and behavioral problems needing further evaluation; single response form used for all ages; may be useful as a surveillance tool.

Modified Checklist for Autism in Toddlers (MCHAT)

Parent-completed questionnaire designed to identify children at risk for autism in the general population.

Screening Tool for Autism in Toddlers and Young Children (STAT)

This is an interactive screening tool designed for children when developmental concerns are suspected. It consists of 12 activities assessing play, communication, and imitation skills and takes 20 minutes to administer.

Diagnostic Tools

There are many tools to assess ASD in young children, but no single tool should be used as the basis for diagnosis. Diagnostic tools usually rely on two main sources of information—parents' or caregivers' descriptions of their child's development and a professional's observation of the child's behavior.

In some cases, the primary care provider might choose to refer the child and family to a specialist for further assessment and diagnosis.

Such specialists include neurodevelopmental pediatricians, developmental-behavioral pediatricians, child neurologists, geneticists, and early intervention programs that provide assessment services.

Selected examples of diagnostic tools:

Autism Diagnosis Interview – Revised (ADI-R)

A clinical diagnostic instrument for assessing autism in children and adults. The instrument focuses on behavior in three main areas: reciprocal social interaction; communication and language; and restricted and repetitive, stereotyped interests and behaviors. The ADI-R is appropriate for children and adults with mental ages about 18 months and above.

Autism Diagnostic Observation Schedule – Generic (ADOS-G)

A semi-structured, standardized assessment of social interaction, communication, play, and imaginative use of materials for individuals suspected of having ASD. The observational schedule consists of four 30-minute modules, each designed to be administered to different individuals according to their level of expressive language.

Childhood Autism Rating Scale (CARS)

Brief assessment suitable for use with any child over 2 years of age. CARS includes items drawn from five prominent systems for diagnosing autism; each item covers a particular characteristic, ability, or behavior.

Gilliam Autism Rating Scale – Second Edition (GARS-2)

Assists teachers, parents, and clinicians in identifying and diagnosing autism in individuals ages 3 through 22. It also helps estimate the severity of the child's disorder.

In addition to the tools above, the American Psychiatric Association's *Diagnostic and Statistical Manual, Fifth Edition* (DSM-5) provides standardized criteria to help diagnose ASD.

Myths about Developmental Screening

Myth 1: There are no adequate screening tools for preschoolers.

Fact: Although this may have been true decades ago, today sound screening measures exist. Many screening measures have sensitivities and specificities greater than 70%.

Myth 2: A great deal of training is needed to administer screening correctly.

Fact: Training requirements are not extensive for most screening tools. Many can be administered by paraprofessionals.

Myth 3: Screening takes a lot of time.

Fact: Many screening instruments take less than 15 minutes to administer, and some require only about 2 minutes of professional time.

Myth 4: Tools that incorporate information from the parents are not valid.

Fact: Parents' concerns are generally valid and are predictive of developmental delays. Research has shown that parental concerns detect 70% to 80% of children with disabilities.

Section 17.5

Audiological Screening

Text in this section is excerpted from "Hearing Loss in Children," Centers for Disease Control and Prevention (CDC), October 23, 2015.

What is Hearing Loss?

A hearing loss can happen when any part of the ear is not working in the usual way. This includes the outer ear, middle ear, inner ear, hearing (acoustic) nerve, and auditory system.

Signs and Symptoms

The signs and symptoms of hearing loss are different for each child. If you think that your child might have hearing loss, ask the child's doctor for a hearing screening as soon as possible. Don't wait!

Even if a child has passed a hearing screening before, it is important to look out for the following signs.

Signs in Babies

- Does not startle at loud noises.

- Does not turn to the source of a sound after 6 months of age.

- Does not say single words, such as "dada" or "mama" by 1 year of age.

- Turns head when he or she sees you but not if you only call out his or her name. This sometimes is mistaken for not paying attention or just ignoring, but could be the result of a partial or complete hearing loss.

- Seems to hear some sounds but not others.

Signs in Children

- Speech is delayed.

- Speech is not clear.

- Does not follow directions. This sometimes is mistaken for not paying attention or just ignoring, but could be the result of a partial or complete hearing loss.

- Often says, "Huh?"

- Turns the TV volume up too high.

Babies and children should reach milestones in how they play, learn, communicate and act. A delay in any of these milestones could be a sign of hearing loss or other developmental problem. Visit our web page to see milestones that children should reach from 2 months to 5 years of age.

Screening and Diagnosis

Hearing screening can tell if a child might have hearing loss. Hearing screening is easy and is not painful. In fact, babies are often asleep while being screened. It takes a very short time—usually only a few minutes.

Babies

All babies should have a hearing screening no later than 1 month of age. Most babies have their hearing screened while still in the hospital. If a baby does not pass a hearing screening, it's very important to get a full hearing test as soon as possible, but no later than 3 months of age.

Children

Children should have their hearing tested before they enter school or any time there is a concern about the child's hearing. Children who do not pass the hearing screening need to get a full hearing test as soon as possible.

Treatments and Intervention Services

No single treatment or intervention is the answer for every person or family. Good treatment plans will include close monitoring, follow-ups and any changes needed along the way. There are many different types of communication options for children with hearing loss and for their families. Some of these options include:

- Learning other ways to communicate, such as sign language

- Technology to help with communication, such as hearing aids and cochlear implants

- Medicine and surgery to correct some types of hearing loss

- Family support services

Causes and Risk Factors

Hearing loss can happen any time during life–from before birth to adulthood.

Following are some of the things that can increase the chance that a child will have hearing loss:

- A genetic cause: About 1 out of 2 cases of hearing loss in babies is due to genetic causes. Some babies with a genetic cause for their hearing loss might have family members who also have a hearing loss. About 1 out of 3 babies with genetic hearing loss have a "syndrome." This means they have other conditions in addition to the hearing loss, such as Down syndrome or Usher syndrome. Learn more about the genetics of hearing loss.

- 1 out of 4 cases of hearing loss in babies is due to maternal infections during pregnancy, complications after birth, and head trauma. For example, the child:

- Was exposed to infection, such as cytomegalovirus (CMV) infection, before birth

- Spent 5 days or more in a hospital neonatal intensive care unit (NICU) or had complications while in the NICU

- Needed a special procedure like a blood transfusion to treat bad jaundice

- Has head, face or ears shaped or formed in a different way than usual

- Has a condition like a neurological disorder that may be associated with hearing loss

- Had an infection around the brain and spinal cord called meningitis

- Received a bad injury to the head that required a hospital stay

- For about 1 out of 4 babies born with hearing loss, the cause is unknown.

Prevention

Following are tips for parents to help prevent hearing loss in their children:

- Have a healthy pregnancy.

- Learn how to prevent cytomegalovirus (CMV) infection during pregnancy.

- Make sure your child gets all the regular childhood vaccines.

- Keep your child away from high noise levels, such as from very loud toys. Visit the National Institutes of Health's website to learn more about preventing noise-induced hearing loss.

Get Help!

- If you think that your child might have hearing loss, ask the child's doctor for a **hearing screening** as soon as possible. Don't wait!

- If your child does not pass a hearing screening, ask the child's doctor for a **full hearing test** as soon as possible.

- If your child has hearing loss, talk to the child's doctor about **treatment and intervention services**.

Hearing loss can affect a child's ability to develop speech, language, and social skills. The earlier children with hearing loss start getting services, the more likely they are to reach their full potential. If you are a parent and you suspect your child has hearing loss, trust your instincts and speak with your child's doctor.

Chapter 18

Getting Help for Developmental Delay

Chapter Contents

Section 18.1

If You Are Concerned, Act Early

This section includes excerpts from "If You're Concerned," Centers for Disease Control and Prevention (CDC), February 18, 2015; text from "What to Say," Centers for Disease Control and Prevention (CDC), March 27, 2014; and text from "While You Wait," Centers for Disease Control and Prevention (CDC), October 9, 2014.

Talk to Your Child's Doctor

As a parent, you know your child best. If your child is not meeting the milestones for his or her age, or if you think there could be a problem with the way your child plays, learns, speaks, acts, and moves talk to your child's doctor and share your concerns. Don't wait.

Milestones Checklist

Use the milestone checklist to track your child's development. These checklists are not a substitute for standardized, validated developmental screening tools.

Ask about Developmental Screening

The American Academy of Pediatrics recommends that children be screened for general development using standardized, validated tools at 9, 18, and 24 or 30 months and for autism at 18 and 24 months or whenever a parent or provider has a concern. Ask your child's doctor about your child's developmental screening.

Ask for a Referral

If you or the doctor thinks there might be a delay, ask the doctor for a referral to a specialist who can do a more in-depth evaluation of your child.

Doctors your child might be referred to include:

- Developmental pediatricians. These doctors have special training in child development and children with special needs.

- Child neurologists. These doctors work on the brain, spine, and nerves.

- Child psychologists or psychiatrists. These doctors know about the human mind.

Get an Evaluation

At the same time as you ask the doctor for a referral to a specialist, call your state's public early childhood system to request a free evaluation to find out if your child qualifies for intervention services. This is sometimes called a Child Find evaluation. You do not need to wait for a doctor's referral or a medical diagnosis to make this call.

Where to call for a free evaluation from the state depends on your child's age:

Children 0–3 Years Old

If your child is younger than 3 years old, contact your local early intervention system.

Children 3 Years Old or Older

If your child is 3 years old or older, contact your local public school system.

Even if your child is not old enough for kindergarten or enrolled in a public school, call your local elementary school or board of education and ask to speak with someone who can help you have your child evaluated.

Tips and Tools

What to Say

The following tips will help you talk with your child's doctor's office and the evaluation centers.

Doctor's Office

When you call your child's doctor's office, say, "I would like to make an appointment to see the doctor because I am concerned about my child's development."

Be ready to share your specific concerns about your child when you call. If you wrote down notes about your concerns, keep them. Your notes will be helpful during your visit with the doctor.

National Dissemination Center for Children with Disabilities

When you call the National Dissemination Center for Children with Disabilities, say, "My child is (child's age) and I live in (state). I am concerned about my child's development and would like to request a developmental evaluation. Can you tell me who to call and give me the phone number?"

- Write down all the information you are given and keep it; you might need it another time

Early Intervention Services Office

When you call your state's early intervention services office (if your child is not yet 3 years old), say, "I am concerned about my child's development and would like to request an evaluation. Can you help me or let me speak with someone who can?"

- Be ready to share your specific concerns about your child. You will also be asked for some general information about yourself and your child (your name, your child's name and age, where you live, and more).

- Write down who you speak to, the date, and what was said; you might need this information later.

Elementary School or Board of Education

When you call your local elementary school or board of education (if your child is 3 or older), say, "I am concerned about my child's development and would like to talk with someone about having my child evaluated. Can you help me or let me speak with someone who can?"

- Be ready to share your specific concerns about your child. You will also be asked for some general information about yourself and your child (your name, your child's name and age, where you live, and more).

- Write down who you speak to, the date, and what was said; you might need this information later.

While You Wait

Unfortunately, families may have to wait many weeks or sometimes months before they are able to get an appointment to see a specialist or start intervention services for their child's developmental problem. This can be a frustrating time for parents who want answers and help now.

If you find yourself in this situation, know that there are some simple things you can do today and everyday to help your child's development.

Make the Most of Playtime

Interact with your child as much as possible. Read books, sing songs, play with toys, make crafts, do household chores, and play outside together. Talk to your child: label items, point out interesting things, tell stories, comment about what you see and how you feel, and explain how things work and why things happen. Your child may not always seem to be listening, but he or she may be hearing more than you think.

Section 18.2

Sharing Concerns with Your Child's Physician

Text in this section is excerpted from "Concerned about Development? How to Talk with the Doctor," Centers for Disease Control and Prevention (CDC), October 5, 2014.

A first step toward getting help for your child when you are concerned about his or her development (how your child plays, learns, speaks, acts and moves) is to talk with your child's doctor.

1. Prepare for your visit.

- When you make the appointment, tell the doctor's staff you have concerns about your child's development that you want to discuss.

- Write down your questions, concerns, and some examples; take these to the appointment.

- Fill out a milestones checklist for your child's age from www. cdc.gov/milestones and take it with you to share with the doctor.

- Have other adults who know your child well fill out a milestone checklist, too.

- If you can, take another adult with you to play with your child so you can better focus on what the doctor says.

2. **Ask all of your questions during the visit; you know your child best and your concerns are important!**

- Tell the doctor you have concerns at the start of the visit and share the milestones checklist and any questions you might have written down.

- If the doctor seems to be in a hurry, ask if you should schedule another visit.

- Ask about your child's most recent developmental screening results.

- If a screening has not been done, ask for one.

- Take notes to help you remember what the doctor says and what to do next

3. **Make sure you understand what the doctor says and what to do next.**

- Before you leave, make sure all of your questions have been answered.

- If you do not understand something, ask the doctor to explain it again or in a different way.

- Review your notes and ask the doctor, nurse or office staff for any information you will need to do what the doctor has told you. For example, "What is the phone number for my local early intervention program?"

- When you get home, review your notes and call the doctor's office if you have any questions.

- Take the steps the doctor has told you and remember to follow up with the doctor about how it went.

Chapter 19

ASD Assessment

Children who have been diagnosed with an autism spectrum disorder (ASD) typically undergo a series of assessments to help parents and educators gain a better understanding of the children's abilities and deficits. Autism specialists analyze the results of various assessments and use the information to organize interventions, services, and resources to maximize the children's growth and development. The assessment process can be complicated, time consuming, stressful, and often disheartening for parents since the results tend to focus on the children's disabilities. Yet such evaluations are critical to understanding the social and communication challenges children with ASDs must overcome in order to reach their potential.

It is important to keep in mind that each type of assessment has different strengths and weaknesses, which has implications for accurately interpreting and applying the results. Parents should make an effort to understand the purpose and goals of the various types of ASD assessments so that they can use the results proactively to benefit their children. A thorough knowledge of the assessment process enables parents to glean relevant and useful information to help them serve as effective advocates for their children.

What Is Assessment?

Assessment is a comprehensive process that involves various methods of gathering information about a child's skills, abilities, challenges, and deficits across multiple functional areas. This information is typically used by autism specialists to determine the type of treatment and services that would most benefit the child. There are many different types of assessment tools, instruments, and methods available to measure different aspects of a child's level of functioning, performance, and progress toward meeting developmental goals. The results of the various assessments can help parents, teachers, and medical professionals determine the following in relation to a child with an ASD:

- The accuracy of an initial diagnosis;

- Strengths, deficits, and levels of functioning across skill areas;

- Performance as compared to other children of a similar age;

- Performance in relation to goals, standards, or desired outcomes;

- Needs or problem areas in terms of development;

- Measures of progress at home or at school;

- Effectiveness of intervention, instruction, or behavior support strategies;

- Objectives to include in the Individualized Education Program (IEP), a written document that outlines the special education services provided by a school district under the Individuals with Disabilities Education Act of 2004 (IDEA);

- Eligibility for other services.

Ideally, the assessments should be conducted by a team of professionals from various disciplines working in collaboration in order to provide a full evaluation of the child. This team may include psychologists, neurologists, speech-language pathologists, occupational and physical therapists, and behavior analysts. To ensure accurate results, the individuals performing the assessments should have expertise and experience evaluating children with ASDs. Parents can locate qualified professionals through searchable databases on autism-related websites or through recommendations from parents of children with ASDs.

Purpose of Assessment

The main purpose of ASD assessment is gathering detailed information about a child's abilities and deficits in order to tailor goals and interventions to his or her individual needs. The initial diagnostic assessment is the most comprehensive, and it is used to diagnose an ASD and provide a baseline that can be refined through further testing. In order to receive a diagnosis of ASD, the child must meet the criteria established by the American Psychiatric Association (APA) in its *Diagnostic and Statistical Manual of Mental Disorders* (DSM).

Following the formal diagnosis, different types of assessments are used to evaluate a child's level of functioning in specific areas, such as speech and language abilities, social skills, independent living skills, and emotional well-being. It is important to note than any assessment provides a snapshot of a child's strengths and challenges at a specific point in time. As the child develops, additional assessments should be used to re-evaluate skills and abilities and track progress toward meeting objectives. The results of these assessments can then be used to review and revise goals and design new treatments and interventions.

Re-evaluation assessments are typically conducted every three years under the IEP review process to enable school districts to target special education programming to a child's needs. Such assessments can occur more frequently, however, at the request of parents or on the recommendation of medical professionals, teachers, or the IEP team. Re-evaluation assessments are often conducted to answer emerging questions about a child's skills in a specific area of functioning, such as reading comprehension or ability to ride a bus independently.

Types of Assessments

Initial Diagnostic Assessment

When a child shows signs of having an ASD, the first step in the assessment process is getting a referral for a formal diagnostic assessment. The diagnostic assessment involves a variety of methods of gathering information and measuring abilities, and it can be a long and complex process for families. Parents may be asked to provide a complete developmental history of their child, including social skills, communication skills, and behavioral development. They may also be asked to bring medical records and questionnaires completed by the child's pediatrician, teachers, and caregivers.

The next part of the diagnostic assessment is likely to involve extensive interviews with a psychologist for both the parents and the child. The psychologist may also observe the child as he or she performs everyday tasks in several settings, such as the home, the classroom, or the playground. The diagnostic assessment may also include a standardized test, such as the Autism Diagnostic Observation Schedule (ADOS) or the Autism Diagnostic Interview-Revised (ADI-R).

The following additional assessments may be conducted as part of the initial diagnostic assessment or later as part of an effort to evaluate a specific skill set:

Cognitive

A cognitive assessment evaluates the child's strengths and difficulties in such areas as problem solving, memory, attention, and concentration. Many children with ASDs have deficits in these areas, which are important to identify and address in educational planning.

Speech and Language

Deficits in verbal and nonverbal communication are central to the diagnosis of ASD. A speech and language assessment evaluates the child's communication skills, including his or her abilities to use and understand language as well as communicate with gestures and symbols. The results of the speech and language assessment are used to develop interventions to increase the child's ability to communicate.

Adaptive Behavior

An adaptive behavior assessment examines skills related to daily living and independent functioning, such as eating, dressing, using the toilet, and riding a bus. Although the skills will vary depending on the age of the child, the assessment provides information about the level of supervision the child requires at home and at school, as well as areas of deficit that should be targeted for improvement.

Functional Behavior

This type of assessment attempts to determine the purpose of challenging or unwanted behavior in order to develop interventions to decrease its occurrence and replace it with appropriate behavior. A trained behavior specialist conducts the assessment by observing the child in various settings over time and recording information about the circumstances that lead to the unwanted behavior and the results the child gets from the behavior.

Occupational or Physical Therapy

This type of assessment is designed to identify deficits in motor skills, visual perception, and sensory modulation that may limit the child's ability to function independently. The results are used to design interventions to improve physical strength, hand-eye coordination, and other skills needed in daily life.

Social-Emotional

Since children with ASDs may experience depression, bipolar disorder, or anxiety disorder, social-emotional assessments look for symptoms of mood disorders and measure emotional well-being. The results of these assessments are useful in developing behavior support plans.

The Assessment Process

Sometimes parents seek ASD assessments due to concerns about their child not reaching age-appropriate social or developmental milestones. In other cases, the process begins after a pediatrician raises questions about a child's development and provides a referral for an ASD assessment. Teachers or schools may also suggest that a child be evaluated for an ASD based on his or her behavior or educational progress. Whatever the source of the referral, parents should make sure they understand why the assessment is being recommended and what information it is intended to provide.

Although the process varies depending on the type of assessment being conducted, most assessments include interviews, a review of school and medical records, a developmental history, the completion of behavior checklists, and standardized measures of adaptive behavior, social functioning, or emotional status. Many assessments also involve a period of observation by the professional as the child completes tasks. Some assessments may take a few hours, while others may last several days.

At the end of the assessment, the professional will interpret the results of the testing and offer a diagnosis. Parents are encouraged to ask questions if there is anything they do not understand. Finally, the professional will provide a written report of the results and observations, along with treatment recommendations. After receiving the written report, parents should schedule a meeting with the evaluation team to discuss the recommendations and clarify the next steps in the process. Parental input is important in establishing behavioral and educational goals for the child and determining what interventions and support services are needed to reach them.

References

1. "Life Journey through Autism: A Parent's Guide to Assessment." Organization for Autism Research, 2008.

2. "A Parent's Guide to Psychological Assessments for ASD." Vanderbilt Kennedy Center, 2013.

Chapter 20

Genetic Test for Autism

Genetic Testing for Developmental Disabilities

Genetic abnormalities have been linked to many DDs. Studies suggest that up to 40 percent of DDs may be caused by some genetic aberration. Conventional G-banded karyotyping has been used for decades to confirm the diagnosis of DDs (e.g., aneuploidies) that have a well-defined genetic etiology. More recently, new genetic methods (e.g., microarray-based comparative genomic hybridization [aCGH], whole genome or exome sequencing) have been developed and used to detect genetic abnormalities associated with DDs. These newer tests support the examination of genetic information at a higher resolution and may show genetic abnormalities not seen on G-banded karyotyping. In Appendix B, we provide a detailed technical overview to help illustrate how these genetic testing methods work and the main differences between them.

As previously discussed, clinical diagnosis of ID, ASD, or GDD is typically based on clinical manifestations and cognitive and developmental assessment using standardized measures. ID, ASD, and GDD are "functional diagnoses," which are phenotype-oriented descriptions of DDs. Each of these functional diagnoses includes multiple disorders of different etiologies (e.g., Angelman syndrome, fragile X syndrome, Prader-Willi syndrome, Rett syndrome, Rubinstein-Taybi syndrome,

Text in this chapter is excerpted from "Genetic Testing for Developmental Disabilities, Intellectual Disability, and Autism Spectrum Disorder," Agency for Healthcare Research and Quality (AHRQ), June 2015.

Smith-Magenis syndrome, velocardiofacial syndrome, and Williams syndrome). When genetic tests are used to assess patients diagnosed with ID, ASD, or GDD, they are not used to confirm these functional diagnoses. Instead, these tests are used to establish an "etiologic diagnosis," that is, whether a patient who has an apparent functional diagnosis carries a specific genetic variant.

Etiologic diagnosis is a genotype-oriented description of genetic disorders and may be viewed as an early stage of defining a clinical disorder that has not yet been well understood or defined. A new etiologic diagnosis (i.e., the new genetic variant identified) can be further evaluated among individuals with the genotype in common to determine whether or not they share a common phenotype. If they share a common phenotype, a new genetic disorder may be defined and the genotype becomes part of the clinical definition of the disorder (e.g., fragile X syndrome).

Proposed benefits of establishing an etiologic diagnosis in patients with ID, ASD, or GDD include the following:

- Clarifying a genetic cause and improving the psychosocial outcomes (e.g., improved knowledge and sense of empowerment) for patients and their families

- Providing prognosis or expected clinical course

- Evaluating recurrence risks and helping families in reproductive decisionmaking

- Refining treatment options

- Avoiding unnecessary and redundant diagnostic tests

- Identifying associated medical risks to prevent morbidity

- Providing condition-specific family support

- Facilitating acquisition of needed services and improving access to research treatment protocols

Because of these potential benefits, genetic tests are being used at an increasingly rapid rate. Medical genetics groups now recommend chromosomal microarray analysis (CMA) as a firstline genetic test to identify genetic mutations in children with multiple anomalies not specific to well-delineated syndromes, nonsyndromic DD/ID, and ASD. Payers have seen a significant number of claims for genetic testing in children with suspected or proven DDs.

However, little evidence from controlled studies exists to directly link genetic testing to health outcomes. Published studies have reported superior diagnostic yields of newer genetic tests (e.g., aCGH) in identifying DD-related genetic abnormalities, and some have identified the impact of the tests on medical management (e.g., medical referrals, diagnostic imaging, further laboratory testing). However, these findings are not sufficient for drawing a conclusion that use of the tests will lead to improved health outcomes

The impact of increased use of genetic tests, such as CMA, on health care costs is unclear. Advanced genetic tests are generally more expensive to perform than conventional G-banded karyotyping or other clinical tests. Identification of genetic abnormalities on germline cells may also lead to genetic testing in patients' relatives, which further expands the pool of children for testing and magnifies the potential cost impact. Conversely, the potential increased diagnostic yield of advanced genetic tests may reduce the number of other clinical tests or services used to identify genetic causes of DDs. Besides the uncertain clinical utility and concerns about economic impact, ethical issues—such as how to deal with genetic abnormalities unrelated to DD that are detected in genome-wide CMA—also remain controversial.

Availability of Genetic Tests for Developmental Disabilities in the United States

Genetic tests become clinically available in the United States via one of two pathways. A genetic test may reach the market as a commercially distributed test kit approved or cleared by the U.S. Food and Drug Administration (FDA) or as a laboratory-developed test (LDT). Test kits cleared or approved by FDA include all reagents and instructions needed to complete the test procedure and interpret the results. These test kits can be used in multiple laboratories. LDTs are developed in laboratories using either FDA-regulated or self-developed analyte-specific reagents and are intended for performance solely in the test developer's laboratory.

The U.S. Centers for Medicare and Medicaid Services regulates laboratories that perform LDTs under the Clinical Laboratory Improvement Amendments of 1988 (CLIA). Under CLIA regulations, facilities that perform tests on "materials derived from the human body for the purpose of providing information for the diagnosis, prevention, or treatment of any disease or impairment of, or the assessment of the health of, human beings" must obtain a certificate from the CLIA program. The requirements for CLIA certification are based on the complexity of the tests. LDTs compose the majority of the genetic tests that have become available to clinical practice. Laboratories offering

LDTs must be licensed as high-complexity clinical laboratories under CLIA regulations. A technology assessment report suggested that genetic tests for diagnosing DDs are primarily available as LDTs.

Historically, FDA has exercised regulatory enforcement discretion over LDTs because they were relatively simple lab tests. As LDTs become more complex and proliferate in clinical use, the agency is taking steps to actively regulate LDTs. On October 3, 2014, FDA published two draft guidance documents regarding oversight of LDTs, titled "Framework for Regulatory Oversight of Laboratory Developed Tests (LDTs)" and "FDA Notification and Medical Device Reporting for Laboratory Developed Tests (LDTs)." Under the proposed regulatory framework, LDTs will fall into one of the three categories: LDTs subject to full enforcement discretion; LDTs subject to partial enforcement discretion; and LDTs subject to full FDA regulation. Once the proposed FDA guidance documents are finalized, it will become clearer how genetic tests for DDs will be regulated.

Chapter 21

Language in Children with ASD

Chapter Contents

Section 21.1

Specific Language Impairment

Text in this section is excerpted from "Specific Language
Impairment," National Institute on Deafness and Other
Communication Disorders (NIDCD), April 24, 2015.

What Is Specific Language Impairment?

Specific language impairment (SLI) is a language disorder that
delays the mastery of language skills in children who have no hearing
loss or other developmental delays. SLI is also called developmental
language disorder, language delay, or developmental dysphasia. It
is one of the most common childhood learning disabilities, affecting
approximately 7 to 8 percent of children in kindergarten. The impact
of SLI persists into adulthood.

What Causes Specific Language Impairment?

The cause of SLI is unknown, but recent discoveries suggest it has
a strong genetic link. Children with SLI are more likely than those
without SLI to have parents and siblings who also have had difficulties
and delays in speaking. In fact, 50 to 70 percent of children with SLI
have at least one other family member with the disorder.

What Are the Symptoms of Specific Language Impairment?

Children with SLI are often late to talk and may not produce any
words until they are 2 years old. At age 3, they may talk, but may not be
understood. As they grow older, children with SLI will struggle to learn
new words and make conversation. Having difficulty using verbs is a
hallmark of SLI. Typical errors that a 5-year-old child with SLI would
make include dropping the "s" from the end of present-tense verbs,
dropping past tense, and asking questions without the usual "be" or
"do" verbs. For example, instead of saying "She rides the horse," a child
with SLI will say, "She ride the horse." Instead of saying "He ate the

cookie," a child with SLI will say, "He eat the cookie." Instead of saying "Why does he like me?," a child with SLI will ask, "Why he like me?"

How Is Specific Language Impairment Diagnosed in Children?

The first person to suspect a child might have SLI is often a parent or preschool or school teacher. A number of speech-language professionals might be involved in the diagnosis, including a speech-language pathologist (a health professional trained to evaluate and treat children with speech or language problems).

Language skills are tested using assessment tools that evaluate how well the child constructs sentences and keeps words in their proper order, the number of words in his or her vocabulary, and the quality of his or her spoken language. There are a number of tests commercially available that can specifically diagnose SLI.

Some of the tests use interactions between the child and puppets and other toys to focus on specific rules of grammar, especially the misuse of verb tenses. These tests can be used with children between 3 and 8 years of age and are especially useful for identifying children with SLI once they enter school.

What Treatments Are Available for Specific Language Impairment?

Because SLI affects reading it also affects learning. If it is not treated early, it can affect a child's performance in school. Since the early signs of SLI are often present in children as young as 3 years old, the preschool years can be used to prepare them for kindergarten with special programs designed to enrich language development. This kind of classroom program might enlist normally developing children to act as role models for children with SLI and feature activities that encourage role-playing and sharing time, as well as hands-on lessons to explore new, interesting vocabulary. Some parents also might want their child to see a speech-language pathologist, who can assess their child's needs, engage him or her in structured activities, and recommend home materials for at-home enrichment.

What Kinds of Research Are Being Conducted?

The National Institute on Deafness and Other Communication Disorders (NIDCD) supports a wide variety of research to understand the genetic underpinnings of SLI, the nature of the language deficits that cause it, and better ways to diagnose and treat children with it.

Genetic Research: An NIDCD-supported investigator recently has identified a mutation in a gene on chromosome 6, called the KIAA0319 gene, that appears to play a key role in SLI. The mutation plays a supporting role in other learning disabilities, such as dyslexia, some cases of autism, and speech sound disorders (conditions in which speech sounds are either not produced or produced or used incorrectly). This finding lends support to the idea that difficulties in learning language may be coming from the same genes that influence difficulties with reading and understanding printed text. Other potentially influential genes also are being explored.

Bilingual Research: The standardized tests that speech-language pathologists use in schools to screen for language impairments are based on typical language development milestones in English. Because bilingual children are more likely to score in the at-risk range on these tests, it becomes difficult to distinguish between children who are struggling to learn a new language and children with true language impairments.

After studying a large group of Hispanic children who speak English as a second language, NIDCD-funded researchers have developed a dual language diagnostic test to identify bilingual children with language impairments. It's now being tested in a group of children 4 to 6 years old, and will eventually be expanded to children 7 to 9 years old. The same research team is also trying out an intervention program with a small group of bilingual first graders with SLI to find techniques and strategies to help them succeed academically.

Diagnostic Research: Children with SLI have significant communication problems, which are also characteristic of most children with autism spectrum disorders (ASD). Impairments in understanding and the onset of spoken language are common in both groups. No one knows yet if there are early developmental signs that could signal or predict language difficulties and might potentially allow for early identification and intervention with these children. The NIDCD is currently funding researchers looking for risk markers associated with SLI and ASD that could signal later problems in speech and communication. In a group of children 6 months to 1 year old who, because of family history, are at risk for SLI or ASD, the investigators are collecting data using behavioral, eye-tracking, and neurophysiological measures, as well as general measures of cognitive and brain development. They will then follow these children until they are 3 years old to see if there are indicators that are specific to SLI or ASD or that could predict the development of either disorder. Findings from this research could have a major influence in developing new approaches to early screening and diagnosis for SLI and ASD.

Section 21.2

Speech and Language Developmental Milestones

Text in this section is excerpted from "Speech and Language Developmental Milestones," National Institute on Deafness and Other Communication Disorders (NIDCD), April 30, 2014.

How Do Speech and Language Develop?

The first 3 years of life, when the brain is developing and maturing, is the most intensive period for acquiring speech and language skills. These skills develop best in a world that is rich with sounds, sights, and consistent exposure to the speech and language of others.

There appear to be critical periods for speech and language development in infants and young children when the brain is best able to absorb language. If these critical periods are allowed to pass without exposure to language, it will be more difficult to learn.

What Are the Milestones for Speech and Language Development?

The first signs of communication occur when an infant learns that a cry will bring food, comfort, and companionship. Newborns also begin to recognize important sounds in their environment, such as the voice of their mother or primary caretaker. As they grow, babies begin to sort out the speech sounds that compose the words of their language.

By 6 months of age, most babies recognize the basic sounds of their native language.

Children vary in their development of speech and language skills. However, they follow a natural progression or timetable for mastering the skills of language. A list of milestones for the normal development of speech and language skills in children from birth to 5 years of age are there. These milestones help doctors and other health professionals determine if a child is on track or if he or she may need extra help. Sometimes a delay may be caused by hearing loss, while other times it may be due to a speech or language disorder.

What Is the Difference between a Speech Disorder and a Language Disorder?

Children who have trouble understanding what others say (receptive language) or difficulty sharing their thoughts (expressive language) may have a language disorder. Specific language impairment (SLI) is a language disorder that delays the mastery of language skills. Some children with SLI may not begin to talk until their third or fourth year.

Children who have trouble producing speech sounds correctly or who hesitate or stutter when talking may have a speech disorder. Apraxia of speech is a speech disorder that makes it difficult to put sounds and syllables together in the correct order to form words.

What Should I Do If My Child's Speech or Language Appears to Be Delayed?

Talk to your child's doctor if you have any concerns. Your doctor may refer you to a speech-language pathologist, who is a health professional trained to evaluate and treat people with speech or language disorders. The speech-language pathologist will talk to you about your child's communication and general development. He or she will also use special spoken tests to evaluate your child.

A hearing test is often included in the evaluation because a hearing problem can affect speech and language development. Depending on the result of the evaluation, the speech-language pathologist may suggest activities you can do at home to stimulate your child's development. They might also recommend group or individual therapy or suggest further evaluation by an audiologist (a healthcare professional trained to identify and measure hearing loss), or a developmental psychologist (a healthcare professional with special expertise in the psychological development of infants and children).

What Research Is Being Conducted on Developmental Speech and Language Problems?

The National Institute on Deafness and Other Communication Disorders (NIDCD) sponsors a broad range of research to better understand the development of speech and language disorders, improve diagnostic capabilities, and fine-tune more effective treatments. Additional genetic studies are looking for matches between different genetic variations and specific speech deficits.

Researchers sponsored by the NIDCD have discovered one genetic variant, in particular, that is linked to specific language impairment (SLI), a disorder that delays children's use of words and slows their mastery of language skills throughout their school years. The finding is the first to tie the presence of a distinct genetic mutation to any kind of inherited language impairment. Further research is exploring the role this genetic variant may also play in dyslexia, autism, and speech-sound disorders.

A long-term study looking at how deafness impacts the brain is exploring how the brain "rewires" itself to accommodate deafness. So far, the research has shown that adults who are deaf react faster and more accurately than hearing adults when they observe objects in motion. This ongoing research continues to explore the concept of "brain plasticity"—the ways in which the brain is influenced by health conditions or life experiences—and how it can be used to develop learning strategies that encourage healthy language and speech development in early childhood.

A workshop convened by the NIDCD drew together a group of experts to explore issues related to a subgroup of children with autism spectrum disorders who do not have functional verbal language by the age of 5. Because these children are so different from one another, with no set of defining characteristics or patterns of cognitive strengths or weaknesses, development of standard assessment tests or effective treatments has been difficult. The workshop featured a series of presentations to familiarize participants with the challenges facing these children and helped them to identify a number of research gaps and opportunities that could be addressed in future research studies.

Chapter 22

Measuring Autistic Intelligence

People with autism spectrum disorders (ASD) were once widely thought to have below-average intellectual abilities. Doctors came to this conclusion based on their generally poor performance on the standard IQ tests used to measure intelligence. In recent years, however, research has shown that the common symptoms of ASD—including difficulties with social interaction, verbal and nonverbal communication, sensory processing, and motor skills—complicate the process of measuring the intelligence of people on the autism spectrum. As a result, their IQ scores do not necessarily reflect their true intellectual potential.

IQ tests like the Stanford-Binet and the Wechsler Scales are often used in psychological assessments to determine whether a person has a developmental disorder or learning disability. The administration of these tests can be problematic for people with ASD, however, because they might have trouble understanding and responding quickly to verbal questions asked by a stranger. They also might have sensory processing challenges that make it hard for them to tolerate a testing room with bright fluorescent lights, or behavioral issues that make it tough for them to sit still long enough to complete the test. IQ test results thus may not provide an accurate measure of their cognitive abilities.

Adaptive Functioning

Given the difficulties of measuring autistic intelligence using standard IQ tests, the American Psychiatric Association's Diagnostic and Statistical Manual of Mental Disorders recommends that assessments of intellectual ability also consider adaptive functioning. Adaptive functioning refers to the practical skills needed for daily living and personal independence, such as the ability to bathe, dress, take medicine, prepare food, cross the street safely, or ride a bus. IQ tests, on the other hand, focus on the sort of intelligence required in an academic setting, such as problem solving and abstract reasoning.

Although adaptive skills vary depending on a person's age and culture, they usually correspond with IQ scores, so that people with high IQ scores would also be expected to score highly in adaptive skills. In people with ASD, however, the opposite may be true. Research suggests that people with higher cognitive abilities and autism tend to have more problems with daily living tasks than expected for their age and IQ. In fact, their adaptive skills are more similar to those of people with mild to moderate intellectual disability.

Researchers are not sure why there appears to be a disconnect between IQ and adaptive skills in people with ASD. This situation can clearly be frustrating, however, for people with autism who have higher cognitive abilities yet struggle with seemingly easier adaptive skills. In fact, they may not function as well in school or work settings as people with intellectual disability but good adaptive skills. Assessing adaptive skills in addition to IQ can lead to interventions that improve functioning in these areas.

Increasing IQ Scores with ASD

Despite the difficulties in measuring autistic intelligence, studies have shown that the average IQ scores of people with ASD have increased dramatically over time. A 1999 study found that only 20 percent of people with ASD had scored in the normal range of intelligence during the previous three decades. In 2014, however, a new study found that nearly 50 percent of children with ASD had average or above average intelligence, and only about 30 percent had intellectual disability.

Researchers have put forth several possible explanations for the increase in IQ scores among people with ASD. Some believe the change reflects an expansion of ASD diagnosis to include people with milder forms of autism, such as Asperger's Syndrome. Others credit earlier diagnosis and treatment, along with the development of more effective interventions, with reducing developmental delays and improving cognitive and communication skills among children with ASD.

As researchers increase their understanding of ASD, they may develop new, more accurate methods of measuring intellectual ability. In the meantime, experts recommend using comprehensive assessments that measure adaptive skills, behavior, attention, and social-emotional functioning in addition to IQ in order to compile a complete picture of the abilities and challenges of people with ASD.

References

1. Sarris, Marina. "Measuring Intelligence in Autism." Interactive Autism Network, October 20, 2015.

2. Sicile-Kira, Chantal. "What IQ Tests Really Tell Us about Children with Autism." Psychology Today, March 2011.

Chapter 23

Moving Forward after A Child Is Diagnosed with ASD

Living With

After your child is diagnosed with autism spectrum disorder (ASD), you may feel unprepared or unable to provide your child with the necessary care and education. Know that there are many treatment options, social services and programs, and other resources that can help.

Some tips that can help you and your child are:

- Keep a record of conversations, meetings with health care providers and teachers, and other sources of information. This will help you remember the different treatment options and decide which would help your child most.

- Keep a record of the doctors' reports and your child's evaluation. This information may help your child qualify for special programs.

- Contact your local health department or autism advocacy groups to learn about the special programs available in your state and local community.

Text in this chapter is excerpted from "Autism Spectrum Disorder," National Institute of Mental Health (NIMH), October 27, 2011, Reviewed February 2016; and "Individualized Education Programs (IEPs)," © 1995–2016. The Nemours Foundation/KidsHealth®. Reprinted with permission.

- Talk with your child's pediatrician, school system, or an autism support group to find an autism expert in your area who can help you develop an intervention plan and find other local resources.

Understanding Teens with ASD

The teen years can be a time of stress and confusion for any growing child, including teenagers with autism spectrum disorder (ASD).

During the teenage years, adolescents become more aware of other people and their relationships with them. While most teenagers are concerned with acne, popularity, grades, and dates, teens with ASD may become painfully aware that they are different from their peers. For some, this awareness may encourage them to learn new behaviors and try to improve their social skills. For others, hurt feelings and problems connecting with others may lead to depression, anxiety, or other mental disorders. One way that some teens with ASD may express the tension and confusion that can occur during adolescence is through increased autistic or aggressive behavior. Teens with ASD will also need support to help them understand the physical changes and sexual maturation they experience during adolescence.

If your teen seems to have trouble coping, talk with his or her doctor about possible co-occurring mental disorders and what you can do. Behavioral therapies and medications often help.

Preparing for Your Child's Transition to Adulthood

The public schools' responsibility for providing services ends when a child with ASD reaches the age of 22. At that time, some families may struggle to find jobs to match their adult child's needs. If your family cannot continue caring for an adult child at home, you may need to look for other living arrangements. For more information, see the section, "Living Arrangements for Adults with ASD."

Long before your child finishes school, you should search for the best programs and facilities for young adults with ASD. If you know other parents of adults with ASD, ask them about the services available in your community. Local support and advocacy groups may be able to help you find programs and services that your child is eligible to receive as an adult.

Another important part of this transition is teaching youth with ASD to self-advocate. This means that they start to take on more responsibility for their education, employment, healthcare, and living arrangements. Adults with ASD or other disabilities must self-advocate for their rights under the Americans with Disabilities Act at work, in higher education, in the community, and elsewhere.

Living Arrangements for Adults with ASD

There are many options for adults living with ASD. Helping your adult child choose the right one will largely depend on what is available in your state and local community, as well as your child's skills and symptoms. Below are some examples of living arrangements you may want to consider:

- **Independent living**. Some adults with ASD are able to live on their own. Others can live in their own home or apartment if they get help dealing with major issues, such as managing personal finances, obtaining necessary health care, and interacting with government or social service agencies. Family members, professional agencies, or other types of providers can offer this assistance.

- **Living at home**. Government funds are available for families who choose to have their adult child with ASD live at home. These programs include Supplemental Security Income, Social Security Disability Insurance, and Medicaid waivers. Information about these programs and others is available from the Social Security Administration (SSA). Make an appointment with your local SSA office to find out which programs would be right for your adult child.

- **Other home alternatives**. Some families open their homes to provide long-term care to adults with disabilities who are not related to them. If the home teaches self-care and housekeeping skills and arranges leisure activities, it is called a "skill-development" home.

- **Supervised group living.** People with disabilities often live in group homes or apartments staffed by professionals who help with basic needs. These needs often include meal preparation, housekeeping, and personal care. People who are more independent may be able to live in a home or apartment where staff only visit a few times a week. Such residents generally prepare their own meals, go to work, and conduct other daily activities on their own.

- **Long-term care facilities**. This alternative is available for those with ASD who need intensive, constant supervision.

Educating Your Child

Parents have the right to choose where their kids will be educated. This choice includes public or private elementary schools and secondary schools, including religious schools. It also includes charter schools and home schools.

However, it is important to understand that the rights of children with disabilities who are placed by their parents in private elementary schools and secondary schools are not the same as those of kids with disabilities who are enrolled in public schools or placed by public agencies in private schools when the public school is unable to provide a free appropriate public education (FAPE).

Two major differences that parents, teachers, other school staff, private school representatives, and the kids need to know about are:

- Children with disabilities who are placed by their parents in private schools may not get the same services they would receive in a public school.

- Not all kids with disabilities placed by their parents in private schools will receive services.

You know your child best and should play a central role in creating a learning plan tailored to his or her specific needs.

Part Four

Conditions That May Accompany Autism Spectrum Disorders

Chapter 24

ASD and Communication Difficulties

Chapter Contents

Section 24.1

Communication Problems Associated with Autism

Text in this section is excerpted from "Communication
Problems in Children with Autism Spectrum Disorder,"
National Institute of Deafness and Other Communication
Disorders (NIDCD), July 13, 2015.

What Is Autism Spectrum Disorder?

Autism spectrum disorder (ASD) covers a set of developmental disabilities that can cause significant social, communication, and behavioral challenges. People with ASD process information in their brain differently than other people.

ASD affects people in different ways and can range from mild to severe. People with ASD share some symptoms, such as difficulties with social interaction, but there are differences in when the symptoms start, how severe they are, how many symptoms there are, and whether other problems are present.

The signs of ASD begin before the age of 3, although some children may show hints of future problems within the first year of life.

Who Is Affected by ASD?

ASD affects people of every race, ethnic group, and socioeconomic background, but it is five times more common among boys than among girls. The Centers for Disease Control and Prevention (CDC) estimates that about 1 out of every 88 children will be identified with ASD.

How Does ASD Affect Communication?

The word "autism" has its origin in the Greek word "autos," which means "self." Children with ASD often are self-absorbed and seem to exist in a private world where they are unable to successfully communicate and interact with others. Children with ASD may have difficulty developing language skills and understanding what others say to them.

They also may have difficulty communicating nonverbally, such as through hand gestures, eye contact, and facial expressions.

Not every child with ASD will have a language problem. A child's ability to communicate will vary, depending upon his or her intellectual and social development. Some children with ASD may be unable to speak. Others may have rich vocabularies and be able to talk about specific subjects in great detail. Most children with ASD have little or no problem pronouncing words. The majority, however, have difficulty using language effectively, especially when they talk to other people. Many have problems with the meaning and rhythm of words and sentences. They also may be unable to understand body language and the nuances of vocal tones.

Below are some patterns of language use and behaviors that are often found in children with ASD.

- **Repetitive or rigid language**. Often, children with ASD who can speak will say things that have no meaning or that seem out of context in conversations with others. For example, a child may count from one to five repeatedly. Or a child may repeat words he or she has heard over and over, a condition called echolalia. Immediate echolalia occurs when the child repeats words someone has just said. For example, the child may respond to a question by asking the same question. In delayed echolalia, the child will repeat words heard at an earlier time. The child may say "Do you want something to drink?" whenever he or she asks for a drink. Some children with ASD speak in a high-pitched or singsong voice or use robot-like speech. Other children may use stock phrases to start a conversation. For example, a child may say "My name is Tom," even when he talks with friends or family. Still others may repeat what they hear on television programs or commercials.

- **Narrow interests and exceptional abilities**. Some children may be able to deliver an in-depth monologue about a topic that holds their interest, even though they may not be able to carry on a two-way conversation about the same topic. Others have musical talents or an advanced ability to count and do math calculations. Approximately 10 percent of children with ASD show "savant" skills, or extremely high abilities in specific areas, such as calendar calculation, music, or math.

- **Uneven language development**. Many children with ASD develop some speech and language skills, but not to a normal level of ability, and their progress is usually uneven. For example, they may develop a strong vocabulary in a particular area of interest very quickly. Many children have good memories for information just heard or seen. Some children may be able to read words before 5 years of age, but they may not comprehend what they have read. They often do not respond to the speech of others and may not respond to their own names. As a result, these children sometimes are mistakenly thought to have a hearing problem.

- **Poor nonverbal conversation skills**. Children with ASD often are unable to use gestures—such as pointing to an object—to give meaning to their speech. They often avoid eye contact, which can make them seem rude, uninterested, or inattentive. Without meaningful gestures or the language to communicate, many children with ASD become frustrated in their attempts to make their feelings and needs known. They may act out their frustrations through vocal outbursts or other inappropriate behaviors.

How Are the Speech and Language Problems of ASD Treated?

If a doctor suspects a child has ASD or another developmental disability, he or she usually will refer the child to a variety of specialists, including a speech-language pathologist. This is a health professional trained to treat individuals with voice, speech, and language disorders. The speech-language pathologist will perform a comprehensive evaluation of the child's ability to communicate and design an appropriate treatment program. In addition, the pathologist might make a referral for audiological testing to make sure the child's hearing is normal.

Teaching children with ASD how to communicate is essential in helping them reach their full potential. There are many different approaches to improve communication skills. The best treatment program begins early, during the preschool years, and is tailored to the child's age and interests. It also will address both the child's behavior and communication skills and offer regular reinforcement of positive actions. Most children with ASD respond well to highly structured, specialized programs. Parents or primary caregivers as well as other family members should be involved in the treatment program so it will become part of the child's daily life.

For some younger children, improving verbal communication is a realistic goal of treatment.

Parents and caregivers can increase a child's chance of reaching this goal by paying attention to his or her language development early on. Just as toddlers learn to crawl before they walk, children first develop pre-language skills before they begin to use words. These skills include using eye contact, gestures, body movements, and babbling and other vocalizations to help them communicate. Children who lack these skills may be evaluated and treated by a speech-language pathologist to prevent further developmental delays.

For slightly older children with ASD, basic communication training often emphasizes the functional use of language, such as learning to hold a conversation with another person, which includes staying on topic and taking turns speaking.

Some children with ASD may never develop verbal language skills. For them, the goal may be to acquire gestured communication, such as the use of sign language. For others, the goal may be to communicate by means of a symbol system in which pictures are used to convey thoughts. Symbol systems can range from picture boards or cards to sophisticated electronic devices that generate speech through the use of buttons that represent common items or actions.

What Research Is Being Conducted to Improve Communication in Children with ASD?

The federal government's Combating Autism Act of 2006 brought attention to the need to expand research and improve coordination among all of the components of the National Institutes of Health (NIH) that fund research. These include the National Institute of Mental Health (NIMH), which is the principal institute for research at the NIH, along with the National Institute on Deafness and Other Communication Disorders (NIDCD), the *Eunice Kennedy Shriver* National Institute on Child Health and Human Development (NICHD), the National Institute of Environmental Health Sciences (NIEHS), and the National Institute of Neurological Disorders and Stroke (NINDS).

Together, these five institutes have established the Autism Centers of Excellence (ACE), a program of research centers and networks at universities across the country. Here, scientists study a broad range of topics, from basic science investigations that explore the molecular and genetic components of ASD to translational research studies that test new types of behavioral interventions. Some of these studies, which could be testing new treatments or interventions, might be of interest to parents of children with ASD.

The NIDCD supports additional research to improve the lives of people with ASD and their families. Recently, a group of NIDCD-funded researchers developed recommendations calling for a standardized approach to evaluating language skills. The new benchmarks will make it easier, and more accurate, to compare the effectiveness of different intervention strategies.

NIDCD-funded researchers in universities and organizations across the country also are looking at:

- How to better predict early in infancy if a child is at risk for ASD.

- Whether or not treatment interventions for at-risk infants can influence the development of speech perception and speech preferences.

- How infants with ASD "visually" scan their environment during their earliest social interactions and how this influences their development of language and communication skills.

- How genes and other potential factors predispose individuals to ASD.

Section 24.2

Auditory Processing Disorder in Children

Text in this section is excerpted from "Auditory Processing Disorder,"
© 1995–2016. The Nemours Foundation/KidsHealth®.
Reprinted with permission.

What Is APD?

Auditory processing disorder (APD), also known as central auditory processing disorder (CAPD), is a hearing problem that affects about 5% of school-aged children.

Kids with this condition can't process what they hear in the same way other kids do because their ears and brain don't fully coordinate.

Something interferes with the way the brain recognizes and interprets sounds, especially speech.

With the right therapy, kids with APD can be successful in school and life. Early diagnosis is important, because when the condition isn't caught and treated early, a child can have speech and language delays or problems learning in school.

Trouble Understanding Speech

Kids with APD are thought to hear normally because they can usually hear sounds that are delivered one at a time in a very quiet environment (such as a sound-treated room). The problem is that they usually don't recognize slight differences between sounds in words, even when the sounds are loud and clear enough to be heard.

These kinds of problems usually happen when there is background noise, which is often the case in social situations. So kids with APD can have trouble understanding what is being said to them when they're in noisy places like a playground, sports events, the school cafeteria, and parties.

Symptoms

Symptoms of APD can range from mild to severe and can take many different forms. If you think your child might have a problem processing sounds, ask yourself these questions:

- Is your child easily distracted or unusually bothered by loud or sudden noises?
- Are noisy environments upsetting to your child?
- Does your child's behavior and performance improve in quieter settings?
- Does your child have difficulty following directions, whether simple or complicated?
- Does your child have reading, spelling, writing, or other speech-language difficulties?
- Are verbal (word) math problems difficult for your child?
- Is your child disorganized and forgetful?
- Are conversations hard for your child to follow?

APD is often misunderstood because many of the behaviors noted above also can accompany other problems, like learning

179

disabilities, attention deficit hyperactivity disorder (ADHD), and even depression.

Causes

Often, the cause of a child's APD isn't known. Evidence suggests that head trauma, lead poisoning, and chronic ear infections could play a role. Sometimes, there can be multiple causes.

Diagnosis

If you think your child is having trouble hearing or understanding when people talk, have an audiologist (hearing specialist) exam your child. Only audiologists can diagnose auditory processing disorder.

Audiologists look for five main problem areas in kids with APD:

1. **Auditory figure-ground problems:** This is when a child can't pay attention if there's noise in the background. Noisy, loosely structured classrooms could be very frustrating.

2. **Auditory memory problems:** This is when a child has difficulty remembering information such as directions, lists, or study materials. It can be immediate ("I can't remember it now") and/or delayed ("I can't remember it when I need it for later").

3. **Auditory discrimination problems:** This is when a child has difficulty hearing the difference between words or sounds that are similar (COAT/BOAT or CH/SH). This can affect following directions and reading, spelling, and writing skills, among others.

4. **Auditory attention problems:** This is when a child can't stay focused on listening long enough to complete a task or requirement (such as listening to a lecture in school). Kids with CAPD often have trouble maintaining attention, although health, motivation, and attitude also can play a role.

5. **Auditory cohesion problems:** This is when higher-level listening tasks are difficult. Auditory cohesion skills—drawing inferences from conversations, understanding riddles, or comprehending verbal math problems—require heightened auditory processing and language levels. They develop best when all the other skills (levels 1 through 4 above) are intact.

Since most of the tests done to check for APD require a child to be at least 7 or 8 years old, many kids aren't diagnosed until then or later.

Helping Your Child

A child's auditory system isn't fully developed until age 15. So, many kids diagnosed with APD can develop better skills over time as their auditory system matures. While there is no known cure, speech-language therapy and assistive listening devices can help kids make sense of sounds and develop good communication skills.

A frequency modulation (FM) system is a type of assistive listening device that reduces background noise and makes a speaker's voice louder so a child can understand it. The speaker wears a tiny microphone and a transmitter, which sends an electrical signal to a wireless receiver that the child wears either on the ear or elsewhere on the body. It's portable and can be helpful in classroom settings.

A crucial part of making the FM system effective is ongoing therapy with a speech-language pathologist, who will help the child develop speaking and hearing skills. The speech-language pathologist or audiologist also may recommend tutoring programs.

Several computer-assisted programs are geared toward children with APD. They mainly help the brain do a better job of processing sounds in a noisy environment. Some schools offer these programs, so if your child has APD, be sure to ask school officials about what may be available.

At Home

Strategies applied at home and school can ease some of the problem behaviors associated with APD.

Kids with APD often have trouble following directions, so these suggestions may help:

- Reduce background noise whenever possible at home and at school.

- Have your child look at you when you're speaking.

- Use simple, expressive sentences.

- Speak at a slightly slower rate and at a mildly increased volume.

- Ask your child to repeat the directions back to you and to keep repeating them aloud (to you or to himself or herself) until the directions are completed.

- For directions that are to be completed later, writing notes, wearing a watch, or maintaining a household routine can help. So can general organization and scheduling.

- It can be frustrating for kids with APD when they're in a noisy setting and they need to listen. Teach your child to notice noisy environments and move to quieter places when listening is necessary.

Other tips that might help:

- Provide your child with a quiet study place (not the kitchen table).

- Maintain a peaceful, organized lifestyle.

- Encourage good eating and sleeping habits.

- Assign regular and realistic chores, including keeping a neat room and desk.

- Build your child's self-esteem.

At School

It's important for the people caring for your child to know about APD. Be sure to tell teachers and other school officials about the APD and how it may affect learning. Kids with APD aren't typically put in special education programs, but you may find that your child is eligible for a 504 plan through the school district that would outline any special needs for the classroom.

Some things that may help:

- changing seating plans so your child can sit in the front of the classroom or with his or her back to the window

- study aids, like a tape recorder or notes that can be viewed online

- computer-assisted programs designed for kids with APD

Keep in regular contact with school officials about your child's progress. One of the most important things that both parents and teachers can do is to acknowledge that APD is real. Its symptoms and behaviors are not something that a child can control. What the child can control is recognizing the problems associated with APD and using the strategies recommended both at home and school.

A positive, realistic attitude and healthy self-esteem in a child with APD can work wonders. And kids with APD can go on to be just as successful as other classmates. Coping strategies and techniques learned in speech therapy can help them go far.

Chapter 25

ASD, Seizures, and Epilepsy

What Are the Epilepsies?

The epilepsies are chronic neurological disorders in which clusters of nerve cells, or neurons, in the brain sometimes signal abnormally and cause seizures. Neurons normally generate electrical and chemical signals that act on other neurons, glands, and muscles to produce human thoughts, feelings, and actions. During a seizure, many neurons fire (signal) at the same time – as many as 500 times a second, much faster than normal. This surge of excessive electrical activity happening at the same time causes involuntary movements, sensations, emotions, and behaviors and the temporary disturbance of normal neuronal activity may cause a loss of awareness.

Epilepsy can be considered a spectrum disorder because of its different causes, different seizure types, its ability to vary in severity and impact from person to person, and its range of co-existing conditions. Some people may have convulsions (sudden onset of repetitive general contraction of muscles) and lose consciousness. Others may simply stop what they are doing, have a brief lapse of awareness, and stare into space for a short period. Some people have seizures very infrequently, while other people may experience hundreds of seizures each day. There also are many different types of epilepsy, resulting

---

Text in this chapter is excerpted from "The Epilepsies and Seizures: Hope Through Research," National Institute of Neurological Disorders and Stroke (NINDS), December 18, 2015.

from a variety of causes. Recent adoption of the term "the epilepsies" underscores the diversity of types and causes.

In general, a person is not considered to have epilepsy until he or she has had two or more unprovoked seizures separated by at least 24 hours. In contrast, a provoked seizure is one caused by a known precipitating factor such as a high fever, nervous system infections, acute traumatic brain injury, or fluctuations in blood sugar or electrolyte levels.

Anyone can develop epilepsy. About 2.3 million adults and more than 450,000 children and adolescents in the United States currently live with epilepsy. Each year, an estimated 150,000 people are diagnosed with epilepsy. Epilepsy affects both males and females of all races, ethnic backgrounds, and ages. In the United States alone, the annual costs associated with the epilepsies are estimated to be $15.5 billion in direct medical expenses and lost or reduced earnings and productivity.

The majority of those diagnosed with epilepsy have seizures that can be controlled with drug therapies and surgery. However, as much as 30 to 40 percent of people with epilepsy continue to have seizures because available treatments do not completely control their seizures (called intractable or medication resistant epilepsy).

While many forms of epilepsy require lifelong treatment to control the seizures, for some people the seizures eventually go away. The odds of becoming seizure-free are not as good for adults or for children with severe epilepsy syndromes, but it is possible that seizures may decrease or even stop over time. This is more likely if the epilepsy starts in childhood, has been well-controlled by medication, or if the person has had surgery to remove the brain focus of the abnormal cell firing.

Many people with epilepsy lead productive lives, but some will be severely impacted by their epilepsy. Medical and research advances in the past two decades have led to a better understanding of the epilepsies and seizures. More than 20 different medications and a variety of dietary treatments and surgical techniques (including two devices) are now available and may provide good control of seizures. Devices can modulate brain activity to decrease seizure frequency. Advanced neuroimaging can identify brain abnormalities that give rise to seizures which can be cured by neurosurgery. Even dietary changes can effectively treat certain types of epilepsy. Research on the underlying causes of the epilepsies, including identification of genes for some forms of epilepsy, has led to a greatly improved understanding of these disorders that may lead to more effective treatments or even to new ways of preventing epilepsy in the future.

What Causes the Epilepsies?

The epilepsies have many possible causes, but for up to half of people with epilepsy a cause is not known. In other cases, the epilepsies are clearly linked to genetic factors, developmental brain abnormalities, infection, traumatic brain injury, stroke, brain tumors, or other identifiable problems. Anything that disturbs the normal pattern of neuronal activity from illness to brain damage to abnormal brain development can lead to seizures.

The epilepsies may develop because of an abnormality in brain wiring, an imbalance of nerve signaling in the brain (in which some cells either over-excite or over-inhibit other brain cells from sending messages), or some combination of these factors. In some pediatric conditions abnormal brain wiring causes other problems such as intellectual impairment.

In other persons, the brain's attempts to repair itself after a head injury, stroke, or other problem may inadvertently generate abnormal nerve connections that lead to epilepsy. Brain malformations and abnormalities in brain wiring that occur during brain development also may disturb neuronal activity and lead to epilepsy.

Genetics

Genetic mutations may play a key role in the development of certain epilepsies. Many types of epilepsy affect multiple blood-related family members, pointing to a strong inherited genetic component. In other cases, gene mutations may occur spontaneously and contribute to development of epilepsy in people with no family history of the disorder (called "de novo" mutations). Overall, researchers estimate that hundreds of genes could play a role in the disorders.

Several types of epilepsy have been linked to mutations in genes that provide instructions for ion channels, the "gates" that control the flow of ions in and out of cells to help regulate neuronal signaling. For example, most infants with Dravet syndrome, a type of epilepsy associated with seizures that begin before the age of one year, carry a mutation in the SCN1A gene that causes seizures by affecting sodium ion channels.

Genetic mutations also have been linked to disorders known as the progressive myoclonic epilepsies, which are characterized by ultra-quick muscle contractions (myoclonus) and seizures over time. For example, Lafora disease, a severe, progressive form of myoclonic epilepsy that begins in childhood, has been linked to a gene that helps to break down carbohydrates in brain cells.

Mutations in genes that control neuronal migration – a critical step in brain development – can lead to areas of misplaced or abnormally formed neurons, called cortical dysplasia, in the brain that can cause these mis-wired neurons to misfire and lead to epilepsy.

Other genetic mutations may not cause epilepsy, but may influence the disorder in other ways. For example, one study showed that many people with certain forms of epilepsy have an abnormally active version of a gene that results in resistance to anti-seizure drugs. Genes also may control a person's susceptibility to seizures, or seizure threshold, by affecting brain development.

Other Disorders

Epilepsies may develop as a result of brain damage associated with many types of conditions that disrupt normal brain activity. Seizures may stop once these conditions are treated and resolved. However, the chances of becoming seizure-free after the primary disorder is treated are uncertain and vary depending on the type of disorder, the brain region that is affected, and how much brain damage occurred prior to treatment. Examples of conditions that can lead to epilepsy include:

- Brain tumors, including those associated with neurofibromatosis or tuberous sclerosis complex, two inherited conditions that cause benign tumors called hamartomas to grow in the brain

- Head trauma

- Alcoholism or alcohol withdrawal

- Alzheimer's disease

- Strokes, heart attacks, and other conditions that deprive the brain of oxygen (a significant portion of new-onset epilepsy in elderly people is due to stroke or other cerebrovascular disease)

- Abnormal blood vessel formation (arteriovenous malformations) or bleeding in the brain (hemorrhage)

- Inflammation of the brain

- Infections such as meningitis, HIV, and viral encephalitis

Cerebral palsy or other developmental neurological abnormalities may also be associated with epilepsy. About 20 percent of seizures in children can be attributed to developmental neurological conditions. Epilepsies often co-occur in people with abnormalities of brain development or other neurodevelopmental disorders. Seizures are more common, for example, among individuals with autism spectrum disorder or intellectual impairment. In one study, fully a third of children with autism spectrum disorder had treatment-resistant epilepsy.

Seizure Triggers

Seizure triggers do not cause epilepsy but can provoke first seizures in those who are susceptible or can cause seizures in people with epilepsy who otherwise experience good seizure control with their medication. Seizure triggers include alcohol consumption or alcohol withdrawal, dehydration or missing meals, stress, and hormonal changes associated with the menstrual cycle. In surveys of people with epilepsy, stress is the most commonly reported seizure trigger. Exposure to toxins or poisons such as lead or carbon monoxide, street drugs, or even excessively large doses of antidepressants or other prescribed medications also can trigger seizures.

Sleep deprivation is a powerful trigger of seizures. Sleep disorders are common among people with the epilepsies and appropriate treatment of co-existing sleep disorders can often lead to improved control of seizures. Certain types of seizures tend to occur during sleep, while others are more common during times of wakefulness, suggesting to physicians how to best adjust a person's medication. For some people, visual stimulation can trigger seizures in a condition known as photosensitive epilepsy. Stimulation can include such things as flashing lights or moving patterns.

What is the impact of the epilepsies on daily life?

The majority of people with epilepsy can do the same things as people without the disorder and have successful and productive lives. In most cases it does not affect job choice or performance. One-third or more of people with epilepsy, however, may have cognitive or neuropsychiatric co-concurring symptoms that can negatively impact their quality of life.

Many people with epilepsy are significantly helped by available therapies, and some may go months or years without having a seizure. However, people with treatment-resistant epilepsy can have as many as hundreds of seizures a day or they can have one seizure a year with sometimes disabling consequences. On average, having treatment-resistant epilepsy is associated with an increased risk of cognitive impairment, particularly if the seizures developed in early childhood. These impairments may be related to the underlying conditions associated with the epilepsy rather than to the epilepsy itself.

Mental Health and Stigmatization

Depression is common among people with epilepsy. It is estimated that one of every three persons with epilepsy will have depression in the course of his or her lifetime, often with accompanying symptoms of anxiety disorder. In adults, depression and anxiety are the two most frequent mental health-related diagnoses. In adults, a depression screening questionnaire, specifically designed for epilepsy helps healthcare professionals, identify people who need treatment.

Depression or anxiety in people with epilepsy can be treated with counseling or most of the same medications used in people who don't have epilepsy. People with epilepsy should not simply accept that depression is part of having epilepsy and should discuss symptoms and feelings with health care professionals.

Children with epilepsy also have a higher risk of developing depression and/or attention deficit hyperactivity disorder compared with their peers. Behavioral problems may precede the onset of seizures in some children.

Children are especially vulnerable to the emotional problems caused by ignorance or the lack of knowledge among others about epilepsy. This often results in stigmatization, bullying, or teasing of a child who has epilepsy. Such experiences can lead to behaviors of avoidance in school and other social settings. Counseling services and support groups can help families cope with epilepsy in a positive manner.

Driving and Recreation

Most states and the District of Columbia will not issue a driver's license to someone with epilepsy unless the person can document that she/he has been seizure-free for a specific amount of time (the waiting period varies from a few months to several years). Some states make exceptions for this policy when seizures don't impair consciousness, occur only during sleep, or have long auras or other warning signs that allow the person to avoid driving when a seizure is likely to occur. Studies show that the risk of having a seizure-related accident decreases as the length of time since the last seizure increases. Commercial drivers' licenses have additional restrictions. In addition, people with epilepsy should take extra care if a job involves operation of machinery or vehicles.

The risk of seizures also limits people's recreational choices. Individuals may need to take precautions with activities such as climbing, sailing, swimming, or working on ladders. Studies have not shown any increase in seizures due to sports, although these studies have not focused on any activity in particular. There is some evidence that regular exercise may improve seizure control in some people, but this should be done under a doctor's supervision. The benefits of sports participation may outweigh the risks and coaches or other leaders can take appropriate safety precautions. Steps should be taken to avoid dehydration, overexertion, and hypoglycemia, as these problems can increase the risk of seizures.

Education and Employment

By law, people with epilepsy (or disabilities) in the United States cannot be denied employment or access to any educational, recreational, or other activity because of their epilepsy. However, significant barriers still exist for people with epilepsy in school and work. Anti-seizure drugs may cause side effects that interfere with concentration and memory.

Children with epilepsy may need extra time to complete schoolwork, and they sometimes may need to have instructions or other information repeated for them. Teachers should be told what to do if a child in their classroom has a seizure, and parents should work with the school system to find reasonable ways to accommodate any special needs their child may have.

Pregnancy and Motherhood

Women with epilepsy are often concerned about whether they can become pregnant and have a healthy child. Epilepsy itself does not interfere with the ability to become pregnant. With the right planning, supplemental vitamin use, and medication adjustments prior to pregnancy, the odds of a woman with epilepsy having a healthy pregnancy and a healthy child are similar to a woman without a chronic medical condition.

Children of parents with epilepsy have about 5 percent risk of developing the condition at some point during life, in comparison to about a 1 percent risk in a child in the general population. However, the risk of developing epilepsy increases if a parent has a clearly hereditary form of the disorder. Parents who are worried that their epilepsy may be hereditary may wish to consult a genetic counselor to determine their risk of passing on the disorder.

Other potential risks to the developing child of a woman with epilepsy or on anti seizure medication include increased risk for major congenital malformations (also known as birth defects) and adverse

191

effects on the developing brain. The types of birth defects that have been most commonly reported with antiseizure medications include cleft lip or cleft palate, heart problems, abnormal spinal cord development (spina bifida), urogenital defects, and limb-skeletal defects. Some antiseizure medications, particularly valproate, are known to increase the risk of having a child with birth defects and/or neurodevelopmental problems, including learning disabilities, general intellectual disabilities, and autism spectrum disorder. It is important that a woman work with a team of providers that includes her neurologist and her obstetrician to learn about any special risks associated with her epilepsy and the medications she may be taking.

Although planned pregnancies are essential to ensuring a healthy pregnancy, effective birth control is also essential. Some antiseizure medications that induce the liver's metabolic capacity can interfere with the effectiveness of hormonal contraceptives (e.g., birth control pills, vaginal ring). Women who are on these enzyme-inducing antiseizure medications and using hormonal contraceptives may need to switch to a different kind of birth control that is more effective (such as different intrauterine devices, progestin implants, or long-lasting injections).

Prior to a planned pregnancy, a woman with epilepsy should meet with her healthcare team to reassess the current need for anti seizure medications and to determine a) the optimal medication to balance seizure control and avoid birth defects and b) the lowest dose for going into a planned pregnancy. Any transitions to either a new medication or dosage should be phased in prior to the pregnancy, if possible. If a woman's seizures are controlled for the 9 months prior to pregnancy, she is more likely to continue to have seizure control during pregnancy.

For all women with epilepsy during pregnancy, approximately 15-25 percent will have seizure worsening, but another 15-25 percent will have seizure improvement. As a woman's body changes during pregnancy, the dose of seizure medication may need to be increased. For most medicines, monthly monitoring of blood levels of the antiseizure medicines can help to assure continued seizure control. Many of the birth defects seen with anti seizure medications occur in the first six weeks of pregnancy, often before a woman is aware she is pregnant. In addition, up to 50 percent of pregnancies in the U.S. are unplanned. For these reasons, the discussion about the medications should occur early between the health care professional and any woman with epilepsy who is in her childbearing years.

For all women thinking of becoming pregnant, using supplemental folic acid beginning prior to conception and continuing the supplement during pregnancy is an important way to lower the risk for birth defects and developmental delays. Prenatal multivitamins should also be used prior to the beginning of pregnancy. Pregnant women with epilepsy should get plenty of sleep and avoid other triggers or missed medications to avoid worsening of seizures.

Most pregnant women with epilepsy can deliver with the same choices as women without any medical complications. During the labor and delivery, it is important that the woman be allowed to take her same formulations and doses of anti seizure drugs at her usual times; it is often helpful for her to bring her medications from home. If a seizure does occur during labor and delivery, intravenous short-acting medications can be given if necessary. It is unusual for the newborns of women with epilepsy to experience symptoms of withdrawal from the mother's antiseizure medication (unless she is on phenobarbital or a standing dose of benzodiazepines), but the symptoms resolve quickly and there are usually no serious or long-term effects.

The use of anti seizure medications is considered safe for women who choose to breastfeed their child. On very rare occasions, the baby may become excessively drowsy or feed poorly, and these problems should be closely monitored. However, experts believe the benefits of breastfeeding outweigh the risks except in rare circumstances. One large study showed that the children who were breastfed by mothers with epilepsy on anti seizure medications performed better on learning and developmental scales than the babies who were not breastfed. It is common for the antiseizure medication dosing to be adjusted again in the postpartum setting, especially if the dose was altered during pregnancy.

With the appropriate selection of safe antiseizure medicines during pregnancy, use of supplemental folic acid, and ideally, with pre-pregnancy planning, most women with epilepsy can have a healthy pregnancy with good outcomes for themselves and their developing child.

Chapter 26

Co-Occurring Genetic Disorders in People with ASD

Chapter Contents

Section 26.1

Angelman Syndrome

Text in this section is excerpted from
"Angelman Syndrome," U.S. National Library of
Medicine (NLM), January 11, 2016.

What Is Angelman Syndrome?

Angelman syndrome is a complex genetic disorder that primarily affects the nervous system. Characteristic features of this condition include delayed development, intellectual disability, severe speech impairment, and problems with movement and balance (ataxia). Most affected children also have recurrent seizures (epilepsy) and a small head size (microcephaly). Delayed development becomes noticeable by the age of 6 to 12 months, and other common signs and symptoms usually appear in early childhood.

Children with Angelman syndrome typically have a happy, excitable demeanor with frequent smiling, laughter, and hand-flapping movements. Hyperactivity, a short attention span, and a fascination with water are common. Most affected children also have difficulty sleeping and need less sleep than usual.

With age, people with Angelman syndrome become less excitable, and the sleeping problems tend to improve. However, affected individuals continue to have intellectual disability, severe speech impairment, and seizures throughout their lives. Adults with Angelman syndrome have distinctive facial features that may be described as "coarse." Other common features include unusually fair skin with light-colored hair and an abnormal side-to-side curvature of the spine (scoliosis). The life expectancy of people with this condition appears to be nearly normal.

How Common Is Angelman Syndrome?

Angelman syndrome affects an estimated 1 in 12,000 to 20,000 people.

What Are the Genetic Changes Related to Angelman Syndrome?

Many of the characteristic features of Angelman syndrome result from the loss of function of a gene called UBE3A. People normally inherit one copy of the UBE3A gene from each parent. Both copies of this gene are turned on (active) in many of the body's tissues. In certain areas of the brain, however, only the copy inherited from a person's mother (the maternal copy) is active. This parent-specific gene activation is caused by a phenomenon called genomic imprinting. If the maternal copy of the UBE3A gene is lost because of a chromosomal change or a gene mutation, a person will have no active copies of the gene in some parts of the brain.

Several different genetic mechanisms can inactivate or delete the maternal copy of the UBE3A gene. Most cases of Angelman syndrome (about 70 percent) occur when a segment of the maternal chromosome 15 containing this gene is deleted. In other cases (about 11 percent), Angelman syndrome is caused by a mutation in the maternal copy of the UBE3A gene.

In a small percentage of cases, Angelman syndrome results when a person inherits two copies of chromosome 15 from his or her father (paternal copies) instead of one copy from each parent. This phenomenon is called paternal uniparental disomy. Rarely, Angelman syndrome can also be caused by a chromosomal rearrangement called a translocation, or by a mutation or other defect in the region of DNA that controls activation of the UBE3A gene. These genetic changes can abnormally turn off (inactivate) UBE3A or other genes on the maternal copy of chromosome 15.

The causes of Angelman syndrome are unknown in 10 to 15 percent of affected individuals. Changes involving other genes or chromosomes may be responsible for the disorder in these cases.

In some people who have Angelman syndrome, the loss of a gene called OCA2 is associated with light-colored hair and fair skin. The OCA2 gene is located on the segment of chromosome 15 that is often deleted in people with this disorder. However, loss of the OCA2 gene does not cause the other signs and symptoms of Angelman syndrome. The protein produced from this gene helps determine the coloring (pigmentation) of the skin, hair, and eyes.

Can Angelman Syndrome Be Inherited?

Most cases of Angelman syndrome are not inherited, particularly those caused by a deletion in the maternal chromosome 15 or by paternal uniparental disomy. These genetic changes occur as random events during the formation of reproductive cells (eggs and sperm) or in early embryonic development. Affected people typically have no history of the disorder in their family.

Rarely, a genetic change responsible for Angelman syndrome can be inherited. For example, it is possible for a mutation in the UBE3A gene or in the nearby region of DNA that controls gene activation to be passed from one generation to the next.

Section 26.2

Fragile X Syndrome

Text in this section is excerpted from "Fragile X Syndrome,"
U.S. National Library of Medicine (NLM), January 11, 2016.

What Is Fragile X Syndrome?

Fragile X syndrome is a genetic condition that causes a range of developmental problems including learning disabilities and cognitive impairment. Usually, males are more severely affected by this disorder than females.

Affected individuals usually have delayed development of speech and language by age 2. Most males with fragile X syndrome have mild to moderate intellectual disability, while about one-third of affected females are intellectually disabled. Children with fragile X syndrome may also have anxiety and hyperactive behavior such as fidgeting or impulsive actions. They may have attention deficit disorder (ADD), which includes an impaired ability to maintain attention and difficulty focusing on specific tasks. About one-third of individuals with fragile X syndrome have features of autism spectrum disorders that affect communication and social interaction. Seizures occur in about 15 percent of males and about 5 percent of females with fragile X syndrome.

Most males and about half of females with fragile X syndrome have characteristic physical features that become more apparent with age. These features include a long and narrow face, large ears, a prominent jaw and forehead, unusually flexible fingers, flat feet, and in males, enlarged testicles (macroorchidism) after puberty.

How Common Is Fragile X Syndrome?

Fragile X syndrome occurs in approximately 1 in 4,000 males and 1 in 8,000 females.

What Genes Are Related to Fragile X Syndrome?

Mutations in the FMR1 gene cause fragile X syndrome. The FMR1 gene provides instructions for making a protein called FMRP. This protein helps regulate the production of other proteins and plays a role in the development of synapses, which are specialized connections between nerve cells. Synapses are critical for relaying nerve impulses.

Nearly all cases of fragile X syndrome are caused by a mutation in which a DNA segment, known as the CGG triplet repeat, is expanded within the FMR1 gene. Normally, this DNA segment is repeated from 5 to about 40 times. In people with fragile X syndrome, however, the CGG segment is repeated more than 200 times. The abnormally expanded CGG segment turns off (silences) the FMR1 gene, which prevents the gene from producing FMRP. Loss or a shortage (deficiency) of this protein disrupts nervous system functions and leads to the signs and symptoms of fragile X syndrome.

Males and females with 55 to 200 repeats of the CGG segment are said to have an FMR1 gene premutation. Most people with a premutation are intellectually normal. In some cases, however, individuals with a premutation have lower than normal amounts of FMRP. As a result, they may have mild versions of the physical features seen in fragile X syndrome (such as prominent ears) and may experience emotional problems such as anxiety or depression. Some children with a premutation may have learning disabilities or autistic-like behavior.

The premutation is also associated with an increased risk of disorders called fragile X-associated primary ovarian insufficiency (FXPOI) and fragile X-associated tremor/ataxia syndrome (FXTAS).

How Do People Inherit Fragile X Syndrome?

Fragile X syndrome is inherited in an X-linked dominant pattern. A condition is considered X-linked if the mutated gene that causes the disorder is located on the X chromosome, one of the two sex chromosomes. (The Y chromosome is the other sex chromosome.)

The inheritance is dominant if one copy of the altered gene in each cell is sufficient to cause the condition. X-linked dominant means that in females (who have two X chromosomes), a mutation in one of the two copies of a gene in each cell is sufficient to cause the disorder. In males (who have only one X chromosome), a mutation in the only copy of a gene in each cell causes the disorder. In most cases, males experience more severe symptoms of the disorder than females.

In women, the FMR1 gene premutation on the X chromosome can expand to more than 200 CGG repeats in cells that develop into eggs. This means that women with the premutation have an increased risk of having a child with fragile X syndrome. By contrast, the premutation in men does not expand to more than 200 repeats as it is passed to the next generation. Men pass the premutation only to their daughters. Their sons receive a Y chromosome, which does not include the FMR1 gene.

Section 26.3

Landau-Kleffner Syndrome

Text in this section is excerpted from "NINDS Landau-Kleffner Syndrome Information Page," National Institute of Neurological Disorders and Stroke (NINDS), June 30, 2015.

What Is Landau-Kleffner Syndrome?

Landau-Kleffner Syndrome (LKS) is a rare, childhood neurological disorder characterized by the sudden or gradual development of aphasia (the inability to understand or express language) and an abnormal electro-encephalogram (EEG). LKS affects the parts of the brain that control comprehension and speech. The disorder usually occurs in children between the ages of 5 and 7 years. Typically, children with LKS develop normally but then lose their language skills for no apparent reason. While many of the affected individuals have seizures, some do not. The disorder is difficult to diagnose and may be misdiagnosed as autism, pervasive developmental disorder, hearing impairment, learning disability, auditory/verbal processing disorder, attention deficit disorder, childhood schizophrenia, or emotional/behavioral problems.

Is There Any treatment?

Treatment for LKS usually consists of medications, such as anticonvulsants and corticosteroids, and speech therapy, which should be started early. A controversial treatment option involves a surgical technique called multiple subpial transection in which the pathways of abnormal electrical brain activity are severed.

What Is the Prognosis?

The prognosis for children with LKS varies. Some affected children may have a permanent severe language disorder, while others may regain much of their language abilities (although it may take months or years). In some cases, remission and relapse may occur. The prognosis is improved when the onset of the disorder is after age 6 and when speech therapy is started early. Seizures generally disappear by adulthood.

What Research Is Being Done?

The NINDS supports broad and varied programs of research on epilepsy and developmental disorders. This research is aimed at discovering new ways to prevent, diagnose, and treat epilepsy and developmental disorders and, ultimately, to find cures for them.

Section 26.4

Mitochondrial Disease

Text in this section is excerpted from "Mitochondrial Disease – Frequently Asked Questions," Centers for Disease Control and Prevention (CDC), August 12, 2015.

What Are Mitochondrial Diseases or Disorders?

Mitochondria are tiny parts of almost every cell in your body. Mitochondria are like the power house of the cells. They turn sugar and oxygen into energy that the cells need to work.

In mitochondrial diseases, the mitochondria cannot efficiently turn sugar and oxygen into energy, so the cells do not work correctly.

There are many types of mitochondrial disease, and they can affect different parts of the body: the brain, kidneys, muscles, heart, eyes, ears, and others. Mitochondrial diseases can affect one part of the body or can affect many parts. They can affect those part(s) mildly or very seriously.

Not everyone with a mitochondrial disease will show symptoms. However, when discussing the group of mitochondrial diseases that tend to affect children, symptoms usually appear in the toddler and preschool years.

Mitochondrial diseases and disorders are the same thing.

Is There a Relationship between Mitochondrial Disease and Autism?

A child with a mitochondrial disease:

• may also have an autism spectrum disorder,

• may have some of the symptoms/signs of autism, or

• may not have any signs or symptoms related to autism.

A child with autism may or may not have a mitochondrial disease. When a child has both autism and a mitochondrial disease, they sometimes have other problems as well, including epilepsy, problems with muscle tone, and/or movement disorders.

What Is Regressive Encephalopathy?

Encephalopathy is a medical term for a disease or disorder of the brain. It usually means a slowing down of brain function.

Regression happens when a person loses skills that they used to have like walking or talking or even being social.

Regressive encephalopathy means there is a disease or disorder in the brain that makes a person lose skills they once had.

We know that sometimes children with mitochondrial diseases seem to be developing as they should, but around toddler or preschool age, they regress. The disease was there all the time, but something happens that "sets it off." This could be something like malnutrition, an illness such as flu, a high fever, dehydration, or it could be something else.

Is There a Relationship Between Autism and Encephalopathy?

Most children with an autism spectrum disorder do not and have not had an encephalopathy. Some children with an autism spectrum disorder have had regression and some have had a regressive encephalopathy.

What Do We Know about the Relationship between Mitochondrial Disease and Other Disorders Related to the Brain?

Different parts of the brain have different functions. The area of the brain that is damaged by a mitochondrial disease determines how the person is impacted. This means that a person could have seizures; trouble talking or interacting with people; difficulty eating; muscle weakness, or other problems. They could have one issue or several.

Do Vaccines Cause or Worsen Mitochondrial Diseases?

As of now, there are no scientific studies that say vaccines cause or worsen mitochondrial diseases. We do know that certain illnesses that can be prevented by vaccines, such as the flu, can trigger the regression that is related to a mitochondrial disease. More research is needed to determine if there are rare cases where underlying mitochondrial disorders are triggered by anything related to vaccines. However, we know that for most children, vaccines are a safe and important way to prevent them from getting life-threatening diseases.

Are All Children Routinely Tested for Mitochondrial Diseases? What about Children with Autism?

Children are not routinely tested for mitochondrial diseases. This includes children with autism and other developmental delays.

Testing is not easy and may involve getting multiple samples of blood, and often samples of muscle. Doctors decide whether testing for mitochondrial diseases should be done based on a child's signs and symptoms.

Should I Have My Child Tested for a Mitochondrial Disease?

If you are worried that your child might have a mitochondrial disease, talk to your child's doctor.

Section 26.5

Moebius Syndrome

Text in this section is excerpted from "Moebius Syndrome,"
U.S. National Library of Medicine (NLM), January 4, 2016.

What Is Moebius Syndrome?

Moebius syndrome is a rare neurological condition that primarily affects the muscles that control facial expression and eye movement. The signs and symptoms of this condition are present from birth.

Weakness or paralysis of the facial muscles is one of the most common features of Moebius syndrome. Affected individuals lack facial expressions; they cannot smile, frown, or raise their eyebrows. The muscle weakness also causes problems with feeding that become apparent in early infancy.

Many people with Moebius syndrome are born with a small chin (micrognathia) and a small mouth (microstomia) with a short or unusually shaped tongue. The roof of the mouth may have an abnormal opening (cleft palate) or be high and arched. These abnormalities contribute to problems with speech, which occur in many children with Moebius syndrome. Dental abnormalities, including missing and misaligned teeth, are also common.

Moebius syndrome also affects muscles that control back-and-forth eye movement. Affected individuals must move their head from side to side to read or follow the movement of objects. People with this disorder have difficulty making eye contact, and their eyes may not look in the same direction (strabismus). Additionally, the eyelids may not close completely when blinking or sleeping, which can result in dry or irritated eyes.

Other features of Moebius syndrome can include bone abnormalities in the hands and feet, weak muscle tone (hypotonia), and hearing loss. Affected children often experience delayed development of motor skills (such as crawling and walking), although most eventually acquire these skills.

Some research studies have suggested that children with Moebius syndrome are more likely than unaffected children to have characteristics of autism spectrum disorders, which are a group of conditions characterized by impaired communication and social interaction. However, recent studies have questioned this association. Because people with Moebius syndrome have difficulty with eye contact and speech due to their physical differences, autism spectrum disorders can be difficult to diagnose in these individuals. Moebius syndrome may also be associated with a somewhat increased risk of intellectual disability; however, most affected individuals have normal intelligence.

How Common Is Moebius Syndrome?

The exact incidence of Moebius syndrome is unknown. Researchers estimate that the condition affects 1 in 50,000 to 1 in 500,000 newborns.

What Genes Are Related to Moebius Syndrome?

The causes of Moebius syndrome are unknown, although the condition probably results from a combination of environmental and genetic factors. Researchers have not identified any specific genes related to this condition. However, the disorder appears to be associated with changes in particular regions of chromosomes 3, 10, or 13 in some families. Certain medications taken during pregnancy and abuse of drugs such as cocaine may also be risk factors for Moebius syndrome.

Many of the signs and symptoms of Moebius syndrome result from the absence or underdevelopment of cranial nerves VI and VII. These nerves, which emerge from the brainstem at the back of the brain, control back-and-forth eye movement and facial expressions. The disorder can also affect other cranial nerves that are important for speech, chewing, and swallowing. Abnormal development of cranial nerves leads to the facial muscle weakness or paralysis that is characteristic of Moebius syndrome.

Researchers speculate that Moebius syndrome may result from changes in blood flow to the brainstem during early stages of embryonic development. However, it is unclear what causes these changes to occur and why they specifically disrupt the development of cranial nerves VI and VII. Even less is known about the causes of some other signs and symptoms of this condition, including hand and foot abnormalities.

How Do People Inherit Moebius Syndrome?

Most cases of Moebius syndrome are sporadic, which means they occur in people with no history of the disorder in their family. A small percentage of all cases have been reported to run in families; however, the condition does not have a single clear pattern of inheritance.

Section 26.6

Prader-Willi Syndrome

Text in this section is excerpted from "Prader-Willi Syndrome (PWS): Condition Information," National Institute of Child Health and Human Development (NICHD), January 14, 2014.

What Is PWS?

The term PWS refers to a genetic disorder that affects many parts of the body. Genetic testing can successfully diagnose 99% of infants with PWS.

The syndrome usually results from deletions or partial deletions on chromosome 15 that affect the regulation of gene expression, or how genes turn on and off. Andrea Prader and Heinrich Willi first described the syndrome in the 1950s.

One of the main symptoms of PWS is the inability to control eating. In fact, PWS is the leading genetic cause of life-threatening obesity. Other symptoms include low muscle tone and poor feeding as an infant, delays in intellectual development, and difficulty controlling emotions.

There is no cure for PWS, but people with the disorder can benefit from a variety of treatments to improve their symptoms. These treatments depend on the individual's needs, but they often include strict dietary supervision, physical therapy, behavioral therapy, and treatment with growth hormone, among others. As adults, people with PWS usually do best in special group homes for people with this disorder. Some can work in sheltered environments.

What Are the Symptoms of Prader-Willi Syndrome (PWS)?

Scientists think that the symptoms of PWS may be caused by a problem in a portion of the brain called the hypothalamus. The hypothalamus lies in the base of the brain. When it works normally, it controls hunger or thirst, body temperature, pain, and when it is time to awaken and to sleep. Problems with the hypothalamus can affect various body functions and pathways, leading to a variety of symptoms.

Individuals with PWS may have mild to severe symptoms, which often include the following:

Feeding and Metabolic Symptoms

An important early symptom of PWS is an infant's inability to suck, which affects the ability to feed. Nearly all infants with PWS need help with feeding. Infants may require feeding support for several months. Without assistance, they will not grow. Nursing systems with one-way valves and manual sucking assistive devices, similar to those used with cleft palate (such as bottles with special nipples for babies who do not have the sucking reflex), often are needed. Occasionally, feeding tubes are required, but generally for no more than the first 6 months after birth. The infants may need fewer calories because of the reduced metabolism associated with PWS and may not demand

207

feeding on their own. Frequent weight checks will help in adjusting the infant's diet to maintain a suitable weight gain.

As the infants grow into toddlers and children, compulsive overeating replaces the need for feeding support. Because the metabolic rate of individuals with PWS is lower than normal, their caloric intake must be restricted to maintain a healthy weight, often to 60% of the caloric requirement of comparably sized children without the syndrome.

Feeding and metabolic symptoms persist into adulthood. Unless individuals with PWS live in environments that limit access to food (such as locked cabinets and a locked refrigerator), they will eat uncontrollably, even food that is rotten or sitting in the garbage. Uncontrollable eating can cause choking, a ruptured esophagus, and blockages in the digestive system. It can also lead to extreme weight gain and morbid obesity. Because of their inability to stop eating, people with PWS are at increased risk for diabetes, trouble breathing during sleep, and other health risks. For these reasons, people with PWS need to be monitored by a health care professional their entire lives.

Physical Symptoms

Many physical symptoms of PWS arise from poor regulation of various hormones, including growth hormone, thyroid hormone, and possibly adrenalin. Individuals with PWS grow slowly and experience delays in reaching physical activity milestones (e.g., standing, walking).

Children with PWS tend to be substantially shorter than other children of similar age. They may have small hands and feet and a curvature of the back, called scoliosis (pronounced skoh-lee-OH-sis). In addition, they frequently have difficulty making their eyes work together to focus, a condition called strabismus (pronounced struh-BIZ-muhs).

Infants with PWS are often born with underdeveloped sex organs, including a small penis and scrotum or a small clitoris and vaginal lips. Most individuals with PWS are infertile.

Intellectual Symptoms

Individuals with PWS have varying levels of intellectual disabilities. Learning disabilities are common, as are delays in starting to talk and in the development of language.

Behavioral and Psychiatric Symptoms

Imbalances in hormone levels may contribute to behavioral and psychiatric problems. Behavioral problems may include temper tantrums, extreme stubbornness, obsessive-compulsive symptoms, picking the skin, and general trouble in controlling emotions. The individual will often repeat questions or statements. Sleep disturbances may include excessive daytime sleepiness and disruptions of sleep. Many individuals with PWS have a high pain threshold.

Stages of PWS Symptoms

The appearance of PWS symptoms occurs in two recognized stages:

1.   Stage 1 (Infancy to age 2 years)

     - "Floppiness" and poor muscle tone

     - Weak cries and a weak sucking reflex

     - Inability to breastfeed, which may require feeding support, such as tube feeding

     - Developmental delays

     - Small genital organs

2.   Stage 2 (Ages 2 to 8)

     - Unable to feel satisfied with normal intake of food

     - Inability to control eating, which can lead to overeating if not monitored

     - Food-seeking behaviors

     - Low metabolism

     - Weight gain and obesity

     - Daytime sleepiness and sleep problems

     - Intellectual disabilities

     - Small hands and feet

     - Short stature

     - Curvature of the spine (scoliosis)

     - High pain threshold

     - Behavioral problems, including the display of obsessive-compulsive symptoms, picking the skin, and difficulty controlling emotions

     - Small genitals, often resulting in infertility in later life

How Many People Are Affected/at Risk for Prader-Willi Syndrome (PWS)?

Prader-Willi syndrome, which occurs in about one in every 15,000 to 25,000 live births, is the most common genetic disorder that can lead to life-threatening obesity in children. Boys and girls are equally affected.

Scientists do not know what increases the risk for Prader-Willi syndrome. The genetic error that leads to Prader-Willi syndrome occurs at random, usually around the time of conception or during early fetal development. The syndrome is usually not hereditary.

Genetic testing can identify the chance that a second sibling will develop Prader-Willi syndrome, a possibility that is usually less than 1%.

What Causes Prader-Willi Syndrome (PWS)?

Prader-Willi syndrome is caused by genetic changes on an "unstable" region of chromosome 15 that affects the regulation of gene expression, or how genes turn on and off. This part of the chromosome is called unstable because it is prone to being shuffled around by the cell's genetic machinery before the chromosome is passed on from parent to child.

The genetic changes that cause Prader-Willi syndrome occur in a portion of the chromosome, referred to as the Prader-Willi Critical Region (PWCR), around the time of conception or during early fetal development. This region was identified in 1990 using genetic DNA probes. Although Prader-Willi syndrome is genetic, it usually is not inherited and generally develops due to deletions or partial deletions on chromosome 15.

Specific changes to the chromosome can include the following:

- Deletions. A section of a chromosome may be lost or deleted, along with the functions that this section supported. About 65% to 75% of Prader-Willi syndrome cases result from the loss of function of several genes in one region of the father's chromosome 15, due to deletion. The corresponding mother's genes on chromosome 15 are always inactive and thus cannot make up for the deletion on the father's chromosome 15. The missing paternal genes normally play a fundamental role in regulating hunger and fullness.

- Maternal uniparental disomy. A cell usually contains one set of chromosomes from the father and another set from the mother.

In ordinary cases, a child has two chromosome 15s, one from each parent. In 20% to 30% of Prader-Willi syndrome cases, the child has two chromosome 15s from the mother and none from the father. Because genes located in the PWCR are normally inactive in the chromosome that comes from the mother, the child's lack of active genes in this region leads to Prader-Willi syndrome.

- An imprinting center defect. Genes in the PWCR on the chromosome that came from the mother are normally inactivated, due to a process known as "imprinting" that affects whether the cell is able to "read" a gene or not. In less than 5% of Prader-Willi syndrome cases, the chromosome 15 inherited from the father is imprinted in the same way as the mother's. This can be caused by a small deletion in a region of the father's chromosome that controls the imprinting process, called the imprinting center. In these cases, both of the child's copies of chromosome 15 have inactive PWCRs, leading to Prader-Willi syndrome.

How Do Health Care Providers Diagnose Prader-Willi Syndrome (PWS)?

In many cases of Prader-Willi syndrome, diagnosis is prompted by physical symptoms in the newborn.

If a newborn is unable to suck or feed for a few days and has a "floppy" body and weak muscle tone, a health care provider may conduct genetic testing for Prader-Willi syndrome. Formal diagnostic criteria for recognizing Prader-Willi syndrome depend on the age of the individual-specifically, whether the third birthday has been reached. Before age 3, the most important symptom is extremely poor muscle tone, called hypotonia, which makes infants feel floppy. In affected children 3 years of age and older, other symptoms become apparent, such as obesity, intellectual delays, learning disabilities, or behavior problems, especially connected with food and eating.

- Children younger than 3 years must have at least four major criteria and at least one minor criterion for a Prader-Willi syndrome diagnosis.

- Those older than 3 years must have at least five major criteria and at least three minor criteria for a diagnosis of Prader-Willi syndrome.

Major Clinical Criteria of Prader-Willi Syndrome

- Extremely weak muscles in the body's torso
- Difficulty sucking, which improves after the first few months
- Feeding difficulties and/or failure to grow, requiring feeding assistance, such as feeding tubes or special nipples to aid in sucking
- Beginning of rapid weight gain, between ages 1 and 6, resulting in severe obesity
- Excessive, uncontrollable overeating
- Specific facial features, including narrow forehead and down-turned mouth
- Reduced development of the genital organs, including small genitalia (vaginal lips and clitoris in females and small scrotum and penis in males); incomplete and delayed puberty; infertility
- Developmental delays, mild-to-moderate intellectual disability, multiple learning disabilities

Minor Clinical Criteria of Prader-Willi Syndrome

- Decreased movement and noticeable fatigue during infancy
- Behavioral problems-specifically, temper tantrums, obsessive-compulsive behavior, stubbornness, rigidity, stealing, and lying (especially related to food)
- Sleep problems, including daytime sleepiness and sleep disruption
- Short stature, compared with other members of the family, noticeable by age 15
- Light color of skin, eyes, and hair
- Small hands and feet in comparison to standards for height and age
- Narrow hands
- Nearsightedness and/or difficulty focusing both eyes at the same time
- Thick saliva
- Poor pronunciation
- Picking of the skin

Additional Findings

- High pain threshold
- Inability to vomit
- Curvature of the spine (scoliosis)
- Earlier-than-usual activity in the adrenal glands, which can lead to early puberty
- Especially brittle bones (called osteoporosis),

Genetic testing must confirm the Prader-Willi syndrome diagnosis. More than 99% of individuals with Prader-Willi syndrome have an abnormality within a specific area of chromosome 15. Early diagnosis is best because it enables affected individuals to begin early intervention/special needs programs and treatment specifically for Prader-Willi symptoms.

Genetic testing can confirm the chance that a sibling might be born with Prader-Willi syndrome. Prenatal diagnosis also is available for at-risk pregnancies-that is, pregnancies among women with a family history of Prader-Willi syndrome abnormalities.

Genetic Counseling and Testing of At-Risk Relatives

Genetic counseling and testing provide individuals and families with information about the nature, inheritance, and implications of genetic disorders so that they can make informed medical and personal decisions about having children. Genetic counseling helps people understand their risks. The risk of occurrence in siblings of patients with Prader-Willi syndrome depends on what caused the disorder to occur.

Is There a Cure for Prader-Willi Syndrome (PWS)?

Prader-Willi syndrome has no cure. However, early diagnosis and treatment may help prevent or reduce the number of challenges that individuals with Prader-Willi syndrome may experience, and which may be more of a problem if diagnosis or treatment is delayed.

What Are the Treatments for Prader-Willi Syndrome (PWS)?

Parents can enroll infants with PWS in early intervention programs. However, even if a PWS diagnosis is delayed, treatments are valuable at any age.

The types of treatment depend on the individual's symptoms. The health care provider may recommend the following:

- **Use of special nipples or tubes for feeding difficulties**. Difficulty in sucking is one of the most common symptoms of newborns with Prader-Willi syndrome. Special nipples or tubes are used for several months to feed newborns and infants who are unable to suck properly, to make sure that the infant is fed adequately and grows. To ensure that the child is growing properly, the health care provider will monitor height, weight, and body mass index (BMI) monthly during infancy.

- **Strict supervision of daily food intake**. Once overeating starts between ages 2 and 4 years, supervision will help to minimize food hoarding and stealing and prevent rapid weight gain and severe obesity. Parents should lock refrigerators and all cabinets containing food. No medications have proven beneficial in reducing food-seeking behavior. A well-balanced, low-calorie diet and regular exercise are essential and must be maintained for the rest of the individual's life. People with PWS rarely need more than 1,000 to 1,200 calories per day. Height, weight, and BMI should be monitored every 6 months during the first 10 years of life after infancy and once a year after age 10 for the rest of the person's life to make sure he or she is maintaining a healthy weight. Ongoing consultation with a dietitian to guarantee adequate vitamin and mineral intake, including calcium and vitamin D, might be needed.

- **Growth Hormone (GH) therapy**. GH therapy has been demonstrated to increase height, lean body mass, and mobility; decrease fat mass; and improve movement and flexibility in individuals with PWS from infancy through adulthood. When given early in life, it also may prevent or reduce behavioral difficulties. Additionally, GH therapy can help improve speech, improve abstract reasoning, and often allow information to be processed more quickly. It also has been shown to improve sleep quality and resting energy expenditure. GH therapy usually is started during infancy or at diagnosis with PWS. This therapy often continues during adulthood at 20% to 25% of the recommended dose for children.

- **Treatment of eye problems by a pediatric ophthalmologist**. Many infants have trouble getting their eyes to focus together. These infants should be referred to a pediatric

214

ophthalmologist who has expertise in working with infants with disabilities.

- **Treatment of curvature of the spine by an orthopedist**. An orthopedist should evaluate and treat, if necessary, curvature of the spine (scoliosis). Treatment will be the same as that for people with scoliosis who do not have PWS.

- **Sleep studies and treatment**. Sleep disorders are common with PWS. Treating a sleep disorder can help improve the quality of sleep. The same treatments that health care providers use with the general population can apply to individuals with PWS.

- **Physical therapy**. Muscle weakness is a serious problem among individuals with PWS. For children younger than age 3, physical therapy may increase muscular strength and help such children achieve developmental milestones. For older children, daily exercise will help build lean body mass.

- **Behavioral therapy**. People with PWS have difficulty controlling their emotions. Using behavioral therapy can help. Stubbornness, anger, and obsessive-compulsive behavior, including obsession with food, should be handled with behavioral management programs using firm limit-setting strategies. Structure and routines also are advised.

- **Medications**. Medications, especially serotonin reuptake inhibitors (SRIs), may reduce obsessive-compulsive symptoms. SRIs also may help manage psychosis.

- **Early interventions / Special needs programs**. Individuals with PWS have varying degrees of intellectual difficulty and learning disabilities. Early intervention programs, including speech therapy for delays in acquiring language and for difficulties with pronunciation, should begin as early as possible and continue throughout childhood. Special education is almost always necessary for school-age children. Groups that offer training in social skills may also prove beneficial. An individual aide is often useful in helping PWS children focus on schoolwork.

- **Sex hormone treatments and/or corrective surgery**. These treatments are used to treat small genitals (penis, scrotum, clitoris).

- **Replacement of sex hormones**. Replacement of sex hormones during puberty may result in development of adequate secondary sex characteristics (e.g., breasts, pubic hair, a deeper voice).

• **Placement in group homes during adulthood**. Group homes offer necessary structure and supervision for adults with PWS, helping them avoid compulsive eating, severe obesity, and other health problems.

Section 26.7

Smith-Lemli-Opitz Syndrome

Text in this section is excerpted from "Smith-Lemli-Opitz Syndrome," Social Security Administration (SSA), August 10, 2012. Reviewed February 2016.

What Is Smith-Lemli-Opitz Syndrome?

Smith-Lemli-Opitz Syndrome (SLOS) is an inherited genetic disorder that results in an enzyme deficiency (7-dehydrocholesterol reductase, or 7-DHC reductase) necessary for cholesterol metabolism. Toxic byproducts of disrupted cholesterol synthesis build up in the blood, nervous system, and other tissues, disrupting the growth and development of many body systems.

SLOS is characterized by multiple congenital malformations that are so severe that the fetus is often miscarried or still-born, or the infant dies within the first weeks of life. Surviving infants have dysmorphic facial features, microcephaly, toe abnormalities, and developmental delay. Many affected children have features of autism, and physical malformations of the heart, lungs, kidneys, gastrointestinal tract, and genitalia. Feeding difficulties and failure to thrive are common. Vision loss due to cataracts and optic nerve abnormalities, and hearing loss may also occur.

Diagnostic Testing

A definitive diagnosis of SLOS is by the measurement of plasma sterols, including cholesterol and genetic testing for evidence of mutations in the DHCR7 gene.

Physical Findings

Microcephaly, characteristic facial features such as broad nose, small lower jaw, and low set ears; and hypotonia, These infants may also have webbing of the second and third toes (syndactyly); extra fingers or toes (polydactyly); cleft palate, heart and lung defects, brain malformations, and hearing loss.

SLOS is a genetic condition that is present prior to birth but has signs that are so subtle that detection is not made until later childhood. Most cases identified at birth or shortly after birth are due to obvious birth defects. Mildly affected individuals may have only minor physical abnormalities with learning and behaviour problems. Some children with SLOS may have more severe intellectual impairments, multi-organ system failure, and behaviour problems that can include antisocial, self-destructive, violent acts; or withdrawal, self-stimulation, and autism.

There is no current cure for SLOS. Treatment is supportive and may include surgery to repair physical conditions, such as heart defects, cleft palate, or foot deformities. Hearing aids may benefit those with hearing loss. Gastrostomy feeding may be necessary for nutritional needs.

Section 26.8

Tourette Syndrome

Text in this section is excerpted from "Tourette Syndrome Fact Sheet," National Institute of Neurological Disorders and Stroke (NINDS), April 16, 2014.

What is Tourette syndrome?

Tourette syndrome (TS) is a neurological disorder characterized by repetitive, stereotyped, involuntary movements and vocalizations called tics. The disorder is named for Dr. Georges Gilles de la Tourette, the pioneering French neurologist who in 1885 first described the condition in an 86-year-old French noblewoman.

The early symptoms of TS are typically noticed first in childhood, with the average onset between the ages of 3 and 9 years. TS occurs in people from all ethnic groups; males are affected about three to four times more often than females. It is estimated that 200,000 Americans have the most severe form of TS, and as many as one in 100 exhibit milder and less complex symptoms such as chronic motor or vocal tics. Although TS can be a chronic condition with symptoms lasting a lifetime, most people with the condition experience their worst tic symptoms in their early teens, with improvement occurring in the late teens and continuing into adulthood.

Symptoms of TS ?

Tics are classified as either simple or complex. Simple motor tics are sudden, brief, repetitive movements that involve a limited number of muscle groups. Some of the more common simple tics include eye blinking and other eye movements, facial grimacing, shoulder shrugging, and head or shoulder jerking. Simple vocalizations might include repetitive throat-clearing, sniffing, or grunting sounds. Complex tics are distinct, coordinated patterns of movements involving several muscle groups. Complex motor tics might include facial grimacing combined with a head twist and a shoulder shrug. Other complex motor tics may actually appear purposeful, including sniffing or touching objects, hopping, jumping, bending, or twisting. Simple vocal tics may include throat-clearing, sniffing/snorting, grunting, or barking. More complex vocal tics include words or phrases.

Perhaps the most dramatic and disabling tics include motor movements that result in self-harm such as punching oneself in the face or vocal tics including coprolalia (uttering socially inappropriate words such as swearing) or echolalia (repeating the words or phrases of others). However, coprolalia is only present in a small number (10 to 15 percent) of individuals with TS. Some tics are preceded by an urge or sensation in the affected muscle group, commonly called a premonitory urge. Some with TS will describe a need to complete a tic in a certain way or a certain number of times in order to relieve the urge or decrease the sensation.

Tics are often worse with excitement or anxiety and better during calm, focused activities. Certain physical experiences can trigger or worsen tics, for example tight collars may trigger neck tics, or hearing another person sniff or throat-clear may trigger similar sounds. Tics do not go away during sleep but are often significantly diminished.

Course of TS

Tics come and go over time, varying in type, frequency, location, and severity. The first symptoms usually occur in the head and neck area and may progress to include muscles of the trunk and extremities. Motor tics generally precede the development of vocal tics and simple tics often precede complex tics. Most patients experience peak tic severity before the mid-teen years with improvement for the majority of patients in the late teen years and early adulthood. Approximately 10–15 percent of those affected have a progressive or disabling course that lasts into adulthood.

Can People with TS Control Their Tics?

Although the symptoms of TS are involuntary, some people can sometimes suppress, camouflage, or otherwise manage their tics in an effort to minimize their impact on functioning. However, people with TS often report a substantial buildup in tension when suppressing their tics to the point where they feel that the tic must be expressed (against their will). Tics in response to an environmental trigger can appear to be voluntary or purposeful but are not.

What Causes TS?

Although the cause of TS is unknown, current research points to abnormalities in certain brain regions (including the basal ganglia, frontal lobes, and cortex), the circuits that interconnect these regions, and the neurotransmitters (dopamine, serotonin, and norepinephrine) responsible for communication among nerve cells. Given the often complex presentation of TS, the cause of the disorder is likely to be equally complex.

What Disorders are Associated with Ts?

Many individuals with TS experience additional neurobehavioral problems that often cause more impairment than the tics themselves. These include inattention, hyperactivity and impulsivity (attention deficit hyperactivity disorder—ADHD); problems with reading, writing, and arithmetic; and obsessive-compulsive symptoms such as intrusive thoughts/worries and repetitive behaviors. For example, worries about dirt and germs may be associated with repetitive hand-washing, and concerns about bad things happening may be associated with ritualistic behaviors such as counting, repeating, or ordering and arranging.

People with TS have also reported problems with depression or anxiety disorders, as well as other difficulties with living, that may or may not be directly related to TS. In addition, although most individuals with TS experience a significant decline in motor and vocal tics in late adolescence and early adulthood, the associated neurobehavioral conditions may persist. Given the range of potential complications, people with TS are best served by receiving medical care that provides a comprehensive treatment plan.

How is TS Diagnosed?

TS is a diagnosis that doctors make after verifying that the patient has had both motor and vocal tics for at least 1 year. The existence of other neurological or psychiatric conditions can also help doctors arrive at a diagnosis. Common tics are not often misdiagnosed by knowledgeable clinicians. However, atypical symptoms or atypical presentations (for example, onset of symptoms in adulthood) may require specific specialty expertise for diagnosis. There are no blood, laboratory, or imaging tests needed for diagnosis. In rare cases, neuroimaging studies, such as magnetic resonance imaging (MRI) or computerized tomography (CT), electroencephalogram (EEG) studies, or certain blood tests may be used to rule out other conditions that might be confused with TS when the history or clinical examination is atypical.

It is not uncommon for patients to obtain a formal diagnosis of TS only after symptoms have been present for some time. The reasons for this are many. For families and physicians unfamiliar with TS, mild and even moderate tic symptoms may be considered inconsequential, part of a developmental phase, or the result of another condition. For example, parents may think that eye blinking is related to vision problems or that sniffing is related to seasonal allergies. Many patients are self-diagnosed after they, their parents, other relatives, or friends read or hear about TS from others.

How is TS Treated?

Because tic symptoms often do not cause impairment, the majority of people with TS require no medication for tic suppression. However, effective medications are available for those whose symptoms interfere with functioning. Neuroleptics (drugs that may be used to treat psychotic and non-psychotic disorders) are the most consistently useful medications for tic suppression; a number are available but some are more effective than others (for example, haloperidol and pimozide).

Unfortunately, there is no one medication that is helpful to all people with TS, nor does any medication completely eliminate symptoms. In addition, all medications have side effects. Many neuroleptic side effects can be managed by initiating treatment slowly and reducing the dose when side effects occur. The most common side effects of neuroleptics include sedation, weight gain, and cognitive dulling. Neurological side effects such as tremor, dystonic reactions (twisting movements or postures), parkinsonian-like symptoms, and other dyskinetic (involuntary) movements are less common and are readily managed with dose reduction.

Discontinuing neuroleptics after long-term use must be done slowly to avoid rebound increases in tics and withdrawal dyskinesias. One form of dyskinesia called tardive dyskinesia is a movement disorder distinct from TS that may result from the chronic use of neuroleptics. The risk of this side effect can be reduced by using lower doses of neuroleptics for shorter periods of time.

Other medications may also be useful for reducing tic severity, but most have not been as extensively studied or shown to be as consistently useful as neuroleptics. Additional medications with demonstrated efficacy include alpha-adrenergic agonists such as clonidine and guanfacine. These medications are used primarily for hypertension but are also used in the treatment of tics. The most common side effect from these medications that precludes their use is sedation. However, given the lower side effect risk associated with these medications, they are often used as first-line agents before proceeding to treatment with neuroleptics.

Effective medications are also available to treat some of the associated neurobehavioral disorders that can occur in patients with TS. Recent research shows that stimulant medications such as methylphenidate and dextroamphetamine can lessen ADHD symptoms in people with TS without causing tics to become more severe. However, the product labeling for stimulants currently contraindicates the use of these drugs in children with tics/TS and those with a family history of tics. Scientists hope that future studies will include a thorough discussion of the risks and benefits of stimulants in those with TS or a family history of TS and will clarify this issue. For obsessive-compulsive symptoms that significantly disrupt daily functioning, the serotonin reuptake inhibitors (clomipramine, fluoxetine, fluvoxamine, paroxetine, and sertraline) have been proven effective in some patients.

Behavioral treatments such as awareness training and competing response training can also be used to reduce tics. A recent NIH-funded, multi-center randomized control trial called Cognitive Behavioral Intervention for Tics, or CBIT, showed that training to voluntarily move in response to a premonitory urge can reduce tic symptoms. Other behavioral therapies, such as biofeedback or supportive therapy, have not been shown to reduce tic symptoms. However, supportive therapy can help a person with TS better cope with the disorder and deal with the secondary social and emotional problems that sometimes occur.

Is TS Inherited?

Evidence from twin and family studies suggests that TS is an inherited disorder. Although early family studies suggested an autosomal dominant mode of inheritance (an autosomal dominant disorder is one in which only one copy of the defective gene, inherited from one parent, is necessary to produce the disorder), more recent studies suggest that the pattern of inheritance is much more complex. Although there may be a few genes with substantial effects, it is also possible that many genes with smaller effects and environmental factors may play a role in the development of TS.

Genetic studies also suggest that some forms of ADHD and OCD are genetically related to TS, but there is less evidence for a genetic relationship between TS and other neurobehavioral problems that commonly co-occur with TS. It is important for families to understand that genetic predisposition may not necessarily result in full-blown TS; instead, it may express itself as a milder tic disorder or as obsessive-compulsive behaviors. It is also possible that the gene-carrying offspring will not develop any TS symptoms.

The gender of the person also plays an important role in TS gene expression. At-risk males are more likely to have tics and at-risk females are more likely to have obsessive-compulsive symptoms.

Genetic counseling of individuals with TS should include a full review of all potentially hereditary conditions in the family.

What is the Prognosis?

Although there is no cure for TS, the condition in many individuals improves in the late teens and early 20s. As a result, some may actually become symptom-free or no longer need medication for tic suppression. Although the disorder is generally lifelong and chronic, it is not a degenerative condition. Individuals with TS have a normal life expectancy. TS does not impair intelligence. Although tic symptoms tend to decrease with age, it is possible that neurobehavioral disorders such as ADHD, OCD, depression, generalized anxiety, panic attacks, and mood swings can persist and cause impairment in adult life.

What is the Best Educational Setting for Children with TS?

Although students with TS often function well in the regular classroom, ADHD, learning disabilities, obsessive-compulsive symptoms, and frequent tics can greatly interfere with academic performance or social adjustment. After a comprehensive assessment, students should be placed in an educational setting that meets their individual needs. Students may require tutoring, smaller or special classes, and in some cases special schools.

All students with TS need a tolerant and compassionate setting that both encourages them to work to their full potential and is flexible enough to accommodate their special needs. This setting may include a private study area, exams outside the regular classroom, or even oral exams when the child's symptoms interfere with his or her ability to write. Untimed testing reduces stress for students with TS.

What Research is Being Done?

Within the Federal government, the National Institute of Neurological Disorders and Stroke (NINDS), a part of the National Institutes of Health (NIH), is responsible for supporting and conducting research on the brain and nervous system. The NINDS and other NIH components, such as the National Institute of Mental Health, the *Eunice Kennedy Shriver* National Institute of Child Health and Human Development, the National Institute on Drug Abuse, and the National Institute on Deafness and Other Communication Disorders, support research of relevance to TS, either at NIH laboratories or through grants to major research institutions across the country. Another component of the Department of Health and Human Services, the Centers for Disease Control and Prevention, funds professional education programs as well as TS research.

Knowledge about TS comes from studies across a number of medical and scientific disciplines, including genetics, neuroimaging, neuropathology, clinical trials (medication and non-medication), epidemiology, neurophysiology, neuroimmunology, and descriptive/diagnostic clinical science.

Genetic studies. Currently, NIH-funded investigators are conducting a variety of large-scale genetic studies. Rapid advances in the technology of gene discovery will allow for genome-wide screening approaches in TS, and finding a gene or genes for TS would be a major step toward understanding genetic risk factors. In addition, understanding the genetics of TS genes may strengthen clinical diagnosis, improve genetic counseling, lead to the clarification of pathophysiology, and provide clues for more effective therapies.

Neuroimaging studies. Advances in imaging technology and an increase in trained investigators have led to an increasing use of novel and powerful techniques to identify brain regions, circuitry, and neurochemical factors important in TS and related conditions.

Neuropathology. There has been an increase in the number and quality of donated postmortem brains from TS patients available for research purposes. This increase, coupled with advances in neuropathological techniques, has led to initial findings with implications for neuroimaging studies and animal models of TS.

Clinical trials. A number of clinical trials in TS have recently been completed or are currently underway. These include studies of stimulant treatment of ADHD in TS and behavioral treatments for reducing tic severity in children and adults. Smaller trials of novel approaches to treatment such as dopamine agonists and glutamatergic medications also show promise.

Epidemiology and clinical science. Careful epidemiological studies now estimate the prevalence of TS to be substantially higher than previously thought with a wider range of clinical severity. Furthermore, clinical studies are providing new findings regarding TS and co-existing conditions. These include subtyping studies of TS and OCD, an examination of the link between ADHD and learning problems in children with TS, a new appreciation of sensory tics, and the role of co-existing disorders in rage attacks. One of the most important and controversial areas of TS science involves the relationship between TS and autoimmune brain injury associated with group A beta-hemolytic streptococcal infections or other infectious processes. There are a number of epidemiological and clinical investigations currently underway in this intriguing area.

Section 26.9

Tuberous Sclerosis

Text in this section is excerpted from "Tuberous Sclerosis
Fact Sheet," National Institute of Neurological Disorders and
Stroke (NINDS), July 27, 2015.

What is Tuberous Sclerosis?

Tuberous sclerosis—also called tuberous sclerosis complex (TSC)—
is a rare, multi-system genetic disease that causes benign tumors to
grow in the brain and on other vital organs such as the kidneys, heart,
eyes, lungs, and skin. It usually affects the central nervous system and
results in a combination of symptoms including seizures, developmental delay, behavioral problems, skin abnormalities, and kidney disease.

The disorder affects as many as 25,000 to 40,000 individuals in the
United States and about 1 to 2 million individuals worldwide, with
an estimated prevalence of one in 6,000 newborns. TSC occurs in all
races and ethnic groups, and in both genders.

The name tuberous sclerosis comes from the characteristic **tuber**
or potato-like nodules in the brain, which calcify with age and become
hard or *sclerotic*. The disorder—once known as *epiloia* or *Bourneville's
disease*—was first identified by a French physician more than 100
years ago.

Many TSC patients show evidence of the disorder in the first year
of life. However, clinical features can be subtle initially, and many
signs and symptoms take years to develop. As a result, TSC can be
unrecognized or misdiagnosed for years.

What causes Tuberous Sclerosis?

TSC is caused by defects, or mutations, on two genes-TSC1 and
TSC2. Only one of the genes needs to be affected for TSC to be present.
The TSC1 gene, discovered in 1997, is on chromosome 9 and produces
a protein called *hamartin*. The TSC2 gene, discovered in 1993, is on
chromosome 16 and produces the protein *tuberin*. Scientists believe
these proteins act in a complex as growth suppressors by inhibiting the

225

activation of a master, evolutionarily conserved kinase called mTOR. Loss of regulation of mTOR occurs in cells lacking either hamartin or tuberin, and this leads to abnormal differentiation and development, and to the generation of enlarged cells, as are seen in TSC brain lesions.

Is TSC Inherited?

Although some individuals inherit the disorder from a parent with TSC, most cases occur as sporadic cases due to new, spontaneous mutations in TSC1 or TSC2. In this situation, neither parent has the disorder or the faulty gene(s). Instead, a faulty gene first occurs in the affected individual.

In familial cases, TSC is an autosomal dominant disorder, which means that the disorder can be transmitted directly from parent to child. In those cases, only one parent needs to have the faulty gene in order to pass it on to a child. If a parent has TSC, each offspring has a 50 percent chance of developing the disorder. Children who inherit TSC may not have the same symptoms as their parent and they may have either a milder or a more severe form of the disorder.

Rarely, individuals acquire TSC through a process called **gonadal mosaicism**. These patients have parents with no apparent defects in the two genes that cause the disorder. Yet these parents can have a child with TSC because a portion of one of the parent's reproductive cells (sperm or eggs) can contain the genetic mutation without the other cells of the body being involved. In cases of gonadal mosaicism, genetic testing of a blood sample might not reveal the potential for passing the disease to offspring.

What are the Signs and Symptoms of TSC?

TSC can affect many different systems of the body, causing a variety of signs and symptoms. Signs of the disorder vary depending on which system and which organs are involved. The natural course of TSC varies from individual to individual, with symptoms ranging from very mild to quite severe. In addition to the benign tumors that frequently occur in TSC, other common symptoms include seizures, cognitive impairment, behavior problems, and skin abnormalities. Tumors can grow in nearly any organ, but they most commonly occur in the brain, kidneys, heart, lungs, and skin. Malignant tumors are rare in TSC. Those that do occur primarily affect the kidneys.

Brain involvement in TSC Three types of brain lesions are seen in TSC: *cortical tubers*, for which the disease is named, generally form on the surface of the brain but may also appear in the deep areas of the brain: *subependymal nodules (SEN)*, which form in the walls of the ventricles--the fluid-filled cavities of the brain; and *subependymal giant-call astrocytomas (SEGA)*, which develop from SEN and grow such that they may block the flow of fluid within the brain, causing a buildup of fluid and pressure and leading to headaches and blurred vision.

TSC usually causes the greatest problems for those affected and their family members through effects on brain function. Most individuals with TSC will have seizures at some point during their life. Seizures of all types may occur, including infantile spasms; tonic-clonic seizures (also known as grand mal seizures); or tonic, akinetic, atypical absence, myoclonic, complex partial or generalized squires. Infantile spasms can occur as soon as the day of birth and are often difficult to recognize. Seizures can also be difficult to control by medication, and sometimes surgery or other measures are used.

About one-half to two-thirds of individuals with TSC have developmental delays ranging from mild learning disabilities to severe impairment. Behavior problems, including aggression, sudden rage, attention deficit hyperactivity disorder, acting out, obsessive-compulsive disorder, and repetitive, destructive, or self-harming behavior occur in children with TSC and can be difficult to manage. About one-third of children with TSC meet criteria for autism spectrum disorder.

Kidney problems such as *cysts* and *angiomyolipomas* occur in an estimated 70 to 80 percent of individuals with TSC, usually occurring between ages 15 and 30. Cysts are usually small, appear in limited numbers, and cause no serious problems. Approximately 2 percent of individuals with TSC develop large numbers of cysts in a pattern similar to polycystic kidney disease during childhood. In these cases, kidney function is compromised and kidney failure occurs. In rare instances, the cysts may bleed, leading to blood loss and anemia.

Angiomyolipomas-benign growths consisting of fatty tissue and muscle cells-are the most common kidney lesions in TSC. These growths are seen in the majority of individuals with TSC, but are also found in about one of every 300 people without TSC. Angiomyolipomas caused by TSC are usually found in both kidneys and in most cases they produce no symptoms. However, they can sometimes grow so large that they cause pain or kidney failure. Bleeding from angiomyolipomas may also occur, causing both pain and weakness. If severe bleeding does not stop naturally, there may severe blood loss, resulting in profound anemia and a life-threatening drop in blood pressure, warranting urgent medical attention.

Other rare kidney problems include renal cell carcinoma, developing from an angiomyolipoma, and oncocytomas, benign tumors unique to individuals with TSC.

Tumors called cardiac *rhabdomyomas* are often found in the hearts of infants and young children with TSC, and they are often seen on prenatal fetus ultrasound exams. If the tumors are large or there are multiple tumors, they can block circulation and cause death. However, if they do not cause problems at birth-when in most cases they are at their largest size-they usually become smaller with time and do not affect the individual in later life.

Benign tumors called *phakomas* are sometimes found in the eyes of individuals with TSC, appearing as white patches on the retina. Generally they do not cause vision loss or other vision problems, but they can be used to help diagnose the disease.

Additional tumors and cysts may be found in other areas of the body, including the liver, lung, and pancreas. Bone cysts, rectal polyps, gum fibromas, and dental pits may also occur.

A wide variety of skin abnormalities may occur in individuals with TSC. Most cause no problems but are helpful in diagnosis. Some cases may cause disfigurement, necessitating treatment. The most common skin abnormalities include:

- Hypomelanic macules ("ash leaf spots"), which are white or lighter patches of skin that may appear anywhere on the body and are caused by a lack of skin pigment or melanin-the substance that gives skin its color.

- Reddish spots or bumps called *facial angiofibromas* (also called *adenoma sebaceum*), which appear on the face (sometimes resembling acne) and consist of blood vessels and fibrous tissue.

- Raised, discolored areas on the forehead called forehead plaques, which are common and unique to TSC and may help doctors diagnose the disorder.

- Areas of thick leathery, pebbly skin called shagreen patches, usually found on the lower back or nape of the neck.

- Small fleshy tumors called *ungual* or *subungual fibroma*s that grow around and under the toenails or fingernails and may need to be surgically removed if they enlarge or cause bleeding. These usually appear later in life, ages 20 - 50.

- Other skin features that are not unique to individuals with TSC, including *molluscum fibrosum* or skin tags, which typically occur across the back of the neck and shoulders, *café au lait spots* or flat brown marks, and *poliosis*, a tuft or patch of white hair that may appear on the scalp or eyelids.

Lung lesions are present in about one-third of adult women with TSC and are much less commonly seen in men. Lung lesions include lymphangioleiomyomatosis (LAM) and multinodular multifocal pneumocyte hyperplasia (MMPH). LAM is a tumor-like disorder in which cells proliferate in the lungs, and there is lung destruction with cyst formation. There is a range of symptoms with LAM, with many TSC individuals having no symptoms, while others suffer with breathlessness, which can progress and be severe. MMPH is a more benign tumor that occurs in men and women equally.

How is TSC Diagnosed?

The diagnosis of TSC is based upon clinical criteria. In many cases the first clue to recognizing TSC is the presence of seizures or delayed development. In other cases, the first sign may be white patches on the skin (hypomelanotic macules) or the identification of cardiac tumor rhabdomyoma.

Diagnosis of the disorder is based on a careful clinical exam in combination with computed tomography (CT) or magnetic resonance imaging (MRI) of the brain, which may show tubers in the brain, and an ultrasound of the heart, liver, and kidneys, which may show tumors in those organs. Doctors should carefully examine the skin for the wide variety of skin features, the fingernails and toenails for ungual fibromas, the teeth and gums for dental pits and/or gum fibromas, and the eyes for retinal lesions. A Wood's lamp or ultraviolet light may be used to locate the hypomelantic macules which are sometimes hard to see on infants and individuals with pale or fair skin. Because of the wide variety of signs of TSC, it is best if a doctor experienced in the diagnosis of TSC evaluates a potential patient.

In infants TSC may be suspected if the child has cardiac rhabdomyomas or seizures (infantile spasms) at birth. With a careful examination of the skin and brain, it may be possible to diagnose TSC in a very young infant. However, many children are not diagnosed until later in life when their seizures begin and other symptoms such as facial angiofibromas appear.

How is TSC Treated?

There is no cure for TSC, although treatment is available for a number of the symptoms. Antiepileptic drugs may be used to control seizures. Vigabatrin is a particularly useful medication in TSC, and has been approved by the U.S. Food and Drug Administration (FDA) for treatment of infantile spams in TSC, although it has significant side effects. The FDA has approved the drug everolimus (Afinitor) to treat subependymal giant cell astrocytomas (SEGA brain tumors) and angiomyolipoma kidney tumors. Specific medications may be prescribed for behavior problems. Intervention programs including special schooling and occupational therapy may benefit individuals with special needs and developmental issues. Surgery may be needed in case of complications connected to tubers, SEN or SEGA, as well as in risk of hemorrhage from kidney tumors. Respiratory insufficiency due to LAM can be treated with supplemental oxygen therapy or lung transplantation if severe.

Because TSC is a lifelong condition, individuals need to be regularly monitored by a doctor to make sure they are receiving the best possible treatments. Due to the many varied symptoms of TSC, care by a clinician experienced with the disorder is recommended.

Basic laboratory studies have revealed insight into the function of the TSC genes and has led to recent use of rapamycin and related drugs for treating some manifestations of TSC. Rapamycin has been shown to be effective in treating SEGA, the brain tumor seen in TSC. However, its benefit for a variety of other aspects of and tumors seen in people with TSC is less certain, and clinical trials looking at the benefit carefully are continuing. Rapamycin and related drugs are not yet approved by the FDA for any purpose in individuals with TSC.

What Is the Prognosis?

The prognosis for individuals with TSC is highly variable and depends on the severity of symptoms. Those individuals with mild symptoms usually do well and have a normal life expectancy, while paying attention to TSC-specific issues. Individuals who are severely affected can suffer from severe mental retardation and persistent epilepsy.

All individuals with TSC are at risk for life-threatening conditions related to the brain tumors, kidney lesions, or LAM. Continued monitoring by a physician experienced with TSC is important. With appropriate medical care, most individuals with the disorder can look forward to normal life expectancy.

Chapter 27

Other Conditions That May Accompany ASD

Chapter Contents

Section 27.1

Unhealthy Weight in U.S. Adolescents with Autism

Text in this section is excerpted from "Key Findings: Prevalence and Impact of Unhealthy Weight in a National Sample of US Adolescents with Autism and Other Learning and Behavioral Disorders," Centers for Disease Control and Prevention (CDC), March 4, 2014.

The Maternal and Child Health Journal has published a new study that focuses on unhealthy weight among adolescents with developmental disabilities. Researchers from CDC and the Health Resources and Services Administration found that obesity is high among adolescents with learning and behavioral developmental disabilities and highest among children with autism compared to adolescents without these conditions. This puts these already vulnerable adolescents at risk for lifelong health conditions related to being obese. Currently, there are no specific recommendations for preventing obesity among children or adolescents with developmental disabilities. Obesity prevention and management approaches for this at-risk group need further consideration.

Main Findings from this Study

- Adolescents with learning and behavioral developmental disabilities were about 1.5 times more likely to be obese than adolescents without developmental disabilities.

  - Adolescents with autism were about 2 times more likely to be obese than adolescents without developmental disabilities.

  - Among adolescents with either Attention-Deficit/ Hyperactivity Disorder (ADHD) or learning disorder/other developmental delay, those who were not taking prescription medications were more likely to be obese than adolescents without developmental disabilities.

- About 5.6% of adolescents with learning and behavioral developmental disabilities were underweight, compared with 3.5% of adolescents without developmental disabilities. This means that adolescents with learning and behavioral developmental disabilities were about 1.5 times more likely to be underweight

- Adolescents with intellectual disability were 4 times more likely to be underweight than adolescents without developmental disabilities. However, this likelihood decreased when taking into account whether the adolescent was born too small (less than 5.5 lbs).

- Both obese adolescents (with or without developmental disabilities) and adolescents with developmental disabilities (with or without obesity) were more likely to have health conditions, such as asthma, eczema, and migraine headaches in comparison to non-obese adolescents without developmental disabilities.

  - Adolescents with both obesity and developmental disabilities had the highest number of these same health conditions.

Table 27.1. Percentage of Adolescents Who Are Obese

Without Developmental Disabilities	13.10%
With any Learning Behavioral Developmental Disability	20.40%
With Autism	31.80%
With Intellectual Disability	19.80%
With ADHD	17.60%
With Learning Disorder/Other Developmental Delay	20.30%

Section 27.2

Childhood Vision Impairment, Hearing Loss, and Co-Occurring Autism Spectrum Disorder

Text in this section is excerpted from "Key findings: Childhood Vision Impairment, Hearing Loss and Co-Occurring Autism Spectrum Disorder," Centers for Disease Control and Prevention (CDC), February 12, 2015.

The *Disability and Health Journal* has published a new study: "Childhood vision impairment, hearing loss and co-occurring autism spectrum disorder." This study is based on information from the Metropolitan Atlanta Developmental Disabilities Surveillance Program (MADDSP). The study found that autism spectrum disorder was more common among children who also have vision impairment or hearing loss compared with the overall population of 8-year-old children with an autism spectrum disorder in metro Atlanta. More needs to be done to ensure that all children with autism spectrum disorder are identified as early as possible so that they can get the help they need.

Main Findings

Vision Impairment

- About 1 in 830 children in metro Atlanta has vision impairment.
- Approximately 7% of the children with vision impairment also had autism spectrum disorder compared with about 1% of children in metro Atlanta with autism spectrum disorder overall.
- Compared to children with vision impairment without an autism spectrum disorder, the children with vision impairment and autism spectrum disorder were significantly more likely to:
  - Be born too earl
  - Be born too small
  - Have intellectual disability

- The children with vision impairment and autism spectrum disorder were first evaluated by a community provider at about the same age as children without vision impairment. However, children with vision impairment were diagnosed with autism spectrum disorder later than those without vision impairment (6 years and 7 months compared to 4 years and 8 months).

Hearing Loss

- About 1 in 770 children in metro Atlanta has hearing loss.
- About 6% of the children with hearing loss also had autism spectrum disorder compared with about 1% of children in metro Atlanta with autism spectrum disorder overall.
- Compared to children with hearing loss without an autism spectrum disorder, the children with hearing loss and autism spectrum disorder were more likely to:
  - Be boys
  - Have intellectual disability and/or cerebral palsy
- The children with hearing loss and autism spectrum disorder were first evaluated by a community provider earlier than children without hearing loss (3 years and 4 months compared with 4 years and 2 months, respectively). However, both groups were diagnosed with autism spectrum disorder at about the same age (4 years and 7 months).

What Is the Take Home Message?

- This study highlights the need for:
  - Greater awareness of the signs and symptoms of autism spectrum disorder among doctors and other providers serving children with vision impairment or hearing loss;
  - More tools that can be used to diagnose autism spectrum disorder among children with vision impairment or hearing loss; and
  - Early treatment and improved services to address autism spectrum disorder among children with vision impairment or hearing loss.
- This study found that certain factors, such as being born too early, increase the chance of a child having both autism spectrum disorder and either vision impairment or hearing loss.

Part Five

Interventions and Treatments for Autism Spectrum Disorder

Chapter 28

ASD Interventions

Interventions—also known as procedures, programs, services, strategies, supports, or treatments—are designed to help people with autism spectrum disorders (ASD) and their families negotiate the challenges associated with ASD and achieve positive outcomes. There are many different types of ASD interventions, and they vary in terms of goals, purpose, scope, intensity, timing, duration, and methodology. Some interventions focus on improving communication skills, encouraging social interaction, promoting independence, or increasing educational achievement. Other interventions aim to address challenging or inappropriate behaviors, treat sensory processing issues, or develop adaptive skills.

All interventions are intended to help people with ASD capitalize on their strengths, improve upon their deficits, and maximize their growth and development. Most individuals with ASD receive a combination of interventions from multiple providers, such as psychologists, behavior specialists, speech pathologists, physical therapists, and special education teachers.

Autism is a complex disorder that affects each person differently, so the key is to develop the right combination of interventions and therapies to meet an individual's unique needs. In general, though, research has shown that early intervention is a critical factor in terms of improving social skills and behavior for children with ASD. The biological processes underlying brain systems and functions are most responsive to outside influences during the first few years of life, so the likelihood of interventions leading to significant breakthroughs

"ASD Interventions," © 2016 Omnigraphics, Inc. Reviewed February 2016.

is highest at that time. Appropriate interventions can still produce positive results for older children, teenagers, and adults with ASD, however. Studies have shown that interventions can reduce ASD symptoms and lead to improvements in health, independence, and quality of life for people with ASD.

Effective ASD interventions typically include a predictable schedule, structured activities, and positive reinforcement of behavior. Outcomes are also enhanced when treatment programs break tasks down into simple steps, engage the person's attention and build on their interests, and promote self-esteem and independence. Successful interventions require the involvement of parents and caregivers because they play such a prominent role in shaping the experiences and environment of the person with ASD. The professional who leads the intervention must have the necessary skills and experience in working with people with autism, as well as a style that is a good fit with the patient. Finally, the process works best when professionals work collaboratively and coordinate their efforts across different types of interventions.

The Intervention Process

ASD intervention can be viewed as part of a process. The process begins with screening children for symptoms of autism, diagnosing ASD, and conducting assessments of skills, abilities, challenges, and deficits in functioning. Once an individual's unique needs have been identified through assessments, the next step is planning interventions to help the individual reach his or her goals. After the intervention plan has been developed and implemented, the final step in the process involves monitoring progress and revising the plan as needed.

Assessment

Assessment for intervention planning is typically conducted by a multidisciplinary team of professionals. A thorough assessment of an individual's symptoms, behavior, communication, social competence, and psychological functioning is required to determine what interventions will be most effective. The information gathered in the assessments guides the development of an individualized intervention plan.

Intervention Planning

Once the assessment results have identified the strengths and needs of the person with ASD, the individual and his or her parents and caregivers work with a team of professionals to review and select interventions to meet their goals. Interventions chosen should be supported by evidence-based research findings, reflect the values and preferences of the individual and his or her family, and be accessible given family and community resources. The final part of the intervention plan involves determining procedures to be used for monitoring progress toward meeting objectives.

Monitoring Progress

Once the intervention plan is put in place, data is collected and compared to the initial assessment results to monitor the individual's progress in response to the interventions. This data helps families and professionals determine whether the interventions are working as intended and whether the desired changes or improvements are occurring. If not, adjustments and revisions can be made to the intervention plan.

Types of Interventions

There are many different types of interventions available to address many different aspects of ASD. A few of the more common interventions include:

- Social skills training to help children with ASD express thoughts and feelings appropriately and interact with others in social situations.

- Speech-language therapy to help children with ASD communicate better and interpret the verbal and nonverbal signals of others.

- Sensory integration therapy to help children with ASD develop their motor skills, gain control over their senses, or improve their responses to sensory stimuli.

- Cognitive behavior therapy (CBT) to help people with ASD manage their emotions, fears, and anxieties in order to reduce challenging behaviors and respond more appropriately in various situations.

- Applied behavioral analysis (ABA)—a highly structured method of breaking down skills into small steps and providing positive reinforcement for achieving the desired result—to teach people with ASD communication, social, academic, adaptive, and other skills, as well as to reduce challenging behaviors.

241

- Parent education and training to enable caregivers to incorporate aspects of treatment programs into the daily home life of a child with ASD. Interventions such as social skills and behavior training tend to be more successful when they are reinforced consistently in multiple settings.

References

1. "Autism Spectrum Disorders: Guide to Evidence-Based Interventions." Missouri Autism Guidelines Initiative, 2012.

2. "Interventions and Treatment Options." Autism Speaks, 2016.

Chapter 29

Evidence for ASD Interventions

Effects of Behavioral Interventions on Core and Commonly Associated Symptoms in Children with ASD

Studies of Early Intensive Behavioral and Developmental Interventions

Based on the that studies included five RCTs of good quality, six of fair quality, and one of poor quality. Individual studies using intensive University of California, Los Angeles (UCLA)/Lovaas-based interventions, the Early Start Denver Model (ESDM), the Learning Experiences and Alternate Program for Preschoolers and their Parents (LEAP) program, and eclectic variants reported improvements in outcomes for young children. Improvements were most often seen in cognitive abilities and language acquisition, with less robust and consistent improvements seen in adaptive skills, core ASD symptom severity, and social functioning.

Young children receiving high-intensity applied behavior analysis (ABA)-based interventions over extended timeframes (i.e., 8 months–2 years) displayed improvement in cognitive functioning and language skills relative to community controls. However, the magnitude of these

Text in this chapter is excerpted from "Therapies for Children with Autism Spectrum Disorder: Behavioral Interventions Update," Agency for Healthcare Research and Quality (AHRQ), August 6, 2014.

effects varied across studies. This variation may reflect subgroups showing differential responses to particular interventions. Intervention response is likely moderated by both treatment and child factors, but exactly how these moderators function is not clear. Despite multiple studies of early intensive treatments, intervention approaches still vary substantially, which makes it difficult to tease apart what these unique treatment and child factors may be. Further, the long-term impact of these early skill improvements is not yet clear, and many studies did not follow children beyond late preschool or early school years.

Studies of high-intensity early intervention services also demonstrated improvements in children's early adaptive behavior skills, but these improvements were more variable than those found for early cognitive and language skills. Treatment effects were not consistently maintained over followup assessments across studies. Many studies measured different adaptive behavior domains (creating within-scale variability), and some evidence suggests that adaptive behavior changes may be contingent on baseline child characteristics, such as cognitive/language skills and ASD severity.

Evidence for the impact of early intensive intervention on core ASD symptoms is limited and mixed. Children's symptom severity often decreased during treatment, but these improvements often did not differ from those of children in control groups. Better quality studies reported positive effects of intervention on symptom severity, but multiple lower quality studies did not.

Since our previous review, there have been substantially more studies of well-controlled low-intensity interventions that provide parent training in bolstering social communication skills. Although parent training programs modified parenting behaviors during interactions, data were more limited about their ability to improve broad developmental skills (such as cognition, adaptive behavior, and ASD symptom severity) beyond language gains for some children. Children receiving low-intensity interventions have not demonstrated the same substantial gains in cognitive skills seen in the early intensive intervention paradigms.

Social Skills Studies

We located 13 studies addressing interventions targeting social skills, including 11 RCTs. The overall quality of studies improved in comparison with the previous review, with 2 good-quality and 10 fair-quality studies. Social skills interventions varied widely in terms of scope and intensity. A few studies replicated interventions using the Skillstreaming model, which uses a published treatment manual (i.e., is manualized) to promote a consistent approach. Other studies incorporated peer-mediated and/or group-based approaches, and still others described interventions that focused on emotion identification and Theory of Mind training. The studies also varied in intensity, with most interventions consisting of 1–2 hour sessions/week lasting approximately 4–5 weeks. However, some of the group-based approaches lasted 15–16 weeks.

Most studies reported short-term gains in either parent-rated social skills or directly tested emotion recognition. However, our confidence (strength of evidence) in that effect is low. Although we now have higher quality studies of social skills interventions that demonstrate positive effects, our ability to determine effectiveness continues to be limited by the diversity of the intervention protocols and measurement tools (i.e., no consistent outcome measures used across studies). Studies also included only participants considered "high functioning" and/or with IQ test scores >70, thus limiting generalization of results to children with more significant impairments. Maintenance and generalization of these skills beyond the intervention setting are also inconsistent, with parent and clinician raters noting variability in performance across environments.

Play-/Interaction-Focused Studies

Since our previous review, more studies of well-controlled joint attention interventions across a range of intervention settings (e.g., clinician, parent, teacher delivered) have been published. This growing evidence base includes 11 RCTs of good and fair quality and suggests that joint attention interventions may be associated with positive outcomes for toddler and preschool children with ASD, particularly when targeting joint attention skills themselves as well as related social communication and language skills. Although joint attention intervention studies demonstrated changes within this theoretically important domain, data are more limited about their ability to improve broad developmental skills (such as cognition, adaptive behavior, and ASD symptom severity) beyond direct measures of joint attention and related communication and language gains over time.

Specific training that used naturalistic approaches to promote imitation (e.g., Reciprocal Imitation Training) was associated with some improvements, not only in imitation skills, but also potentially in other social communication skills (such as joint attention). Additionally, parent training in a variety of play-based interventions was associated with enhanced early social communication skills (e.g., joint attention, engagement, play interactions), play skills, and early language skills.

Studies of Interventions Targeting Conditions Commonly Associated with ASD

Six RCTs (five good and one fair quality) of interventions addressing conditions commonly associated with ASD identified for the current update measured anxiety symptoms as a primary outcome. Five of these studies reported significantly greater improvements in anxiety symptoms in the intervention group compared with controls. Two found positive effects of cognitive behavioral therapy (CBT) on the core ASD symptom of socialization, and one reported improvements in executive function in the treatment group. The one RCT that did not find a significant benefit of CBT compared it with social recreational therapy rather than with treatment as usual or a wait-listed control group.

The studies examining the effects of CBT on anxiety had largely consistent methodologies. Six studies provided followup data reflecting treatment effects that lasted beyond the period of direct intervention. Two common factors limit the applicability of the results, however. Due to the nature of CBT, which is often language intensive and requires a certain level of reasoning skills to make abstract connections between concepts, most studies included only children with IQs much greater than 70. These studies report positive results regarding the use of CBT to treat anxiety in children with ASD. They also report some positive results in socialization, executive function, and communication; however, these results were less robust, and it is unclear in some studies if these improvements exceeded improvements related to the impact of ameliorated anxiety itself.

Additional data in the current review relate to parent training to address challenging behavior. Specifically, one fair-quality study combined a parent-training approach with risperidone. This combination significantly reduced irritability, stereotypical behaviors, and hyperactivity, and improved socialization and communication skills. However, these effects were not maintained at 1 year after treatment.

Other Behavioral Studies

Two RCTs (one fair and one poor quality) examined neurofeedback and found some improvements on parent-rated measures of communication and tests of executive function. Three fair-quality RCTs reported on sleep-focused interventions, with little positive effect of a sleep education pamphlet for parents in one, improvements in sleep quality in treatment arms (melatonin alone, melatonin + CBT) in another, and some improvements in time to fall asleep in one short-term RCT of sleep education programs for parents. One poor-quality study of parent education to mitigate feeding problems reported no significant effects.

Modifiers of Treatment Effects

Among the potential modifiers or moderators of early intensive ABA-based interventions, younger age at intake was associated with better outcomes for children in a limited number of studies. Greater baseline cognitive skills and higher adaptive behavior scores were associated with better outcomes across behavioral interventions, but again, these associations were not consistent. In general, children with lower symptom severity or less severe diagnoses improved more than participants with greater impairments.

Many studies (e.g., social skills, CBT) restricted the range of participants' impairment at baseline (e.g., recruiting only participants with IQs >70), limiting understanding of intervention impact on broader populations. Studies assessing parental responsiveness to children's communication typically reported better outcomes in children whose parents were more aligned with the child's communication versus those who attempted to redirect or were less synchronized. Regarding intervention-related factors, duration of treatment had an inconsistent effect. Some studies reported improved outcomes with more intervention time and others reported no association. Overall, most studies were not adequately designed or controlled to identify true moderators of treatment response.

Treatment Effects That Predict Long-Term Outcomes

Few studies assess end-of-treatment effects that may predict outcomes. Several early intensive behavioral and developmental interventions are associated with changes in outcome measures over the course of very lengthy treatments, but such outcomes usually have not been assessed beyond treatment windows. One family of studies attempted to follow young children receiving early joint attention intervention until they were school aged, but this study failed to include adequate followup of control conditions. It also involved children who were receiving many hours of uncontrolled interventions during the course of study.

Generalization of Treatment Effects

The majority of the social skills and behavioral intervention studies targeting associated conditions attempted to collect outcomes based on parent, self, teacher, and peer report of targeted symptoms (e.g., anxiety, externalizing behaviors, social skills, peer relations) at home, at school, and in the community. Although such ratings outside of the clinical setting may be suggestive of generalization in that they improve outcomes in the daily context/life of the child, in most cases, these outcomes are parent reported and not confirmed with direct observation. Behavioral intervention studies rarely measured outcomes beyond the intervention period, and we therefore cannot assume that effects were maintained over time.

Treatment Approaches for Children under Age 2 at Risk for Diagnosis of ASD

In the studies addressing interventions for younger children, children who received behavioral interventions seemed to improve regardless of intervention type (including the comparator interventions, which were also behavioral). None of the fair- or good-quality studies compared treatment groups with a no-treatment control group. Potential modifiers of treatment efficacy include baseline levels of object interest. Most outcome measures of adaptive functioning were based on parent report, and the effect of parental perception of treatment efficacy on perception (and report) of child functioning was generally not explored.

A growing number of studies of improved quality demonstrated positive effects of social skills interventions on at least one outcome measure, but a lack of consistency in the interventions studied and outcome measures used makes it difficult to understand specific effects of different intervention modalities.

A growing evidence base also suggests that children receiving targeted play-based interventions (e.g., joint attention, imitation, play-based interventions) demonstrate improvements in early social communication skills. Children receiving targeted joint attention packages in combination with other interventions show substantial improvements in joint attention and language skills over time. There is also evidence across a variety of play-based interventions that young children may display short-term improvements in early play, imitation, joint attention, and interaction skills. However, evidence that these short-term improvements are linked to broader indexes of change over time is not substantial.

Chapter 30

Early Intervention for Children with Developmental Delays

Chapter Contents

Section 30.1

Early Services for ASD

Text in this section is excerpted from "Treatment," Centers for Disease Control and Prevention (CDC), February 24, 2015.

Treatment

There are no medications that can cure ASD or treat the core symptoms. However, there are medications that can help some people with ASD function better. For example, medication might help manage high energy levels, inability to focus, depression, or seizures.

Medications might not affect all children in the same way. It is important to work with a health care professional who has experience in treating children with ASD. Parents and health care professionals must closely monitor a child's progress and reactions while he or she is taking a medication to be sure that any negative side effects of the treatment do not outweigh the benefits.

It is also important to remember that children with ASD can get sick or injured just like children without ASD. Regular medical and dental exams should be part of a child's treatment plan. Often it is hard to tell if a child's behavior is related to the ASD or is caused by a separate health condition. For instance, head banging could be a symptom of the ASD, or it could be a sign that the child is having headaches. In those cases, a thorough physical exam is needed. Monitoring healthy development means not only paying attention to symptoms related to ASD, but also to the child's physical and mental health, as well.

Early Intervention Services

Research shows that early intervention treatment services can greatly improve a child's development. Early intervention services help children from birth to 3 years old (36 months) learn important skills. Services include therapy to help the child talk, walk, and interact with others. Therefore, it is important to talk to your child's doctor as soon as possible if you think your child has an ASD or other developmental problem.

Even if your child has not been diagnosed with an ASD, he or she may be eligible for early intervention treatment services. The Individuals with Disabilities Education Act (IDEA) says that children under the age of 3 years (36 months) who are at risk of having developmental delays may be eligible for services. These services are provided through an early intervention system in your state. Through this system, you can ask for an evaluation.

In addition, treatment for particular symptoms, such as speech therapy for language delays, often does not need to wait for a formal ASD diagnosis. While early intervention is extremely important, intervention at any age can be helpful.

Types of Treatments

There are many different types of treatments available. For example, auditory training, discrete trial training, vitamin therapy, anti-yeast therapy, facilitated communication, music therapy, occupational therapy, physical therapy, and sensory integration.

The different types of treatments can generally be broken down into the following categories:

- Behavior and Communication Approaches

- Dietary Approaches

- Medication

- Complementary and Alternative Medicine

Behavior and Communication Approaches

According to reports by the American Academy of Pediatrics and the National Research Council, behavior and communication approaches that help children with ASD are those that provide structure, direction, and organization for the child in addition to family participation.

Applied Behavior Analysis (ABA)

A notable treatment approach for people with an ASD is called applied behavior analysis (ABA). ABA has become widely accepted among health care professionals and used in many schools and treatment clinics. ABA encourages positive behaviors and discourages negative behaviors in order to improve a variety of skills. The child's progress is tracked and measured.

There are different types of ABA. Following are some examples:

- **Discrete Trial Training (DTT)**: DTT is a style of teaching that uses a series of trials to teach each step of a desired behavior or response. Lessons are broken down into their simplest parts and positive reinforcement is used to reward correct answers and behaviors. Incorrect answers are ignored.

- **Early Intensive Behavioral Intervention (EIBI)**: This is a type of ABA for very young children with an ASD, usually younger than five, and often younger than three.

- **Pivotal Response Training (PRT)**: PRT aims to increase a child's motivation to learn, monitor his own behavior, and initiate communication with others. Positive changes in these behaviors should have widespread effects on other behaviors.

- **Verbal Behavior Intervention (VBI)**: VBI is a type of ABA that focuses on teaching verbal skills.

Other therapies that can be part of a complete treatment program for a child with an ASD include:

- **Developmental, Individual Differences, Relationship-Based Approach (DIR; also called "Floortime")**. Floortime focuses on emotional and relational development (feelings, relationships with caregivers). It also focuses on how the child deals with sights, sounds, and smells. Treatment and Education of Autistic and related Communication-handicapped Children (TEACCH) uses visual cues to teach skills. For example, picture cards can help teach a child how to get dressed by breaking information down into small steps.

- **Occupational Therapy**. Occupational therapy teaches skills that help the person live as independently as possible. Skills might include dressing, eating, bathing, and relating to people.

- **Sensory Integration Therapy**. Sensory integration therapy helps the person deal with sensory information, like sights, sounds, and smells. Sensory integration therapy could help a child who is bothered by certain sounds or does not like to be touched.

- **Speech Therapy**. Speech therapy helps to improve the person's communication skills. Some people are able to learn verbal communication skills. For others, using gestures or picture boards is more realistic.

- **The Picture Exchange Communication System (PECS).** PECS uses picture symbols to teach communication skills. The person is taught to use picture symbols to ask and answer questions and have a conversation.

Dietary Approaches

Some dietary treatments have been developed by reliable therapists. But many of these treatments do not have the scientific support needed for widespread recommendation. An unproven treatment might help one child, but may not help another.

Many biomedical interventions call for changes in diet. Such changes include removing certain types of foods from a child's diet and using vitamin or mineral supplements. Dietary treatments are based on the idea that food allergies or lack of vitamins and minerals cause symptoms of ASD. Some parents feel that dietary changes make a difference in how their child acts or feels.

If you are thinking about changing your child's diet, talk to the doctor first. Or talk with a nutritionist to be sure your child is getting important vitamins and minerals.

Medication

There are no medications that can cure ASD or even treat the main symptoms. But there are medications that can help some people with related symptoms. For example, medication might help manage high energy levels, inability to focus, depression, or seizures.

Complementary and Alternative Treatments

To relieve the symptoms of ASD, some parents and health care professionals use treatments that are outside of what is typically recommended by the pediatrician. These types of treatments are known as complementary and alternative treatments (CAM). They might include special diets, chelation (a treatment to remove heavy metals like lead from the body), biologicals (e.g., secretin), or body-based systems (like deep pressure).

These types of treatments are very controversial. Recent research shows that as many as one third of parents of children with an ASD may have tried complementary or alternative medicine treatments, and up to 10% may be using a potentially dangerous treatment. Before starting such a treatment, check it out carefully, and talk to your child's doctor.

Section 30.2

Autism Intervention for Toddlers Improves Developmental Outcomes

Text in this section is excerpted from "Autism: Why Act Early?"
Centers for Disease Control and Prevention (CDC), April 13, 2015.

Helping Your Child

If you're concerned about your child's development, don't wait. You know your child best. Use a developmental milestones checklist, talk with your child's doctor, and call your local early intervention program.

Acting early can make a big difference!

Intervention is **likely to be more effective** *and less costly when it is provided earlier in life rather than later.*

- "My doctor said to wait. But having two older children, I knew something wasn't right, and I wasn't willing to wait around hoping it would all get better on its own. I got a second opinion and called the early intervention program, and I'm so thankful that I did! My instincts were right, and now that my daughter is getting help, I'm seeing her make real progress, progress she might not have made if I had waited to act." *Maryland mom*

High-quality early intervention services can **change a child's developmental path** *and improve outcomes for children, families, and communities.*

- "Things are confusing; I needed someone to teach me the 'rules.' The things I learned in early intervention helped the world make sense." *Florida teenager with ASD Autism Spectrum Disorder*

- "Because my parents acted early, I have a brother who I can have a relationship with." *Florida brother of person with ASD Autism Spectrum Disorder*

- "If it's autism, waiting for a child to 'catch up on his own' just won't work. Acting early can help a child communicate, play, and learn from the world now and for the future. It can also prevent frustration—so common in children with communication difficulties—from turning into more difficult behaviors." Pennsylvania clinical psychologist

Connections in the brain (also called neural circuits), which create the foundation for learning, behavior and health, are most adaptable or "plastic" during the **first three years** *of life. Over time, they become increasingly difficult to change.*

- "Every day you delay action is an opportunity missed." *Florida dad*

- "The earlier developmental delays are detected and intervention begins, the greater the chance the young child, because of more brain plasticity, has of eventually achieving typical or near typical development. Unfortunately, the longer we wait to start interventions, the less likely the child will achieve his or her maximal potential. " *Georgia pediatrician."*

- "Your child expects you to meet his needs, and waiting will not solve anything." *Florida teenager with ASD*

- "Action replaced fear and empowered me with knowledge to help my son. He has overcome most of his symptoms and is headed to college next year." *Florida mom.*

- "Acting early gives your child a chance to receive the appropriate therapy, giving him the best chance for a good outcome in the future. I believe that early intervention is the reason my high-functioning son is now able to blend in with his peers and attend kindergarten in a regular classroom with no supports." *Kansas mom*

Chapter 31

Interventions for Individuals with Asperger Syndrome

Helping Your Child

Although Asperger syndrome (AS) presents challenges for kids and their parents, you can help your child adjust and offer support in many ways:

- Look into educational or training programs for parents. You're your child's first teacher and you'll continue to be the cornerstone in supporting his or her development.

- Teach your child self-help skills. Learning these skills helps kids achieve maximum independence.

- Because it's not always obvious that a child has AS, alert others to the fact that your child has special needs. As a parent, you may have to take on the role of educator when dealing with teachers, medical personnel, and other caregivers.

Text in this chapter is excerpted from "Asperger Syndrome," © 1995–2016. The Nemours Foundation/KidsHealth®. Reprinted with permission; and text from "I Have Asperger Syndrome. How Do I Make New Friends?" © 1995–2016. The Nemours Foundation/KidsHealth®. Reprinted with permission; and text from "Interventions for Adolescents and Young Adults with Autism Spectrum Disorders," Agency for Healthcare Research and Quality (AHRQ), August 27, 2012.

- Find a program that addresses your child's specific needs or areas of "deficiency." The Autism Society of America (ASA) encourages family members to talk to the program director to determine if the curriculum or program addresses their child's particular issues.

- Choose special programs or treatments that focus on long-term outcomes and that take the developmental level of your child into consideration.

- Remember that your child is part of a family unit and that his or her needs should be balanced with the those of other family members.

- Get support for yourself and other family members. You can't help your child if you are not meeting your own emotional and physical needs. Your community may offer support groups at a local hospital or mental health center. There is considerable state-to-state variation in the types of government-sponsored services and other programs available to children with autism spectrum disorders and their families.

Your Child's Future

Currently, few facilities are specifically dedicated to providing for the needs of kids with AS. Some children are in mainstream schools where their progress depends on the support and encouragement of parents, caregivers, teachers, and classmates. However, some go to special schools for kids with autism or learning disabilities.

Many people with AS can function well in most aspects of life, so the condition does not have to prevent your child from succeeding academically and socially.

You may feel overwhelmed and discouraged if your child is diagnosed with AS. Remember that your child's treatment team can provide enormous support and encouragement for your child — and your family.

ASD in Adolescence and Young Adulthood

Research conducted to date has suggested that most individuals with ASD will require some sort of intervention, often at very intensive levels, throughout adolescence and adulthood, and the estimated costs of medical and nonmedical care (e.g., special education, daycare) are high. One study estimates that the total yearly societal per capita cost of caring for and treating a person with autism in the United States at \$3.2 million and at about \$35 billion for an entire birth cohort of individuals with autism. A study of health care utilization in a large group health plan revealed increased medication costs in older children with an ASD compared with younger children, as well as similarly aged adolescents without an ASD; other care costs were also higher in this population, including a significantly increased rate of hospitalizations.

Costs of transitional and employment programs are also high for young adults with ASD. In a recent analysis of U.S. Federal- and State-funded vocational rehabilitation programs, enrolled individuals with ASD were among the most costly of nine disability groups, with costs even higher among those with ASD and another concomitant disability. However, those with ASD had a higher rate of employment (40.8%) at the time of case closure compared with those with other disabilities, though with fewer work hours and lower wages than some other disability groups.

There is no cure for ASD and no global consensus regarding which intervention strategies are most effective. Chronic management, often using multiple treatment approaches, may be required to maximize ultimate functional independence and quality of life by minimizing core ASD features, facilitating development and learning, promoting socialization, reducing maladaptive behaviors, and educating and supporting families. Investigators have noted that less data on therapies for adolescents or young adults exist than for younger children, and such research is increasingly important as the prevalence of ASD continues to grow and as children with ASD diagnoses reach adolescence.

Research into educational approaches for adolescents and young adults with ASD is very limited, with only two small crossover studies identified in this population. These studies focused on the impact of highly specified educational strategies and outcomes (e.g., vocabulary development) and ultimately provide little evidence to support selection of either specific or various broad-based educational strategies.

Studies of adaptive/life skills-focused interventions meeting our criteria were of poor quality, addressed disparate interventions, and typically included few participants. Individual studies documented specified short-term gains in learning or successfully executing an adaptive or life skills-focused tasks, but the applicability and generalization of these findings is limited by the highly specified approaches utilized. Additionally, studies were typically uncontrolled and of short duration.

Among five studies of supported employment/vocational interventions, all focused on on-the-job supports as the employment/vocational intervention. No other vocational interventions were reported in the literature meeting our study criteria. Our ability to know the ultimate benefit of supported employment programs is limited given the existing research. No study utilized random assignment, making it difficult to draw conclusions about the effectiveness of the programs, and all studies were poor quality. Three small studies focused on employment as an outcome of interest reported that supported employment interventions increased rates of employment for young adults with ASD. Additional studies reported that supported employment was associated with improvements in quality of life and core symptoms and cognitive functioning in supported employment participants relative to young adults with ASD in sheltered work settings.

Supported employment interventions remain understudied. For example, only one study examined rates of employment for programs that lasted 3 years or longer. Further, this longer term study did not include a control group, making it impossible to determine the rates of employment over time for young adults with ASD who were not participating in the supported employment intervention. Finally, none of the studies examined whether increased employment rates or improvements in other outcomes were sustained after the termination of the supported employment intervention.

The use of medical interventions in adolescents and young adults with ASD is common. However, there is little evidence that supports the use of medical interventions specifically in this population. Overall, most studies focused on the use of medications to address specific challenging behaviors (i.e., aggression or irritability). A crossover study of risperidone also showed a significant reduction of irritability/agitation ratings with risperidone treatment, but the control was indirect. A placebo-controlled crossover study found that haloperidol significantly improved hyperactivity/defiance ratings, but no significant difference was found for irritability/agitation or other symptoms. While limited literature supports the use of risperidone in adolescents or young adults with ASD, the efficacy of risperidone in studies including mostly children has moderate strength of evidence that is consistent with the results of the one fair RCT and one poor crossover study in adults with ASD. There is therefore no evidence to suggest that the effects of risperidone for irritability/agitation in ASD are specific to a particular age range.

A number of studies of SRIs were identified but with limited consistency across studies as a whole. An RCT of fluvoxamine showed decreases in repetitive behavior, aggression, autistic symptoms, and language usage. In contrast, no significant differences were observed in a crossover study of clomipramine versus placebo. Three case series of

SRIs were also identified, including sertraline, fluoxetine, and clomipramine, with each study reporting some benefit to treatment. A recent study not meeting criteria for this review contributes to the limited data on SRIs: the placebo-controlled RCT51 of fluoxetine included individuals with ASD with a mean age of and reported improvements in repetitive behavior and ASD symptoms in the treatment group and mild harms. This study used a different medication than the one fair quality study in our age range, so it would be unlikely to influence the strength of evidence for a specific medication. It is possible, however, that a systematic review of SRIs in the broader age range of adults with ASD could provide data that might increase our confidence in the effect.

A crossover study of the opioid receptor antagonist naltrexone found no significant improvements in problem behavior and showed worsening of stereotyped behavior with naltrexone treatment compared with placebo.

Based upon the published studies in adolescents and adults with ASD, the strength of evidence is insufficient for harms associated with medications tested in this population. As in the case of efficacy, the data on adverse effects associated with risperidone, including sedation and weight gain, are consistent with the high strength of evidence for these adverse effects in children with ASD. The available evidence therefore appears consistent in supporting our understanding of the risk of these adverse events in ASD without being limited to a specific age range.

Of course, this does not mean that other medications tested in ASD are free of adverse effects. It is reasonable to expect that, in contrast to efficacy, which is more likely to be specific to disorder and symptom, adverse effects are more likely to extend across diverse groups of subjects studied. Clinicians evaluating the evidence and sharing information with families routinely take this perspective, as does the Food and Drug Administration in mandating that all adverse events be listed for a drug, rather than just those for a particular indication.

Few studies of allied health interventions met our criteria. One fair quality RCT assessed a 12-month recreation program and reported improved quality of life and lower stress scores in individuals participating in the leisure/recreation program compared with those on a waiting list. Two studies of facilitated communication used approaches designed to assess the effects of facilitation both with and without facilitators' awareness of the word being prompted. Both studies demonstrated some facilitator influence without specific effects on participants' independent ability to communicate. One retrospective study of a music therapy program reported some positive effects on participants' socials skills using largely subjective outcome measures. One poor-quality case series included young adults engaged in a music therapy intervention. Nearly all participants reported making friends during the program and were generally satisfied with the program. Both studies assessed outcomes shortly after treatment, so longer term effects of the interventions are not known.

Chapter 32

Behavior and Communication Therapies for ASD

Chapter Contents

Section 32.1

Occupational Therapy

Introduction

Occupational therapy (OT) treatment focuses on helping people with a physical, sensory, or cognitive disability be as independent as possible in all areas of their lives. OT can help kids with various needs improve their cognitive, physical, sensory, and motor skills and enhance their self-esteem and sense of accomplishment.

Some people may think that occupational therapy is only for adults; kids, after all, do not have occupations. But a child's main job is playing and learning, and occupational therapists can evaluate kids' skills for playing, school performance, and daily activities and compare them with what is developmentally appropriate for that age group.

According to the American Occupational Therapy Association (AOTA), in addition to dealing with an someone's physical well-being, OT practitioners address psychological, social, and environmental factors that can affect functioning in different ways. This approach makes OT a vital part of health care for some kids.

Kids Who Might Need Occupational Therapy

According to the AOTA, kids with these medical problems might benefit from OT:

- birth injuries or birth defects
- sensory processing disorders
- traumatic injuries (brain or spinal cord)
- learning problems
- autism/pervasive developmental disorders

- juvenile rheumatoid arthritis
- mental health or behavioral problems
- broken bones or other orthopedic injuries
- developmental delays
- post-surgical conditions
- burns
- spina bifida
- traumatic amputations
- cancer
- severe hand injuries
- multiple sclerosis, cerebral palsy, and other chronic illnesses

Occupational Therapists Might

- help kids work on fine motor skills so they can grasp and release toys and develop good handwriting skills
- address hand-eye coordination to improve kids' play and school skills (hitting a target, batting a ball, copying from a blackboard, etc.)
- help kids with severe developmental delays learn basic tasks (such as bathing, getting dressed, brushing their teeth, and feeding themselves)
- help kids with behavioral disorders maintain positive behaviors in all environments (e.g., instead of hitting others or acting out, using positive ways to deal with anger, such as writing about feelings or participating in a physical activity)
- teach kids with physical disabilities the coordination skills needed to feed themselves, use a computer, or increase the speed and legibility of their handwriting
- evaluate a child's need for specialized equipment, such as wheelchairs, splints, bathing equipment, dressing devices, or communication aids
- work with kids who have sensory and attentional issues to improve focus and social skills

How Physical Therapy and OT Differ

Although both physical and occupational therapy help improve kids' quality of life, there are differences. Physical therapy (PT) deals with pain, strength, joint range of motion, endurance, and gross motor functioning, whereas OT deals more with fine motor skills, visual-perceptual skills, cognitive skills, and sensory-processing deficits.

Occupational Therapy Practitioners

There are two professional levels of occupational practice — occupational therapist (OT) and occupational therapist assistant (OTA).

Since 2007, an OT must complete a master's degree program (previously, only a bachelor's degree was required). An OTA is only required to complete an associate's degree program and can carry out treatment plans developed by the occupational therapist but can't complete evaluations.

All occupational therapy practitioners must complete supervised fieldwork programs and pass a national certification examination. A license to practice is mandatory in most states, as are continuing education classes to maintain that licensure.

Occupational therapists work in a variety of settings, including:

- hospitals
- schools
- rehabilitation centers
- mental health facilities
- private practices
- children's clinics
- nursing homes

Finding Care for Your Child

If you think your child might benefit from occupational therapy, ask your doctor to refer you to a specialist. The school nurse or guidance counselor also might be able to recommend someone based on your child's academic or social performance.

You also can check your local yellow pages, search online, or contact your state's occupational therapy association or a nearby hospital or rehabilitation center for referrals. However you find an occupational therapist for your child, make sure that your health insurance company covers the program you select.

Section 32.2

Speech-Language Therapy

Text in this section is excerpted from "Speech-Language Therapy," © 1995–2016. The Nemours Foundation/KidsHealth®. Reprinted with permission.

Speech Disorders, Language Disorders, and Feeding Disorders

A speech disorder refers to a problem with the actual production of sounds. A language disorder refers to a problem understanding or putting words together to communicate ideas.

Speech disorders include:

- **Articulation disorders**: difficulties producing sounds in syllables or saying words incorrectly to the point that listeners can't understand what's being said.

- **Fluency disorders**: problems such as stuttering, in which the flow of speech is interrupted by abnormal stoppages, partial-word repetitions ("b-b-boy"), or prolonging sounds and syllables (sssssnake).

- **Resonance or voice disorders**: problems with the pitch, volume, or quality of the voice that distract listeners from what's being said. These types of disorders may also cause pain or discomfort for a child when speaking.

Language disorders can be either receptive or expressive:

- **Receptive disorders**: difficulties understanding or processing language.

- **Expressive disorders**: difficulty putting words together, limited vocabulary, or inability to use language in a socially appropriate way.

- **Cognitive-communication disorders**: difficulty with communication skills that involve memory, attention, perception, organization, regulation, and problem solving.

267

Dysphagia/oral feeding disorders are disorders in the way someone eats or drinks, including problems with chewing, swallowing, coughing, gagging, and refusing foods.

Specialists in Speech-Language Therapy

Speech-language pathologists (SLPs), often informally known as speech therapists, are professionals educated in the study of human communication, its development, and its disorders. They hold at least a master's degree and state certification/licensure in the field, and a certificate of clinical competency from the American Speech-Language-Hearing Association (ASHA).

SLPs assess speech, language, cognitive-communication, and oral/feeding/swallowing skills to identify types of communication problems (articulation; fluency; voice; receptive and expressive language disorders, etc.) and the best way to treat them.

Remediation

In speech-language therapy, an SLP will work with a child one-on-one, in a small group, or directly in a classroom to overcome difficulties involved with a specific disorder.

Therapists use a variety of strategies, including:

- **Language intervention activities**: The SLP will interact with a child by playing and talking, using pictures, books, objects, or ongoing events to stimulate language development. The therapist may also model correct vocabulary and grammar and use repetition exercises to build language skills.

- **Articulation therapy**: Articulation, or sound production, exercises involve having the therapist model correct sounds and syllables in words and sentences for a child, often during play activities. The level of play is age-appropriate and related to the child's specific needs. The SLP will physically show the child how to make certain sounds, such as the "r" sound, and may demonstrate how to move the tongue to produce specific sounds.

- **Oral-motor/feeding and swallowing therapy**: The SLP may use a variety of oral exercises — including facial massage and various tongue, lip, and jaw exercises — to strengthen the muscles of the mouth for eating, drinking, and swallowing. The SLP may also introduce different food textures and temperatures to increase a child's oral awareness during eating and swallowing.

When Is Therapy Needed?

Kids might need speech-language therapy for a variety of reasons, including, but not limited to:

- hearing impairments
- cognitive (intellectual, thinking) or other developmental delays
- weak oral muscles
- chronic hoarseness
- birth defects such as cleft lip or cleft palate
- autism
- motor planning problems
- articulation problems
- fluency disorders
- respiratory problems (breathing disorders)
- feeding and swallowing disorders
- traumatic brain injury

Therapy should begin as soon as possible. Children enrolled in therapy early (before they're 5 years old) tend to have better outcomes than those who begin therapy later.

This does not mean that older kids can't make progress in therapy; they may progress at a slower rate because they often have learned patterns that need to be changed.

Finding a Therapist

It's important to make sure that the speech-language therapist is certified by ASHA. That certification means the SLP has at least a master's degree in the field and has passed a national examination and successfully completed an ASHA-accredited supervised clinical fellowship.

Sometimes, speech assistants (who usually have a 2-year associate's or 4-year bachelor's degree) may assist with speech-language services under the supervision of ASHA-certified SLPs. Your child's SLP should be licensed in your state and have experience working with kids and your child's specific disorder.

You might find a specialist by asking your child's doctor or teacher for a referral or by checking local directories online or in your telephone book. State associations for speech-language pathology and audiology also maintain listings of licensed and certified therapists.

Helping Your Child

Speech-language experts agree that parental involvement is crucial to the success of a child's progress in speech or language therapy.

Parents are an extremely important part of their child's therapy program and help determine whether it is a success. Kids who complete the program quickest and with the longest-lasting results are those whose parents have been involved.

Ask the therapist for suggestions on how you can help your child. For instance, it's important to help your child do the at-home stimulation activities that the SLP suggests to ensure continued progress and carry-over of newly learned skills.

The process of overcoming a speech or language disorder can take some time and effort, so it's important that all family members be patient and understanding with the child.

Chapter 33

Medical and Related Interventions

Medical and Related Interventions

Interventions in this category are those in which a medication, supplement, or other substance is administered to a child with ASDs. Medical treatments for symptoms of ASDs comprise a variety of pharmacologic agents including antipsychotics, psychostimulants, and serotonin reuptake inhibitors (SRIs) that are generally intended to treat common comorbidities of ASDs. Modalities such as therapeutic diets, supplements, hormonal supplements, immunoglobulin, hyperbaric oxygen, and chelating agents also have been employed to treat ASDs symptoms.

Antipsychotics

Antipsychotic medications generally act on the dopamine system, which is involved in regulating emotions, and potentially decrease behavioral outbursts. Whereas the older typical antipsychotic drugs act primarily on the dopamine system, newer atypical antipsychotic drugs interact with a variety of brain chemicals, such as serotonin. Although these medications were developed to treat psychosis, they have also

Text in this chapter is excerpted from "Therapies for Children with Autism Spectrum Disorders," Agency for Healthcare Research and Quality (AHRQ), April 2011. Reviewed February 2016.

been studied extensively for the treatment of other disorders, including mood disorders, obsessive compulsive disorder, and tic disorders.

Among typical antipsychotics, haloperidol has been used since the 1980s to treat challenging behavior in children with ASDs. More recently, risperidone, an atypical antipsychotic that acts on both dopamine D2 and serotonin 5-HT2A receptors, was the first medication to receive Food and Drug Administration (FDA) approval for the treatment of irritability in children with ASDs. Aripiprazole, which has a more complex mechanism of action, also recently received FDA approval for irritability in children with ASDs.

Serotonin Reuptake Inhibitors

Serotonin is associated with mood elevation and reduced anxiety symptoms. SRIs block the serotonin transporter so that increased serotonin stays in the system. SRIs have come into wide use for the treatment of depression and anxiety and are some of the most commonly prescribed medications for children with ASDs. SRIs were tested for use in children with ASDs after it was noted that 30 percent of this population had elevated blood serotonin.

Early RCTs of both comipramine and fluvoxamine showed improvements in multiple behaviors. Open label trials of selective SRIs in the 1990s provided further support for the idea that this class may benefit some children with ASDs, but also revealed common side effects including hyperactivity and decreased sleep. Most recent clinical trials in children with ASDs have focused on changes in repetitive behaviors with SRIs with longer half-lives, including fluoxetine, and citalopram or escitalopram, one of two component drugs contained in citalopram. Longer half lives can be associated with a more stable blood level over time, reducing susceptibility to the effects of missed doses.

Stimulants and Other Medications for Hyperactivity

Psychostimulants treat hyperactivity and inattention in patients diagnosed with attention deficit hyperactivity disorder (ADHD). Stimulants studied in ASDs include methylphenidate (MPH), amphetamine, and dextroamphetamine. All stimulant medications inhibit dopamine uptake from the synapse; amphetamine and dextroamphetamine also cause release of dopamine into the synapse.

Other medications studied for the treatment of ADHD have also been studied for the treatment of hyperactivity in ASDs, including atomoxetine, which inhibits norepinephrine reuptake from the synapse

Guanfacine, a norepinephrine receptor alpha-2a agonist that was orig-inally used for the treatment of high blood pressure, has also been studied for use in ASDs.

Secretin

Secretin is a gastrointestinal polypeptide used to treat peptic ulcers and in the evaluation of pancreatic function. Animal studies have suggested that secretin affects the central nervous system. Interest in secretin for the treatment of symptoms of ASDs derived from a report of 3 children with ASDs given synthetic intravenous secretin during a routine endoscopy evaluation for gastrointestinal problems. The report noted social, cognitive and communicative gains after the first infusion and after a second infusion given weeks later.

Other Medical Interventions

Additional studies in the medical literature addressed medical ther-apies for sleep and gastrointestinal dysfunction as well as the use of hyperbaric oxygen, specialized diets, supplements, and other agents explored to address symptoms of ASDs.

Management of Sleep Issues. Children with ASDs commonly sleep little or fitfully, creating stress for them and their families. Mel-atonin, a hormone associated with regulating circadian rhythms, and iron supplementation have been studied to improve disordered sleep in children with ASDs.

Management of Gastrointestinal Symptoms. Gastrointestinal (GI) symptoms may or may not have an increased prevalence in ASDs, with some evidence supporting increased difficulty with constipation but not other GI symptoms. Oral immunoglobulin has been considered for its potential utility in addressing GI symptoms in ASDs.

Dietary Supplements and Restrictive Diets for Core Symp-toms of ASDs. A range of dietary supplements with potential neuro-logic effects show some benefit in other chronic neurological conditions and have been assessed for use in treatment of ASDs. Magnesium-vi-tamin B6 and two amino acid-related compounds, L-carnosine and dimethylglycine, show some potential anticonvulsant activity in obser-vational studies and have been tried in ASDs for potential positive behavioral effects. Reduced levels of free polyunsaturated fatty acids (PUFAs) have been reported in a range of neuropsychiatric conditions

273

including ASDs. Supplementation with agents containing PUFAs, such as fish oil and evening primrose supplements, have been considered for their possible benefits in ASDs.

Some observational data suggest benefit of a ketogenic diet, a high fat, low carbohydrate diet, in some patients with epilepsy and seizures refractory to standard therapy, and this strategy has also been explored in ASDs.

Other. Amantadine, an antiviral agent, is thought by some to have neurologic effects that may positively affect behavior problems in ASDs. Similarly, the putative cognitive enhancer piracetam has been used in the treatment of dementia and has been considered for potential cognitive benefit in ASDs. Hyperbaric therapy, in which oxygen is administered in special chambers that maintain a higher air pressure, has shown possible effects in other chronic neurologic conditions and has also undergone preliminary exploration in ASDs.

Cholinesterase inhibitors, such as donepezil hydrochloride and rivastigmine tartrate, inhibit an enzyme that breaks down the neurotransmitter acetylcholine; these drugs have been used to prevent further cognitive decline in Alzheimer's disease and have similarly been studied for possible benefit in ASDs.

Dimercaptosuccinic acid (DMSA), used in chelation therapy, was approved by the FDA to treat lead poisoning, and may have similar activity against other heavy metals such as mercury. While no clear evidence suggests that mercury or ability to remove mercury from the body is involved in ASDs in any way, investigators have evaluated the ability of DMSA to affect

ASD symptoms based upon existing off-label use in some children with autism. Pentoxifylline is typically used to improve blood flow in individuals with peripheral arterial disease and also inhibits the production of tumor necrosis factor, suggested as playing a role in neurological disorders; the drug also acts on the release and uptake of serotonin and dopamine and was suggested for use in autism after improvements in autistic behavior were noted in a child with an ASD receiving the medication for suspected post-traumatic brain damage.

Chapter 34

Treatments for Autism Spectrum Disorder (ASD)

What Are the Treatments for Autism Spectrum Disorder (ASD)?

There is currently no one standard treatment for autism. But there are many ways to help minimize the symptoms and maximize abilities. People who have ASD have the best chance of using all of their abilities and skills if they receive appropriate therapies and interventions.

The most effective therapies and interventions are often different for each person. However, most people with ASD respond best to highly structured and specialized programs. In some cases, treatment can help people with autism to function at near-normal levels.

Research shows that early diagnosis and interventions, such as during preschool or before, are more likely to have major positive effects on symptoms and later skills. Read more about early interventions for autism.

Because there can be overlap in symptoms between ASD and other disorders, such as attention deficit hyperactivity disorder (ADHD), it's important that treatment focus on a person's specific needs, rather than the diagnostic label.

Text in this chapter is excerpted from "What Are the Treatments for Autism Spectrum Disorder (ASD)?" National Institute of Child Health and Human Development (NICHD), December 18, 2013.

Types of Therapies for ASD

Behavioral Management Therapy

Behavior management therapy tries to reinforce wanted behaviors and reduce unwanted behaviors. It also suggests what caregivers can do before, during, after, and between episodes of problem behaviors. Behavioral therapy is often based on applied behavior analysis (ABA), a widely accepted approach that tracks a child's progress in improving his or her skills.

Different types of ABA commonly used to treat autism spectrum disorder (ASD) include:

- Positive Behavioral and Support (PBS). PBS aims to figure out why a child does a particular problem behavior. It works to change the environment, teach skills, and make other changes that make a correct behavior more positive for the child. This encourages the child to behave correctly.

- Pivotal Response Training (PRT). PRT takes place in the child's everyday environment. Its goal is to improve a few "pivotal" skills, such as motivation and taking initiative to communicate. These help the child to learn many other skills and deal with many situations.

- Early Intensive Behavioral Intervention (EIBI). EIBI provides individualized, behavioral instruction to very young children with ASD. It requires a large time commitment and provides one-on-one or small-group instruction.

- Discrete Trial Teaching (DTT). DTT teaches skills in a controlled, step-by-step way. The teacher uses positive feedback to encourage the child to use new skills.

Keep in mind that other behavioral therapies, beyond ABA, may also be effective for people with ASD. Talk to your health care provider about the best options for your child.

Cognitive Behavior Therapy

Cognitive behavior therapy focuses on the connection between thoughts, feelings, and behaviors. Together, the therapist, the person with autism spectrum disorder (ASD), and/or the parents come up with specific goals for the course of therapy. Throughout the sessions, the person with autism learns to identify and change thoughts that lead to problem feelings or behaviors in particular situations.

Cognitive behavioral therapy is structured into specific phases of treatment. However, it is also individualized to patients' strengths and weaknesses. Research shows that this therapy helps people with some types of ASD deal with anxiety. It can also help some people with autism cope with social situations and better recognize emotions.

Early Intervention

Research shows that early diagnosis and interventions are more likely to have major positive effects on symptoms and later skills. Early interventions occur at or before preschool age. In this period, a young child's brain is still forming. For this reason, early interventions give children the best start possible and the best chance of developing to their full potential. The sooner a child gets help, the greater the chance for learning and progress.

With early intervention, between 3% and 25% of children with autism make so much progress that they are no longer on the autism spectrum when they are older. Many of the children who later go off the spectrum have some things in common:

- Diagnosis and treatment at younger ages

- A higher intelligence quotient (IQ, a measure of thinking ability) than the average child with autism

- Better language and motor skills

Goals of Early Intervention

Early intervention programs help children gain the basic skills that they usually learn in the first 2 years of life, such as:

- Physical skills
- Thinking skills
- Communication skills
- Social skills
- Emotional skills

Early intervention programs often include:

- Family training
- Speech therapy
- Hearing impairment services

- Physical therapy
- Nutrition services

State-Run Programs

Each state has its own early intervention program for children from birth to age 2 years who are diagnosed with developmental delays or disabilities, including ASD. These programs are specified by Part C of Public Law 108-77: Individuals with Disabilities Education Improvement Act (2004), sometimes called "IDEA." Some states also provide services for children who are at risk for developmental delays and disabilities.

Educational and School-Based Therapies

Children with autism are guaranteed free, appropriate public education under the federal laws of Public Law 108-177: Individuals with Disabilities Education Improvement Act (2004), sometimes called "IDEA."

IDEA ensures that children diagnosed with certain disabilities or conditions, including autism, get free educational services and educational devices to help them to learn as much as they can.

IDEA Covers Children and Young Adults

In most states, each child is entitled to these services from age 3 years through high school, or until age 21, whichever comes first. Some states now offer these types of services beyond age 21. You can find the specific rules of IDEA for each state from the National Early Childhood Technical Assistance Center.

Educational Environment

IDEA states that children must be taught in the "least restrictive environment, appropriate for that individual child." This means the teaching environment should:

- Be designed to meet a child's specific needs and skills
- Minimize restrictions on the child's access to typical learning experiences and interactions

Educating people with autism often includes a combination of one-on-one, small group, and regular classroom instruction.

Individualized Educational Program (IEP)

The special education team in your child's school will work with you to design an individualized educational program (IEP) for your child. An IEP is a written document that:

- Lists individualized goals for your child

- Specifies the plan for services your child will receive

- Lists the developmental specialists who will work with your child

Qualifying for Special Education

To qualify for access to special education services, the child must be evaluated by the school system and meet specific criteria as outlined by federal and state guidelines. To learn how to have your child assessed for special services, you can:

- Contact a local school principal or special education coordinator

- Visit the Parent Technical Assistance Center Network

- Consult a parents' organization to get information on therapeutic and educational services and how to get these services for a child.

Joint Attention Therapy

People with autism usually have difficulty with joint attention. This means that they have trouble following someone's gaze or pointed finger to look at something. Joint attention is important to communication and language learning. Joint attention therapy focuses on improving specific skills related to shared attention, such as:

- Pointing

- Showing

- Coordinating looks between a person and an object

Improvements from such treatments can last for years.

Medication Treatment

Currently, there is no medication that can cure ASD or all of its symptoms. But in many cases, medication can help treat some of the symptoms associated with ASD, especially certain behaviors.

Health care providers often use medications to deal with a specific behavior, such as to reduce self-injury or aggression. Once a symptom is no longer a problem, the person with autism can focus on other things, including learning and communication. Research shows that medication is most effective when used in combination with behavioral therapies.

Approved Medications

In 2006, the U.S. Food and Drug Administration (FDA) approved the drug risperidone for treating irritability in children with autism who are between 5 years and 16 years of age. Risperidone is currently the only FDA-approved drug for the treatment of specific autism symptoms.

Other Medications

Other drugs are often used to help improve symptoms of autism, but they are not approved by the FDA for this specific purpose. Some medications on this list are not approved for those younger than 18 years of age. Please consult the FDA for complete information on the medications listed below.

All medications carry risks, some of them serious. Families should work closely with their children's health care providers to ensure safe use of any medication.

- Selective serotonin re-uptake inhibitors (SSRIs)

  - This group of antidepressants treats some problems that result from imbalances in the body's chemical systems.

  - SSRIs might reduce the frequency and intensity of repetitive behaviors; decrease anxiety, irritability, tantrums, and aggressive behavior; and improve eye contact.

- Tricyclics

  - These medications are another type of antidepressant used to treat depression and obsessive-compulsive behaviors.

  - These drugs seem to cause more minor side effects than do SSRIs. They are sometimes more effective than SSRIs for treating certain people and certain symptoms.

- Psychoactive or anti-psychotic medications

  - These types of medications affect the brain of the person taking them. The anti-psychotic drug risperidone is approved for reducing irritability in 5-to-16-year-olds with autism.

- These medications can decrease hyperactivity, reduce stereo-typed behaviors, and minimize withdrawal and aggression among people with autism.

- Stimulants

- This group of medications can help to increase focus and decrease hyperactivity in people with autism. They are particularly helpful for those with mild ASD symptoms.

- Anti-anxiety medications

- This group of medications can help relieve anxiety and panic disorders, which are often associated with ASD.

- Anti-convulsants

- These medications treat seizures and seizure disorders, such as epilepsy. (Seizures are attacks of jerking or staring and seeming frozen.)

- Almost one-third of people with autism symptoms have seizures or seizure disorders.

Autism Speaks, one of the leading autism science and family support organizations in the United States, offers a tool to help parents and caregivers make informed decisions about medication.

Creating a Medication Plan

Health care providers usually prescribe a medication on a trial basis to see if it helps. Some medications may make symptoms worse at first or take several weeks to work. Your child's health care provider may have to try different dosages or different combinations of medications to find the most effective plan.

Families, caregivers, and health care providers need to work together to make sure that the medication plan is safe and that all medications have some benefit.

Things to remember about medication:

- Health care providers and families should work together to help ensure safe use of medication.

- Not every medication helps every person with symptoms of autism.

- One person with autism might respond to medications differently than another person with autism or than people who don't have autism.

• Some medications have serious risks involved with their use.

Nutritional Therapy

For a variety of reasons, children with autism may not get the nutrition they need. Some children with autism will only eat certain foods because of how the foods feel in their mouths. Other times, they might avoid eating foods because they associate them with stomach pain or discomfort. Some children are put on limited diets in hopes of improving autism symptoms.

It is important that parents and caregivers work with a nutrition specialist—such as a registered dietitian—or health care provider to design a meal plan for a person with autism, especially if they want to try a limited diet. Such providers can help to make sure the child is still getting all the nutrients he or she needs to grow into a healthy adult, even while on the special diet.

For example, many children with ASD are on gluten-free or casein-free diets. (Gluten and casein are types of proteins found in wheat and milk products, respectively.) Available research data do not support the use of a casein-free diet, a gluten-free diet, or a combined gluten-free, casein-free diet as a primary treatment for individuals with ASD.

Good Nutrition Is Important

Research shows that children with autism tend to have thinner bones than children without autism. Restricting access to bone-building foods, such as dairy products, can make it even harder for their bones to grow strong. Working with a health care provider can help ensure that children who are on special diets still get the bone-building and other nutrients they need.

Digestive Problems in ASD

Some people with autism also have digestive problems, such as constipation, abdominal (belly) pain, or vomiting. Some research suggests that digestive problems occur more often in people with autism than in people without autism, but research is still being done on this topic. Working with a health care provider can help ensure that a diet does not make digestive problems worse.

The NICHD and other agencies and organizations will continue research to learn more about how children with autism grow and if they have specific nutritional needs.

Occupational Therapy

Occupational therapy helps people with autism spectrum disorder do everyday tasks by finding ways to work within and make the most of their needs, abilities, and interests.

An occupational therapist might:

- Find a specially designed computer mouse and keyboard to ease communication

- Teach personal care skills such as getting dressed and eating

- Do many of the same types of activities that physical therapists do

Parent-Mediated Therapy

In parent-mediated therapy, parents learn therapy techniques from professionals and provide specific therapies to their own child. This approach gives children with autism spectrum disorder consistent reinforcement and training throughout the day. Parents can also conduct some therapies with children who are at risk of autism but are too young to be diagnosed.

Several types of therapies can be parent-mediated, including:

- Joint attention therapy

- Social communication therapy

- Behavioral therapy

Studies suggest that parent-mediated therapies might be able to improve the child's communication skills and interactions with others. There is currently little evidence supporting one specific parent-mediated therapy over another. Autism Speaks sponsors the Autism Speaks Toddler Treatment Network, which evaluates specific methods for very young children.

Physical Therapy

Physical therapy includes activities and exercises that build motor skills and improve strength, posture, and balance.

For example, this type of therapy aims to help a child build muscle control and strength so that he or she can play more easily with other children.

Problems with movement are common in ASD, and many children with autism receive physical therapy. However, there is not yet solid evidence that particular therapies can improve movement skills in those with autism.

Social Skills Training

This training teaches children the skills they need to interact with their peers. It includes repeating and reinforcing certain behaviors. Social skills training can help improve relationships.

The Children's Friendship Training intervention, for instance, helps elementary school-age children improve several social skills:

- Conversation

- Handling teasing

- Being a good sport

- Showing good host behavior during play dates

Speech-Language Therapy

Speech-language therapy can help people with autism spectrum disorder improve their abilities to communicate and interact with others.

Verbal Skills

This type of therapy can help some people improve their spoken or verbal skills, such as:

- Correctly naming people and things

- Better explaining feelings and emotions

- Using words and sentences better

- Improving the rate and rhythm of speech

Nonverbal Communication

Speech-language therapy can also teach nonverbal communication skills, such as:

- Using hand signals or sign language

- Using picture symbols to communicate (Picture Exchange Communication System)

Speech-language therapy activities can also include social skills and normal social behaviors. For example, a child might learn how to make eye contact or to stand at a comfortable distance from another person. These skills make it a little easier to interact with others.

Chapter 35

Complementary and Alternative Medicine Interventions

According to a national survey, a wide range of complementary health approaches, including dietary supplements, spinal manipulation, and yoga, are used by or given to children. This chapter offers information for parents who may be thinking about or are already using a complementary health approach for their child.

Patterns in the Use of Complementary Health Approaches in Children

According to the 2012 National Health Interview Survey (NHIS), which included a comprehensive survey on the use of complementary health approaches by Americans, 11.6 percent of the more than 10,000 children aged 4 to 17 included in the survey had used or been given some form of complementary health product or practice during the past year.

Text in this chapter is excerpted from "Children and Complementary Health Approaches," National Center for Complementary and Integrative Health (NCCIH), February 2015.

The most frequently used complementary approaches for children were natural products such as fish oil, melatonin, or probiotics and chiropractic or osteopathic manipulation.

For children, complementary approaches were most often used for back or neck pain, other musculoskeletal conditions, head or chest colds, anxiety or stress, attention-deficit hyperactivity disorder (ADHD), and insomnia or trouble sleeping.

Children who use or are given complementary health products or practices vary in age and health status. For example, other studies on use show that:

Up to 10 percent of infants are given teas or botanical supplements, usually for fussiness or stomach problems.

- Between 21 and 42 percent of children take multivitamins, according to a 2012 study. Children aged 2 to 8 were the most likely to take vitamins. However, they were also the only age group who had nutritionally adequate diets whether they took multivitamins or not.

- Teens are particularly likely to use products that claim to enhance sports performance, energy levels, or weight loss.

- More than half of children with chronic medical conditions use some form of complementary health approach, usually along with conventional care.

Safety of Complementary Health Approaches for Children

Many complementary health products and practices aren't tested for safety or effectiveness in children. It's important to note that children may react differently than adults. Also, Federal regulations for dietary supplements are less strict than those for prescription and over-the-counter drugs. Some dietary supplements may be of poor quality or contain contaminants, including drugs, chemicals, or metals.

If You're Considering a Complementary Health Approach for Your Child

- Make sure that your child has received an accurate diagnosis from a licensed health care provider.

- Educate yourself about the potential risks and benefits of complementary health approaches.

- Ask your child's health care provider about the effectiveness and possible risks of approaches you're considering or already using for your child.

- Remind your teenagers to discuss with their health care providers any complementary health approaches they may use.

- Don't use any health product or practice that hasn't been proven safe and effective to replace or delay conventional care or prescribed medications.

- If a health care provider suggests a complementary health approach, don't increase the dose or duration of the treatment beyond what is recommended (more isn't necessarily better).

- If you have any concerns about the effects of a complementary approach, contact your child's health care provider.

- As with all medications, store herbal and other dietary supplements out of the sight and reach of children.

- Tell all your child's health care providers about any complementary health approaches your child uses. Give them a full picture of what you do to manage your child's health. This will help ensure coordinated and safe care.

Selecting a Complementary Health Practitioner

- If you're looking for a complementary health practitioner for your child, be as careful and thorough in your search as you are when looking for conventional care. Be sure to ask about the practitioner's:

- Experience in coordinating care with conventional health care providers

- Experience in delivering care to children

- Education, training, and license. Some states have licensing requirements for certain complementary health practitioners, such as chiropractors, naturopathic doctors, massage therapists, and acupuncturists.

Key Points

- Nearly 12 percent of American children (aged 4 to 17) have used or been given a complementary health product or practice.

- Few studies have examined the effects of complementary health approaches on children.

- Tell all your child's health care providers about any complementary health approaches your child uses or is given. Give them a full picture of what you do to manage your child's health. This will help ensure coordinated and safe care.

Chapter 36

Facts on Medication for Autism Spectrum Disorder

What Medicines Are Used to Treat ASD Symptoms?

- Antipsychotics

- Risperidone (brand name: Risperdal®)

- Aripiprazole (brand name: Abilify®)

- Serotonin-reuptake inhibitors or "SRIs" (antidepressants)

- Examples include Prozac,® Sarafem,® Celexa,® and Cipramil®

- Stimulants and other hyperactivity medicines

- Examples include Ritalin,® Adderall,® and Tenex®

- Secretin. This medicine is used for digestion problems but some researchers thought it might help children with ASD symptoms as well.

- Chelation. This therapy uses substances to remove heavy metals from the body, which some people think causes autism.

Text in this chapter is excerpted from "Therapies for Children with Autism Spectrum Disorder," Agency for Healthcare Research and Quality (AHRQ), September 23, 2014.

Do They Help?

- Research found that two antipsychotic drugs – risperidone (Risperdal®) and aripiprazole (Abilify®) – can help reduce emotional distress, aggression, hyperactivity, and self-injury. Many people who take risperidone and aripiprazole report side effects such as weight gain, sleepiness, tremors, and abnormal movements. Because of these side effects, these medicines may be best only for children who have more severe symptoms or have symptoms that might increase their risk of hurting themselves.

- SRIs and a hyperactivity medicine called methylphenidate (Ritalin®) have not been studied enough to know if they help treat ASD symptoms.

- Research showed that secretin is not effective in improving autistic symptoms.

- According to the U. S. Food and Drug Administration, there are serious safety issues associated with chelation products. Even when used under the care of a doctor, these products can cause serious harm, including dehydration, kidney failure, and death. Research does not support the use of chelation for ASD.

Why Is There so Little Known about ASD and These Treatments?

The research reviewed for this guide showed that some treatments can make specific improvements in the way a child thinks or acts. But researchers do not have enough information to know whether one type of treatment works better than any other. For most treatments, researchers also do not know which treatments will work best for specific children. For example, research does not show whether a program usually works best for older or younger children, or for children with severe or less severe ASD.

This does not mean that a treatment, therapy, or program will not be helpful for your child. It only means that researchers do not have enough information to say so with strong confidence.

Researchers are still studying these treatments and therapies. Check with your doctor or a support group to find out about new research on the programs and treatments in this guide and about new options.

Making a Decision

There are many things for you to consider when choosing therapies or programs for your child. There are many people you should talk to, including your doctor, social worker, school administrator, and health insurance representative. Here are some questions to ask:

What plan is best for my child?

- Do you think an early intensive intervention would help my child?
- What other types of programs might be helpful?
- Do you think my child would benefit from taking medicine?

What is available in my community?

- Are there any early intensive intervention programs in this community?
- Do the schools in this district have programs for children with ASD?
- What support groups are available?

What are the costs?

- How much will it cost for us to participate in these programs?
- Is help available from the schools or other public agencies?
- Does my health insurance plan cover any costs?

What changes to our work schedules and life will we need to make?

- How much time does each option take?
- What are ways that other families have fit these programs into their lives?
- What else can we do to help our child?

Which medicine, if any, is best for my child?

- What symptoms will the medicines help?

- How soon should I see changes in my child's symptoms?
- What are the warning signs that my child may be having a harmful side effect?
- What else is available if my child needs different medicine?

Chapter 37

False or Misleading Claims for Treating Autism

About Autism

According to the Centers for Disease Control (CDC), about 1 in 68 children has been identified with an autism spectrum disorder (ASD). ASDs are reported to occur in all racial, ethnic and socioeconomic groups, and are almost five times more common among boys (1 in 54) than among girls (1 in 252).

The National Institutes of Health (NIH) describe autistic children as having difficulties with social interaction, displaying problems with verbal and nonverbal communication, exhibiting repetitive behaviors and having narrow, obsessive interests. These behaviors can range in impact from mild to disabling.

"Autism varies widely in severity and symptoms," says Amy Taylor, M.D., M.H.S., a pediatrician at FDA. "Existing autism therapies and interventions are designed to remedy specific symptoms and can bring about improvement," she adds.

In addition, FDA has approved medications that can help some people manage related symptoms of ASD. For example, the FDA has approved the use of antipsychotics such as risperidone and aripripazole

---

This chapter includes excerpts from "Beware of False or Misleading Claims for Treating Autism," U.S. Food and Drug Administration (FDA), April 25, 2014; and text from "6 Tip-offs to Rip-offs: Don't Fall for Health Fraud Scams," U.S. Food and Drug Administration (FDA), March 4, 2013.

to treat children 5 or 6 years of age and older who have severe tantrums or aggression and self-injurious behavior. Before using any behavioral intervention or drug therapy (prescription or over-the-counter), check with your health care professional.

The Association for Science in Autism Treatment (ASAT), a not-for-profit organization of parents and professionals committed to improving the education, treatment, and care of people with autism, says that since autism was first identified, there has been a long history of failed treatments and fads.

Autism Therapies Carrying Health Risks

According to Gary Coody, R.Ph., FDA's national health fraud coordinator, the agency has warned a number of companies that they are facing possible legal action if they continue to make false or misleading claims about products and therapies claiming to treat or cure autism. Some of these so-called therapies carry significant health risks and include:

- **Chelation Therapies**. These products claim to cleanse the body of toxic chemicals and heavy metals by binding to them and "removing" them from circulation. They come in a number of forms, including sprays, suppositories, capsules, liquid drops and clay baths. FDA-approved chelating agents are approved for specific uses, such as the treatment of lead poisoning and iron overload, and are available by prescription only. FDA-approved prescription chelation therapy products should only be used under medical supervision. Chelating important minerals needed by the body can lead to serious and life-threatening outcomes.

- **Hyperbaric Oxygen Therapy**. This involves breathing oxygen in a pressurized chamber and has been cleared by FDA for certain medical uses, such as treating decompression sickness suffered by divers. It has not been cleared for autism, among other conditions.

- **Miracle Mineral Solution**. Also known as Miracle Mineral Supplement and MMS, this product becomes a potent chemical that's used as bleach when mixed according to package directions. FDA has received reports of consumers who say they experienced nausea, severe vomiting and life-threatening low blood pressure after drinking the MMS and citrus juice mixture.

- **Detoxifying Clay Baths**. Added to bath water, these products claim to draw out chemical toxins, pollutants and heavy metals from the body, falsely offering "dramatic improvement" for autism symptoms.

- **Coconut kefir and other probiotic products**. These marketed products claim to treat autism and gastrointestinal illnesses associated with autism. They have not been proven safe and effective for these advertised uses.

Coody offers some quick tips to help you identify false or misleading claims.

- Be suspicious of products that claim to treat a wide range of diseases.

- Personal testimonials are no substitute for scientific evidence.

- Few diseases or conditions can be treated quickly, so be suspicious of any therapy claimed as a "quick fix."

- So-called "miracle cures," which claim scientific breakthroughs and secret ingredients, may be a hoax.

The bottom line is this—if it's an unproven or little known treatment, talk to your health care professional before buying or using these products.

Tip-Offs

FDA offers some tip-offs to help you identify rip-offs.

- **One product does it all:** Be suspicious of products that claim to cure a wide range of diseases. A New York firm claimed its products marketed as dietary supplements could treat or cure senile dementia, brain atrophy, atherosclerosis, kidney dysfunction, gangrene, depression, osteoarthritis, dysuria, and lung, cervical and prostate cancer. In October 2012, at FDA's request, U.S. marshals seized these products.

- **Personal testimonials:** Success stories, such as, "It cured my diabetes" or "My tumors are gone," are easy to make up and are not a substitute for scientific evidence.

- **Quick fixes:** Few diseases or conditions can be treated quickly, even with legitimate products. Beware of language such as, "Lose 30 pounds in 30 days" or "eliminates skin cancer in days."

297

- **"All natural."** Some plants found in nature (such as poisonous mushrooms) can kill when consumed. Moreover, FDA has found numerous products promoted as "all natural" but that contain hidden and dangerously high doses of prescription drug ingredients or even untested active artificial ingredients.

- **"Miracle cure."** Alarms should go off when you see this claim or others like it such as, "new discovery," "scientific breakthrough" or "secret ingredient." If a real cure for a serious disease were discovered, it would be widely reported through the media and prescribed by health professionals—not buried in print ads, TV infomercials or on Internet sites.

- **Conspiracy theories:** Claims like "The pharmaceutical industry and the government are working together to hide information about a miracle cure" are always untrue and unfounded. These statements are used to distract consumers from the obvious, common-sense questions about the so-called miracle cure.

Even with these tips, fraudulent health products are not always easy to spot. If you're tempted to buy an unproven product or one with questionable claims, check with your doctor or other health care professional first.

Chapter 38

Research Studies and ASD

Join a Mental Health Research Study

Researchers at the National Institute of Mental Health (NIMH) conduct a large number of research studies with patients and healthy volunteers. The first steps to research participation include: calling the NIMH research study team to learn study details, an evaluation for eligibility to enroll, and consenting to participate.

The studies are conducted at the NIH Clinical Center (CC), a hospital dedicated to the highest quality research, and located in Bethesda, Maryland, near Washington, D.C. Some studies enroll locally, others regionally or nationally. Please contact each research study team to learn more specifics.

Adult, Children and Healthy Volunteer study descriptions and other information provided here can help you decide whether to participate or volunteer. If you qualify for a study, then a study-related evaluation, treatment and, in some cases transportation to NIH is provided without cost to you or your health plan.

Brain Behavior Study in Children

Researchers at the National Institute of Mental Health are seeking children between the ages of 4 years and 8 years who have been

_____

This chapter includes excerpts from "Join A Study," National Institute of Mental Health (NIMH), June 12, 2014; text from "Children: Autism Spectrum Disorders," National Institute of Mental Health (NIMH), June 12, 2014; and text from "Adults: Autism Spectrum Disorders," National Institute of Mental Health (NIMH), June 12, 2014.

diagnosed with either an autism spectrum disorder (ASD) or atten-tion deficit hyperactivity disorder (ADHD) to participate in a study examining the use of Near Infra-Red Spectroscopy (NIRS). A group of children who are typically developing will also be recruited as a comparison group.

The purpose of this study is to test whether the NIRS system, which is a functional imaging technique that can monitor brain activity while allowing for movement, can be used to monitor cognitive brain activity and detect differences in children who are diagnosed with an ASD or ADHD. The study involves an initial screening evaluation that will include a comprehensive caregiver interview and behavioral assess-ment of the child. Eligible participants will then complete a NIRS scan while performing computer generated tasks. One follow-up visit at an 18 month interval will include another administration of the NIRS scan while the participant completes computer generated tasks. This study will involve outpatient visits and will be conducted at the NIH Clinical Center in Bethesda, Maryland.

The results of this study will provide information about the utility of the NIRS technique to detect differences in children with ASD or ADHD and may aid in the understanding of the cognitive functions that underlie these disorders.

Brain Imaging of Autism Biomarker

This research study seeks to detect and measure an immune bio-marker in the brain. Researchers will compare the brain scans of those with Autism to those without Autism.

The causes of autism are not known, but previous research has suggested an association between autism and immune changes in the brain. This study proposes to determine whether the emerging evidence and role of neuroimmune activation (as a biomarker in the brain) will indicate if there are greater immune changes in persons with autism.

This outpatient research study includes 2–4 outpatient visits of 2–6 hours each. There is an initial screening appointment that includes a physical examination, psychological examination, medical history, mood and behavior questions, and blood and urine tests. The research study includes a baseline MRI brain scan, a PET brain scan (with the administration of a drug that attaches to a brain protein), and a fol-low-up visit to provide a final blood sample. Eligibility criteria includes: adults ages 18–45; a diagnosis of autism, Asperger syndrome, or an ASD; and good health (without a serious medical condition).

Chapter 39

Autism Spectrum Disorder—Clinical Trials

Chapter Contents

Section 39.1

What Are Clinical Trials?

Text in this section is excerpted from "Clinical Trials," National
Heart, Lung, and Blood Institute (NHLBI), July 15, 2015.

What Are Clinical Trials?

Clinical trials are research studies that explore whether a medical
strategy, treatment, or device is safe and effective for humans. These
studies also may show which medical approaches work best for certain illnesses or groups of people. Clinical trials produce the best data
available for health care decision making. The purpose of clinical trials
is research, so the studies follow strict scientific standards. These standards protect patients and help produce reliable study results. Clinical
trials are one of the final stages of a long and careful research process.
The process often begins in a laboratory (lab), where scientists first
develop and test new ideas. If an approach seems promising, the next
step may involve animal testing. This shows how the approach affects
a living body and whether it's harmful. However, an approach that
works well in the lab or animals doesn't always work well in people.
Thus, research in humans is needed. For safety purposes, clinical trials
start with small groups of patients to find out whether a new approach
causes any harm. In later phases of clinical trials, researchers learn
more about the new approach's risks and benefits. A clinical trial
may find that a new strategy, treatment, or device improves patient
outcomes; offers no benefit; or causes unexpected harm All of these
results are important because they advance medical knowledge and
help improve patient care.

Why Are Clinical Trials Important?

Clinical trials are a key research tool for advancing medical knowledge and patient care. Clinical research is done only if doctors don't
know whether a new approach works well in people and is safe and
which treatments or strategies work best for certain illnesses or groups
of people.

Some clinical trials show a positive result. The results from other clinical trials show what doesn't work or may cause harm.

Clinical trials, help improve and advance medical care. They also can help health care decisionmakers direct resources to the strategies and treatments that work best.

How Do Clinical Trials Work?

If you take part in a clinical trial, you may get tests or treatments in a hospital, clinic, or doctor's office. In some ways, taking part in a clinical trial is different from having regular care from your own doctor. For example, you may have more tests and medical exams than you would otherwise. The purpose of clinical trials is research, so the studies follow strict scientific standards. These standards protect patients and help produce reliable study results.

Clinical Trial Protocol

Each clinical trial has a master plan called a protocol. This plan explains how the trial will work. The trial is led by a principal investigator (PI), who often is a doctor. The PI prepares the protocol for the clinical trial.

The protocol outlines what will be done during the clinical trial and why. Each medical center that does the study uses the same protocol.

Key information in a protocol includes how many patients will take part in the clinical trial; who is eligible to take part in the clinical trial; what tests patients will get and how often they will get them; what type of data will be collected during the clinical trial; and detailed information about the treatment plan.

Eligibility Criteria

A clinical trial's protocol describes what types of patients are able to take part in the research—that is, who is eligible. Each trial must include only people who fit the patient traits for that study (the eligibility criteria).

Eligibility criteria differ from trial to trial. They include factors such as a patient's age and gender, the type and stage of disease, and whether the patient has had certain treatments or has other health problems.

Eligibility criteria ensure that new approaches are tested on similar groups of people. This makes it clear to whom a clinical trial's results apply. These criteria also are a safety measure. They ensure a trial excludes any people for whom the protocol has known risks that outweigh any possible benefits.

Clinical Trial Phases

Clinical trials of new medicines or medical devices are done in phases. These phases have different purposes and help researchers answer different questions.

For example, phase I clinical trials test new treatments in small groups of people for safety and side effects.

Phase II clinical trials look at how well treatments work and further review these treatments for safety.

Phase III clinical trials use larger groups of people to confirm how well treatments work, further examine side effects, and compare new treatments with other available treatments.

Who Can Participate in Clinical Trials?

Each clinical trial defines who is eligible to take part in the study. Each trial must include only people who fit the patient traits for that study (the eligibility criteria).

Some trials enroll people who have a specific disease or condition. Others enroll healthy people to test new approaches to prevention, diagnosis, or screening.

In the past, clinical trial participants often were White men. Researchers assumed that trial results were valid for other populations as well.

Researchers now realize that women and people in different ethnic groups sometimes respond differently than White men to the same medical approach. As a result, the National Institutes of Health and the National Heart, Lung, and Blood Institute (NHLBI) are committed to sponsoring clinical trials that include women and that are ethnically diverse.

Children also need clinical trials that focus on them, as medical treatments and approaches often differ for children. For example, children may need lower doses of certain medicines or smaller medical devices. Their stage of development also can affect how safe a treatment is or how well it works.

Children (aged 18 and younger) get special protection as research subjects. Almost always, parents must give legal consent for their child to take part in a clinical trial.

When researchers think that a trial's potential risks are greater than minimal, both parents must give permission for their child to enroll. Also, children aged 7 and older often must agree (assent) to take part in clinical trials.

What to Expect during a Clinical Trial?

During a clinical trial, doctors, nurses, social workers, and other health care providers might be part of your treatment team. They will monitor your health closely. You may have more tests and medical exams than you would if you were not taking part in a clinical trial.

Your treatment team also may ask you to do other tasks. For example, you may have to keep a log about your health or fill out forms about how you feel.

Some people will need to travel or stay in hospitals to take part in clinical trials. Many clinical trials take place in medical centers and doctors' offices around the country.

What Are the Possible Benefits and Risks of Clinical Trials?

Possible Benefits

Taking part in a clinical trial can have many benefits. For example, you may gain access to new treatments before they're widely available. If a new treatment is proven to work and you're in the group getting it, you might be among the first to benefit.

If you're in a clinical trial and don't get the new strategy being tested, you may receive the current standard care for your condition. This treatment might be as good as, or better than, the new approach. You also will have the support of a team of health care providers, who will likely monitor your health closely.

In late-phase clinical trials, possible benefits or risks of a treatment can be identified earlier than they would be in general medical practice. This is because late-phase trials have large groups of similar patients taking the same treatment the same way. These patients are closely watched by Data and Safety Monitoring Boards.

Even if you don't directly benefit from the results of the clinical trial you take part in, the information gathered can help others and add to scientific knowledge. People who take part in clinical trials are vital to the process of improving medical care. Many people volunteer because they want to help others.

Possible Risks

Clinical trials do have risks and some downsides, such as the following.

The new strategies and treatments being studied aren't always better than current standard care. Even if a new approach benefits some participants, it may not work for you. A new treatment may have side effects or risks that doctors don't know about or expect. This is especially true during phase I and phase II clinical trials. The risk of side effects might be even greater for trials with cutting-edge approaches, such as gene therapy or new biological treatments. Health insurance and health care providers don't always cover all patient care costs for clinical trials. If you're thinking about taking part in a clinical trial, find out ahead of time about costs and coverage.

You should learn about the risks and benefits of any clinical trial before you agree to take part in the trial. Talk with your doctor about specific trials you're interested in.Talk with your doctor about specific trials you're interested in. For a list of questions to ask your doctor and the research staff, go towww.nhlbi.nih.gov/studies/clinicaltrials/protect

Section 39.2

Autism Spectrum Disorder Research at CDC

Text in this section is excerpted from "Autism Spectrum Disorder (ASD)," Centers for Disease Control and Prevention (CDC), August 12, 2015.

Research

There is still a lot to learn about ASD. Research on ASD has increased a great deal in recent years and CDC is part of the larger group of public and private organizations working to better understand ASD through research. Like the many families living with ASD, CDC considers ASD an important public health concern. CDC is committed to continuing to provide essential data on ASD, search for risk factors and causes, and develop resources that help identify children with ASD as early as possible.

Determining How Many People Have ASD

More people than ever before are being diagnosed with ASD. It is unclear how much of this increase is due to a broader definition of ASD and better efforts in diagnosis. However, a true increase in the number of people with an ASD cannot be ruled out. The increase in ASD diagnosis is likely due to a combination of these factors.

By studying the number of children with ASD at different points in time, CDC can find out if the number is rising, dropping, or staying the same. We also can compare the number of children with ASD in different areas of the country and among different groups of people. This information can help direct our research into potential factors that might put children at risk for ASD, and can help communities direct their outreach efforts to those who need it most.

Following are activities that CDC conducts or funds in order to learn more about the number of people with ASD:

Autism and Developmental Disabilities Monitoring (ADDM) Network

The ADDM Network is a group of programs funded by CDC to estimate the number of children with ASD and other developmental disabilities living in different areas of the United States. The ADDM Network sites all collect data using the same surveillance methods, which are modeled after CDC's Metropolitan Atlanta Developmental Disabilities Surveillance Program (MADDSP).

CDC estimates that 1 in 68 children were identified with an ASD. This data comes from the ADDM Network, which estimated the number of 8-year-old children with ASD living in 11 communities throughout the United States in 2010.

Metropolitan Atlanta Developmental Disabilities Surveillance Program (MADDSP)

MADDSP was established to determine all children who have one or more of four developmental disabilities—intellectual disability, cerebral palsy, hearing loss, and vision impairment—in the metropolitan Atlanta area. Autism spectrum disorder was added as a fifth disability beginning in the 1996 study year.

CDC estimates that about 1 in 64 children were identified with ASD in metropolitan Atlanta in 2010.

Evaluating CDC's Tracking System

CDC evaluated the tracking system that is used to estimate the prevalence of ASD. Validation studies that evaluate tracking systems, such as this one, allow CDC to make informed changes in order to provide the most complete prevalence estimates.

Important findings from the study include:

The CDC tracking system is likely not over-estimating the prevalence of ASD.

Most children found to have an ASD by a clinical examination were also detected by the tracking system.

The CDC tracking system missed 12 of 177 children who were examined and found to have an ASD. This result shows we are likely not counting some children with ASD.

National Surveys

CDC conducts nationally representative surveys that provide data on the health of children in the United States: the National Health and Nutrition Examination Survey (NHANES) III and the National Health Interview Survey (NHIS). These surveys include information on developmental disabilities and delays.

CDC also collaborates on the development and management of other nationally representative surveys sponsored by the Maternal and Child Bureau of the U.S. Health Resources and Services Administration: the National Survey of Children's Health (NSCH) and the National Survey of Children with Special Health Care Needs (NSSHCN). These surveys also provide data on children's health and development.

CDC has used data from these national surveys to conduct a range of studies on the prevalence of developmental disabilities, demographic characteristics of children with developmental disabilities, health and health care needs of children with developmental disabilities, and family impacts of parenting a child with special needs.

Evaluating Changes in the Prevalence of Autism Spectrum Disorder (ASD)

To provide a forum for sharing the latest information on ASD prevalence changes, CDC and Autism Speaks co-hosted the "Workshop on U.S. Data to Evaluate Changes in the Prevalence of Autism Spectrum

Disorders (ASDs)" on February 1, 2011. The workshop brought together scientists and stakeholders from the autism community to increase knowledge about ASD prevalence, to learn from other conditions, and to share ideas on how to move forward to better understand ASD trends.

Brick Autism Project (Project Completed)

In late 1997, a citizen's group in Brick Township, New Jersey, told the state Department of Health and Senior Services about what seemed to be a larger than expected number of children with autism spectrum disorder (ASD) in Brick Township. CDC and the Agency for Toxic Substances and Disease Registry (ATSDR) worked together to find out how common ASD were in Brick Township and to study the possible relationship of environmental factors to ASD in the community.

The prevalence of ASD in Brick Township was 6.7 per 1,000 children. This was higher than prevalence estimates from other studies conducted at that time, particularly studies conducted in the United States. However, the prevalence of ASD in Brick Township was within the range of studies that used more thorough case-finding methods among smaller populations.

Understanding Risk Factors and Causes

We do not know all of the causes of ASD. However, we have learned that there are likely many causes for multiple types of ASD. There may be many different factors that make a child more likely to have an ASD, including environmental and genetic factors.

Most scientists agree that genes are one of the risk factors that can make a person more likely to develop ASD.

Children who have a sibling with ASD are at a higher risk of also having ASD.

ASD tends to occur more often in people who have certain genetic or chromosomal conditions, such as fragile X syndrome or tuberous sclerosis.

When taken during pregnancy, the prescription drugs valproic acid and thalidomide have been linked with a higher risk of ASD.

There is some evidence that the critical period for developing ASD occurs before, during, and immediately after birth.

Children born to older parents are at greater risk for having ASD

Study to Explore Early Development (SEED)

SEED is a multi-year study funded by CDC. It is currently the largest study in the United States to help identify factors that may put children at risk for ASD and other developmental disabilities. Understanding the risk factors that make a person more likely to develop an ASD will help us learn more about the causes.

The six SEED study sites and a data coordinating center are part of the Centers for Autism and Developmental Disabilities Research and Epidemiology (CADDRE) network.

Vaccines Safety

Many studies have looked at whether there is a relationship between vaccines and autism spectrum disorder (ASD). To date, the studies continue to show that vaccines are not associated with ASD.

However, CDC knows that some parents and others still have concerns. To address these concerns, CDC is part of the Inter-Agency Autism Coordinating Committee (IACC), which is working with the National Vaccine Advisory Committee (NVAC) on this issue. The job of the NVAC is to advise and make recommendations regarding the National Vaccine Program.

International Research

The CDC-Denmark Program (Project Completed)

The CDC–Denmark Program was set up to look at many public health issues. The program highlights the work done using Danish national public health data systems. These systems are not found anywhere else. They include more than 200 long-term disease and administrative registries. They also include the stored newborn blood samples of all children born in Denmark from 1982 onward. These systems are linked with one another. Thus, they can be used to make data sets with information on very large numbers of people. These data sets cover long periods of time. Therefore, they can be used to look at health trends and disease traits. They can also be used to study less common risk factors or diseases in more detail and with more accuracy than can be done anywhere else.

Section 39.3

NIH-supported Clinical Trials

Text in this section is excerpted from "NIH-supported NeuroBioBank
Joins Autism BrainNet in Brain Donation Initiative," National
Institute of Mental Health (NIMH), November 17, 2015; text from
"NIH Joins Public-Private Partnership to Fund Research on Autism
Biomarkers," National Institute of Mental Health (NIMH), July 16,
2015; and text from "Disorganized Cortical Patches Suggest Prenatal
Origin of Autism," National Institute of Mental Health (NIMH),
March 26, 2014.

The National Institute of Mental Health (NIMH) has signed an
agreement to establish a collaborative, nationwide effort for the collection, storage, and distribution of postmortem human brain tissue
for the benefit of autism research. The agreement with Foundation
Associates LLC will coordinate the efforts of two independent networks
of human brain tissue repositories, the National Institutes of Health
(NIH) NeuroBioBank (NBB) and the Autism BrainNet (ABN).

The pace of research is dependent on the availability of high-quality brain tissue, and the need for donor tissue from individuals both
with and without an autism spectrum disorder (ASD) has never been
greater. This collaboration will leverage the advantages of public and
private efforts to collect vital brain specimens to advance our understanding of ASD and related disorders.

Since its 2013 launch, the NIH NBB has increased the quality and
quantity of human brain tissue available for neurological, neurodevelopmental, and psychiatric research. Multiple brain tissue repositories
in the NIH NBB network, located in academic research sites across
the country, have accomplished this feat by working in unison to raise
public awareness of brain donation and its benefits to human brain
disease research.

Now, the NIH NBB and ABN—a consortium of academic research
sites that collect, store, and distribute tissue specifically for ASD
research—will jointly redouble their efforts to ensure best practices
around the collection and distribution of these precious resources.
The ABN initiative is directed by David Amaral, Ph.D., research
director of the MIND Institute at the University of California, Davis,

311

and supported by Autism Speaks and the Simons Foundation Autism Research Initiative.

"One of the best ways for us to fully understand the molecular and cellular characteristics associated with the development and progression of ASD is to study brain tissue from individuals with ASD," said NIMH Acting Director Bruce Cuthbert, Ph.D. "This unified effort will allow researchers to generate new data, which will enhance our understanding of this disorder and ultimately speed progress toward new and personalized interventions for individuals across the autism spectrum."

A key aspect of the collaboration involves developing standardized brain donation protocols for use by personnel at tissue collection and research sites across the United States. These include procedures for obtaining consent, ensuring privacy protection, processing and maintaining donor tissue, and collecting donors' clinical, medical, and education records.

Both the NIH NBB and the ABN will maintain a catalog of all available samples and data from both repositories and enforce fair tissue distribution rules. NIMH and Foundation Associates anticipate that this joint effort will facilitate the distribution of high quality human brain tissue to ASD researchers worldwide.

NBB is supported by NIMH, the National Institute of Neurological Disorders and Stroke, and the Eunice Kennedy Shriver National Institute of Child Health and Human Development.

NIH Joins Public-Private Partnership to Fund Research on Autism Biomarkers

Government, non-profit and other private partners will fund a multi-year project to develop and improve clinical research tools for studying autism spectrum disorder (ASD). The project will receive a total of $28 million over the next four years to test and refine clinical measures of social impairment in ASD in order to better evaluate potential behavioral and drug therapies. It is supported by the National Institutes of Health (NIH), the Foundation for the NIH (FNIH), the Simons Foundation Autism Research Initiative (SFARI), and others. NIH funding comes from the National Institute of Mental Health (NIMH), the National Institute of Neurological Disorders and Stroke, and the Eunice Kennedy Shriver National Institute of Child Health and Human Development.

The effort is the latest addition to the prestigious list of projects supported by the Biomarkers Consortium, a large public-private partnership that aims to accelerate biomedical research progress. James McPartland Ph.D. of Yale School of Medicine, New Haven, Connecticut, serves as principal investigator. The Consortium supports research to identify disease-specific biomarkers and develop targeted technologies and treatments. Its ultimate goal is precision medicine —an emerging approach to prevention and treatment that takes into account an individual's disease-related variations in genes, environment, and lifestyle.

ASD is a group of neurodevelopmental disorders that affects social interaction and communication skills and can cause restricted and repetitive behaviors. Approximately 1 percent of children throughout the world have an ASD, each with his or her own unique combination of symptoms and levels of impairment. It is this extensive spectrum of symptoms and severity that has proven to be particularly challenging for clinical research.

"The heterogeneity in people with an ASD makes it imperative that we find more precisely diagnosed groups of research subjects so that we can objectively evaluate the clinical effects of an intervention," said NIMH Director Thomas R. Insel, M.D. "This consortium project will develop reliable tools and measures that clinical researchers can use to assess potential treatments."

McPartland and his team will conduct a multi-site study of preschool (3-5 years) and school aged (6-11 years) children, both with and without ASD, over the course of several months. Research sites include Yale University, Duke University, Durham, North Carolina, the University of California, Los Angeles, the University of Washington, Seattle, and Boston Children's Hospital.

The research team will begin by comparing lab-based measures of domains of social impairment to commonly used, standardized clinician and caregiver assessments of social function. Specifically, they will investigate the sensitivity and reliability of these unique measures in terms of how well they indicate changes in a participant's core social impairment symptoms over time.

The researchers will then evaluate the potential utility of eye tracking responses and measures of brain activity via electroencephalogram (EEG) as biomarkers for future clinical trials. They will investigate how these two noninvasive and relatively inexpensive biomarker measures relate to their recently validated lab-based measures of social function. Together, these findings will lay the groundwork for ASD researchers to objectively select meaningful subgroups of children and reliably measure the clinical effects of interventions.

In addition to the behavioral measures and biomarker data, this community resource will also include blood samples from subjects and their parents for use in future genetic studies. Data and resource sharing are key components of this Consortium project. All data generated in the project will be made available for other researchers to view and analyze through the NIH-funded National Database for Autism Research and the NIMH Repository and Genomics Resource.

Disorganized Cortical Patches Suggest Prenatal Origin of Autism

The architecture of the autistic brain is speckled with patches of abnormal neurons, according to research partially funded by the National Institute of Mental Health (NIMH), part of the National Institutes of Health. Published in the New England Journal of Medicine on March 27, 2014, this study suggests that brain irregularities in children with autism can be traced back to prenatal development.

"While autism is generally considered a developmental brain disorder, research has not identified a consistent or causative lesion," said Thomas R. Insel, M.D., director of NIMH. "If this new report of disorganized architecture in the brains of some children with autism is replicated, we can presume this reflects a process occurring long before birth. This reinforces the importance of early identification and intervention."

Eric Courchesne, Ph.D. and Rich Stoner, Ph.D., of the Autism Center of Excellence at the University of California, San Diego joined colleagues from the Allen Institute for Brain Science to investigate the cellular architecture of the brain's outermost structure, the cortex, in children with autism. Courchesne recently reported an overabundance of neurons in the prefrontal cortex of children with autism.

For the current study, the researchers analyzed gene expression in postmortem brain tissue from children with and without autism, all between 2 and 15 years of age.

As the prenatal brain develops, neurons in the cortex differentiate into six layers. Each is composed of particular types of brain cells with specific patterns of connections. The research team focused on genes that serve as cellular markers for each of the cortical layers as well as genes that are associated with autism.

The study found that the markers for several layers of the cortex were absent in 91 percent of the autistic case samples, as compared to 9 percent of control samples. Further, these signs of disorganization were not found all over the brain's surface, but instead were localized in focal patches that were 5-7 millimeters (0.20-0.28 inches) in length and encompassed multiple cortical layers.

These patches were found in the frontal and temporal lobes of the cortex—regions that mediate social, emotional, communication, and language functions. Considering that disturbances in these types of behaviors are hallmarks of autism, the researchers conclude that the specific locations of the patches may underlie the expression and severity of various symptoms in a child with the disorder.

The patchy nature of the defects may explain why early treatments can help young infants and toddlers with autism improve. According to the researchers, since the faulty cell layering does not occur over the entire cortex, the developing brain may have a chance to rewire its connections by sidestepping the pathological patches and recruiting cells from neighboring brain regions to assume critical roles in social and communication functions.

Section 39.4

Skewed Norms Weaken Case for Early Brain Overgrowth in Autism

Text in this section is excerpted from "Skewed Norms Weaken Case for Early Brain Overgrowth in Autism," National Institute of Mental Health (NIMH), June 19, 2013.

Biases in standardized norms used to compare data on head size weaken evidence for early excess brain growth in autism, say NIMH intramural researchers. Their analysis of existing and new data undermines the case that had been building for such early brain enlargement as a potential biomarker that might be used in making treatment decisions.

"Our results show that the most highly replicated aspects of early brain overgrowth in autism are not a feature of the disease, but instead arise through replicable biases in the population growth norms that have been used to define brain overgrowth in autism".explained Armin Raznahan, M.D., Ph.D.

Raznahan and NIMH Child Psychiatry Branch colleagues reported their findings online May 23, 2013, in the journal Biological Psychiatry.

Background

Although still a hypothesis, dramatic early brain overgrowth during the first year of life had become widely-viewed as a likely hallmark feature of autism, raising hopes that it might find application as a biomarker.

Most studies reporting such early brain overgrowth in autism have been based on head circumference as a proxy for brain size. Researchers have typically compared head circumference of children with autism to – as a control group – standardized charts of head circumference published by the Center for Disease Control (CDC), and World Health Organization (WHO).

Ten of 11 long-term studies of head circumference in autism had been published since the last time the topic had been systematically reviewed. Also, discrepancies had emerged between the norms used in autism studies and recent patterns of head growth emerging from several more recent large non-autism studies. Typically-developing young children's heads seemed to be growing faster, so that they looked strikingly similar to the overgrowth – it turns out perhaps erroneously – ascribed to autism. This suggested that previous studies had been based on norms that underestimated typical early brain growth.

Suspecting that the norms might be skewed by various sources of bias, the NIMH researchers reexamined them in light of the updated data from 34 relevant studies. They integrated crosssectional and longitudinal head circumference data between birth and 18 months. They also included 330 head circumference measures from their own longitudinal study that followed 35 children with autism and 22 typically developing controls as they grew up, from birth to 18 years old.

Results of This study

"The most methodologically robust and bias-free sources of evidence are equivocal regarding the presence of abnormally accelerated early brain growth in autism" said Raznahan.

In the few studies that did find evidence of such early brain overgrowth, head circumference in children with autism showed a "subtle divergence" from that in controls during the second year of life, rather than in the first year.

Significance

Earlier studies overestimated early brain growth in children with autism because their head circumference data was compared to published norms that were wrong – based on studies that underestimated typical head circumference/brain growth.

Inconsistencies that turned up in the study suggest the possibility of a more subtle, later emerging pattern of early brain overgrowth among only a subgroup of children with autism. Since some related disorders show brain undergrowth, the results are also consistent with the idea that extreme dysregulation of brain growth—as opposed to brain enlargement per se—may be more relevant to understanding autism spectrum disorders.

What's Next

Use of head circumference as an index of brain size offers practical advantages over more sophisticated measures, such as structural magnetic resonance imaging, in longitudinal studies, provided that the methodological pitfalls can be minimized, say the researchers.

Future studies might compare evidence for extreme versus isolated overgrowth and possible links between aberrant brain size and genetic and environmental influences prior to, or just after, birth, they add.

"These findings have far-reaching implications for use of standardized growth norms extending well beyond autism to decision-making across medicine." said Raznahan, who suggests that widely-used norms be reevaluated in light of the new evidence.

Section 39.5

Autism Risk Unrelated to Total Vaccine Exposure in Early Childhood

Text in this section is excerpted from "Autism Risk Unrelated to Total Vaccine Exposure in Early Childhood," National Institute of Mental Health (NIMH), March 29, 2013.

A child's risk for developing an autism spectrum disorder (ASD) is not increased by receiving "too many vaccines too soon," according to a new study published in The Journal of Pediatrics.

Although previous scientific evidence has shown that vaccines do not cause autism, more than 1 in 10 parents refuse or delay vaccinations

317

for their young children. A main safety concern of these parents is the number of vaccines administered, both on a single day and over the course of a child's first 2 years of life.

In the first study of its kind, researchers from the CDC and Abt Associates, Inc. compared vaccine records for over 1000 children born from 1994–1999, some of whom were later diagnosed with ASD. The researchers calculated the total number of vaccine antigens each child received between birth and age 2, as well as the maximum number of antigens each child received on a single day.

The study found that the total number of vaccine antigens received was the same between children with ASD and those without ASD. Additionally, antigen number was also found to be unrelated to the development of two sub-categories of ASD—autistic disorder and ASD with regression.

The researchers concluded, "The possibility that immunological stimulation from vaccines during the first 1 or 2 years of life could be related to the development of ASD is not well-supported by what is known about the neurobiology of ASDs."

Section 39.6

Prevalence of Parent-reported Autism

Text in this section is excerpted from "Prevalence of Parent-reported Autism," National Institute of Mental Health (NIMH), March 20, 2013.

The U.S. Centers for Disease Control and Prevention (CDC) and Health Resources and Services Administration released a report titled "Changes in Prevalence of Parent-reported Autism Spectrum Disorder in School-aged U.S. Children: 2007 to 2011–2012 ". The report presents data on the prevalence of diagnosed autism spectrum disorder (ASD) as reported by parents of school-aged children ages 6–17 years in 2011–2012. Data was drawn from the 2007 and 2011–2012 National Survey of Children's Health, which comprises independent, nationally representative telephone surveys of households with children.

Last year, the CDC's Autism and Developmental Disabilities Monitoring Network estimated that 1 in 88 children had been identified with ASD. The CDC now estimates that in 2011–2012, about 1 in 50 school-aged children, or 2 percent of children ages 6–17 years have some form of the disorder. Since the average school bus holds 50–55 children, that means, statistically speaking, on average there is one child with parent-reported ASD on every school bus in America.

The agencies conclude that the increase in prevalence of parent-reported ASD was largely due to improved diagnosis of ASD by doctors or other health professional in recent years, especially when the symptoms were mild.

Part Six

Education and Autism Spectrum Disorder

Chapter 40

Understanding the Special Education Process

Chapter Contents

Section 40.1

504 Education Plans

Text in this section is excerpted from "Protecting
Students with Disabilities," U.S. Department of
Education (ED), October 16, 2015.

Introduction

An important responsibility of the Office for Civil Rights (OCR) is
to eliminate discrimination on the basis of disability against students
with disabilities. OCR receives numerous complaints and inquiries
in the area of elementary and secondary education involving Section
504 of the Rehabilitation Act of 1973, as amended, 29 U.S.C. § 794
(Section 504). Most of these concern identification of students who
are protected by Section 504 and the means to obtain an appropriate
education for such students.

Section 504 is a federal law designed to protect the rights of individuals with disabilities in programs and activities that receive Federal
financial assistance from the U.S. Department of Education (ED). Section 504 provides: "No otherwise qualified individual with a disability
in the United States . . . shall, solely by reason of her or his disability,
be excluded from the participation in, be denied the benefits of, or be
subjected to discrimination under any program or activity receiving
Federal financial assistance . . . ."

OCR enforces Section 504 in programs and activities that receive
Federal financial assistance from ED. Recipients of this Federal financial assistance include public school districts, institutions of higher
education, and other state and local education agencies. The regulations implementing Section 504 in the context of educational institutions appear at 34 C.F.R. Part 104.

The Section 504 regulations require a school district to provide a
"free appropriate public education" (FAPE) to each qualified student
with a disability who is in the school district's jurisdiction, regardless
of the nature or severity of the disability. Under Section 504, FAPE
consists of the provision of regular or special education and related

aids and services designed to meet the student's individual educational needs as adequately as the needs of nondisabled students are met.

Interrelationship of IDEA and Section 504

What Is the Jurisdiction of the Office for Civil Rights (OCR), the Office of Special Education and Rehabilitative Services (OSERS) and State Departments of Education / Instruction Regarding Educational Services to Students with Disabilities?

OCR, a component of the U.S. Department of Education, enforces Section 504 of the Rehabilitation Act of 1973, as amended, (Section 504) a civil rights statute which prohibits discrimination against individuals with disabilities. OCR also enforces Title II of the Americans with Disabilities Act of 1990 (Title II), which extends this prohibition against discrimination to the full range of state and local government services, programs, and activities (including public schools) regardless of whether they receive any Federal financial assistance.

The Americans with Disabilities Act Amendments Act of 2008 (Amendments Act), effective January 1, 2009, amended the Americans with Disabilities Act of 1990 (ADA) and included a conforming amendment to the Rehabilitation Act of 1973 (Rehabilitation Act) that affects the meaning of disability in Section 504. The standards adopted by the ADA were designed not to restrict the rights or remedies available under Section 504. The Title II regulations applicable to free appropriate public education issues do not provide greater protection than applicable Section 504 regulations. This guidance focuses primarily on Section 504.

Section 504 prohibits discrimination on the basis of disability in programs or activities that receive Federal financial assistance from the U.S. Department of Education. Title II prohibits discrimination on the basis of disability by state and local governments. The Office of Special Education and Rehabilitative Services (OSERS), also a component of the U.S. Department of Education, administers the Individuals with Disabilities Education Act (IDEA), a statute which funds special education programs.

Each state educational agency is responsible for administering IDEA within the state and distributing the funds for special education programs. IDEA is a grant statute and attaches many specific conditions to the receipt of Federal IDEA funds. Section 504 and the ADA are antidiscrimination laws and do not provide any type of funding.

How Does OCR Get Involved in Disability Issues Within a School District?

OCR receives complaints from parents, students or advocates, conducts agency initiated compliance reviews, and provides technical assistance to school districts, parents or advocates.

Where Can a School District, Parent, or Student Get Information on Section 504 or Find out Information About OCR's Interpretation of Section 504 and Title II?

OCR provides technical assistance to school districts, parents, and students upon request. Additionally, regulations and publicly issued policy guidance is available on OCR's.

What Services Are Available for Students with Disabilities Under Section 504?

Section 504 requires recipients to provide to students with disabilities appropriate educational services designed to meet the individual needs of such students to the same extent as the needs of students without disabilities are met. An appropriate education for a student with a disability under the Section 504 regulations could consist of education in regular classrooms, education in regular classes with supplementary services, and/or special education and related services.

Does OCR Examine Individual Placement or Other Educational Decisions for Students with Disabilities?

Except in extraordinary circumstances, OCR does not review the result of individual placement or other educational decisions so long as the school district complies with the procedural requirements of Section 504 relating to identification and location of students with disabilities, evaluation of such students, and due process. Accordingly, OCR generally will not evaluate the content of a Section 504 plan or of an individualized education program (IEP); rather, any disagreement can be resolved through a due process hearing. The hearing would be conducted under Section 504 or the IDEA, whichever is applicable.

OCR will examine procedures by which school districts identify and evaluate students with disabilities and the procedural safeguards which those school districts provide students. OCR will also examine incidents in which students with disabilities are allegedly subjected to treatment which is different from the treatment to which similarly situated students without disabilities are subjected. Such incidents may involve the unwarranted exclusion of disabled students from educational programs and services.

What Protections Does OCR Provide Against Retaliation?

Retaliatory acts are prohibited. A recipient is prohibited from intimidating, threatening, coercing, or discriminating against any individual for the purpose of interfering with any right or privilege secured by Section 504.

Does OCR Mediate Complaints?

OCR does not engage in formal mediation. However, OCR may offer to facilitate mediation, referred to as "Early Complaint Resolution," to resolve a complaint filed under Section 504. This approach brings the parties together so that they may discuss possible resolution of the complaint immediately. If both parties are willing to utilize this approach, OCR will work with the parties to facilitate resolution by providing each an understanding of pertinent legal standards and possible remedies. An agreement reached between the parties is not monitored by OCR.

What Are the Appeal Rights with OCR?

OCR affords an opportunity to the complainant for appeal of OCR's letters of finding issued pursuant to Section 303(a) of the *OCR Case Processing Manual*. OCR also affords an opportunity to the complainant for appeal of OCR's dismissals or administrative closures of complaints issued pursuant to Sections 108, 110, and 111 of the Manual.

The appeal process provides an opportunity for complainants to bring information to OCR's attention that would change OCR's decision, but it does not involve a de novo review of OCR's decision. The complainant may send a written appeal to the Director of the regional Enforcement Office that issued the determination within 60 days of the date of the determination letter being appealed from.

In an appeal, the complainant must explain why he or she believes the factual information was incomplete, the analysis of the facts was incorrect, and/or the appropriate legal standard was not applied, and how this would change OCR's determination in the case. More information about appeals is found in Section 306 of the Manual.

What Does Noncompliance with Section 504 Mean?

A school district is out of compliance when it is violating any provision of the Section 504 statute or regulations.

What Sanctions Can OCR Impose on a School District That Is out of Compliance?

OCR initially attempts to bring the school district into voluntary compliance through negotiation of a corrective action agreement. If OCR is unable to achieve voluntary compliance, OCR will initiate enforcement action.

OCR may:

1. initiate administrative proceedings to terminate Department of Education financial assistance to the recipient; or

2. refer the case to the Department of Justice for judicial proceedings.

Who Has Ultimate Authority to Enforce Section 504?

In the educational context, OCR has been given administrative authority to enforce Section 504. Section 504 is a Federal statute that may be enforced through the Department's administrative process or through the Federal court system. In addition, a person may at any time file a private lawsuit against a school district. The Section 504 regulations do not contain a requirement that a person file a complaint with OCR and exhaust his or her administrative remedies before filing a private lawsuit.

Section 40.2

Autism Awareness and Acceptance in Early Childhood Education

Text in this section is excerpted from "Autism Awareness and Acceptance in Early Childhood Education," U.S. Department of Health and Human Services (HHS), April 27, 2013.

What Is Autism Spectrum Disorder (ASD)?

ASD is a developmental disability that can affect social communication and behavioral development. ASD is a spectrum disorder which means that each child is affected differently and has unique strengths, challenges, and needs. ASD begins before the age of 3 and lasts throughout a person's life, although symptoms may improve over time. Early identification of ASD is important so children and families can attain the services and support they need as soon as possible. With awareness, acceptance, and the appropriate supports, children with ASD can reach their incredible potential.

What Is the Role of Early Care and Education Providers?

While diagnosing and providing specific interventions for young children with ASD is the role of specialists, early childhood providers can play an active role in supporting children with autism and other developmental disabilities. By using developmentally appropriate practices, tracking developmental milestones, communicating with parents, and being aware of community-based resources, early care and education providers can make important contributions to the lives of young children with ASD and their families.

ACF is dedicated to providing early education providers with the information they need to better understand ASD and support the children in their care.

What Services are Available to Young Children with ASD under IDEA?

The Individuals with Disabilities Education Act (IDEA) is a federal law that requires that all children suspected of having a disability be

329

evaluated without cost to families to determine if they have a disability and are eligible for services under IDEA. For children under 3 years of age, these services are provided through a State's IDEA Part C early intervention system. For children older than 3, IDEA Part B services are available through the public school system.

The National Dissemination Center for Children with Disabilities provides information and resources about IDEA.

Section 40.3

Individualized Education Programs (IEPs)

Text in this section is excerpted from "Individualized Education Programs (IEPs)," © 1995–2016. The Nemours Foundation/ KidsHealth®. Reprinted with permission.

What's an IEP?

Kids with delayed skills or other disabilities might be eligible for special services that provide individualized education programs in public schools, free of charge to families. Understanding how to access these services can help parents be effective advocates for their kids.

The passage of the updated version of the Individuals with Disabilities Education Act (IDEA 2004) made parents of kids with special needs even more crucial members of their child's education team.

Parents can now work with educators to develop a plan — the individualized education program (IEP) — to help kids succeed in school. The IEP describes the goals the team sets for a child during the school year, as well as any special support needed to help achieve them.

Who Needs an IEP?

A child who has difficulty learning and functioning and has been identified as a special needs student is the perfect candidate for an IEP.

Kids struggling in school may qualify for support services, allowing them to be taught in a special way, for reasons such as:

- learning disabilities
- attention deficit hyperactivity disorder (ADHD)
- emotional disorders
- cognitive challenges
- autism
- hearing impairment
- visual impairment
- speech or language impairment
- developmental delay

How Are Services Delivered?

In most cases, the services and goals outlined in an IEP can be provided in a standard school environment. This can be done in the regular classroom (for example, a reading teacher helping a small group of children who need extra assistance while the other kids in the class work on reading with the regular teacher) or in a special resource room in the regular school. The resource room can serve a group of kids with similar needs who are brought together for help.

However, kids who need intense intervention may be taught in a special school environment. These classes have fewer students per teacher, allowing for more individualized attention.

In addition, the teacher usually has specific training in helping kids with special educational needs. The children spend most of their day in a special classroom and join the regular classes for nonacademic activities (like music and gym) or in academic activities in which they don't need extra help.

Because the goal of IDEA is to ensure that each child is educated in the least restrictive environment possible, effort is made to help kids stay in a regular classroom. However, when needs are best met in a special class, then kids might be placed in one.

The Referral and Evaluation Process

The referral process generally begins when a teacher, parent, or doctor is concerned that a child may be having trouble in the classroom, and the teacher notifies the school counselor or psychologist.

331

The first step is to gather specific data regarding the student's progress or academic problems. This may be done through:

- a conference with parents
- a conference with the student
- observation of the student
- analysis of the student's performance (attention, behavior, work completion, tests, classwork, homework, etc.)

This information helps school personnel determine the next step. At this point, strategies specific to the student could be used to help the child become more successful in school. If this doesn't work, the child would be tested for a specific learning disability or other impairment to help determine qualification for special services.

It's important to note, though, that the presence of a disability doesn't automatically guarantee a child will receive services. To be eligible, the disability must affect functioning at school.

To determine eligibility, a multidisciplinary team of professionals will evaluate the child based on their observations; the child's performance on standardized tests; and daily work such as tests, quizzes, classwork, and homework.

Who's on the Team?

The professionals on the evaluation team can include:

- a psychologist
- a physical therapist
- an occupational therapist
- a speech therapist
- a special educator
- a vision or hearing specialist
- others, depending on the child's specific needs

As a parent, you can decide whether to have your child assessed. If you choose to do so, you'll be asked to sign a permission form that will detail who is involved in the process and the types of tests they use. These tests might include measures of specific school skills, such as reading or math, as well as more general developmental skills, such as speech and language. Testing does not necessarily mean that a child will receive services.

Once the team members complete their individual assessments, they develop a comprehensive evaluation report (CER) that compiles their findings, offers an educational classification, and outlines the skills and support the child will need.

The parents then have a chance to review the report before the IEP is developed. Some parents will disagree with the report, and they will have the opportunity to work together with the school to come up with a plan that best meets the child's needs.

Developing an IEP

The next step is an IEP meeting at which the team and parents decide what will go into the plan. In addition to the evaluation team, a regular teacher should be present to offer suggestions about how the plan can help the child's progress in the standard education curriculum.

At the meeting, the team will discuss your child's educational needs — as described in the CER — and come up with specific, measurable short-term and annual goals for each of those needs. If you attend this meeting, you can take an active role in developing the goals and determining which skills or areas will receive the most attention.

The cover page of the IEP outlines the support services your child will receive and how often they will be provided (for example, occupational therapy twice a week). Support services might include special education, speech therapy, occupational or physical therapy, counseling, audiology, medical services, nursing, vision or hearing therapy, and many others.

If the team recommends several services, the amount of time they take in the child's school schedule can seem overwhelming. To ease that load, some services may be provided on a consultative basis. In these cases, the professional consults with the teacher to come up with strategies to help the child but doesn't offer any hands-on instruction. For instance, an occupational therapist may suggest accommodations for a child with fine-motor problems that affect handwriting, and the classroom teacher would incorporate these suggestions into the handwriting lessons taught to the entire class.

Other services can be delivered right in the classroom, so the child's day isn't interrupted by therapy. The child who has difficulty with handwriting might work one on one with an occupational therapist while everyone else practices their handwriting skills. When deciding how and where services are offered, the child's comfort and dignity should be a top priority.

The IEP should be reviewed annually to update the goals and make sure the levels of service meet your child's needs. However, IEPs can be changed at any time on an as-needed basis. If you think your child needs more, fewer, or different services, you can request a meeting and bring the team together to discuss your concerns.

Your Legal Rights

Specific timelines ensure that the development of an IEP moves from referral to providing services as quickly as possible. Be sure to ask about this timeframe and get a copy of your parents' rights when your child is referred. These guidelines (sometimes called procedural safeguards) outline your rights as a parent to control what happens to your child during each step of the process.

The parents' rights also describe how you can proceed if you disagree with any part of the CER or the IEP — mediation and hearings both are options. You can get information about low-cost or free legal representation from the school district or, if your child is in Early Intervention (for kids ages 3 to 5), through that program.

Attorneys and paid advocates familiar with the IEP process will provide representation if you need it. You also may invite anyone who knows or works with your child whose input you feel would be helpful to join the IEP team.

Conclusion

Parents have the right to choose where their kids will be educated. This choice includes public or private elementary schools and secondary schools, including religious schools. It also includes charter schools and home schools.

However, it is important to understand that the rights of children with disabilities who are placed by their parents in private elementary schools and secondary schools are not the same as those of kids with disabilities who are enrolled in public schools or placed by public agencies in private schools when the public school is unable to provide a free appropriate public education (FAPE).

Two major differences that parents, teachers, other school staff, private school representatives, and the kids need to know about are:

Children with disabilities who are placed by their parents in private schools may not get the same services they would receive in a public school.

Not all kids with disabilities placed by their parents in private schools will receive services.

The IEP process is complex, but it's also an effective way to address how your child learns and functions. If you have concerns, don't hesitate to ask questions about the evaluation findings or the goals recommended by the team. You know your child best and should play a central role in creating a learning plan tailored to his or her specific needs.

Section 40.4

Individuals with Disabilities Education Act (IDEA)

Text in this section is excerpted from "Individuals with Disabilities Education Act (IDEA)," Disability.gov, May 20, 2014.

Two of the main laws that help fund special education and protect the rights of students with disabilities are the Individuals with Disabilities Education Act (IDEA) and Section 504 of the Rehabilitation Act (often just called "Section 504."). The IDEA was originally passed in 1975 to make sure that children with disabilities have the opportunity to receive a free, appropriate public education, just like other children. IDEA requires that special education and related services be made available to every eligible child with a disability. Section 504, on the other hand, is a civil rights law that protects children with disabilities from discrimination.

Every year, millions of children receive services under the IDEA. This law governs how states and public agencies provide early intervention, and special education and related services to more than 6.5 million eligible infants, toddlers, children and youth with disabilities. Infants and toddlers (birth-2) with disabilities and their families receive early intervention services under IDEA Part C. Children and youth (ages 3-21) receive special education and related services under IDEA Part B. A couple of good places to help parents better understand this law are the Center for Parent Information and Resources and the National Center on Learning Disabilities' "An Overview of IDEA Parent Guide."

If your child does not receive special education services under IDEA, he or she does not have the protections that are available under the IDEA statute. School districts are required to provide a "free and appropriate public education" (FAPE) to each qualified student with a disability who is in the school district's jurisdiction. Under Section 504, FAPE means regular or special education and related aids and services that meet the student's individual educational needs.

The differences between the IDEA, Section 504 and the ADA, read this comparison chart from the Disability Rights Education and Defense Fund. The National Education Association also has a fact sheet that explains the different protections of these laws.

The services that IDEA requires can be very important in helping children and youth with disabilities develop, learn and succeed in school. Under the law, states are responsible for meeting the needs of eligible children with disabilities. To find out if a child is eligible for services, he or she must first be evaluated. This evaluation is free and can determine if a child has a disability, as defined by IDEA, and what special education and related services he or she may need.

Special education is instruction that is specially designed to meet the specific needs of a child with a disability. Since each child is unique, it's difficult to give an overall example of special education. Special education can be for things like travel training or vocational educa- tion, and it can take place in the classroom, in a home, in a hospital or institution, among other places. This is why you might also hear that "special education is not a place." Where it is provided depends on the child's unique needs as decided by the group of individuals (which includes the parents) that makes the placement decision.

Some students with disabilities may need accommodations and other related services to help them benefit from special education. These related services may include speech-language pathology and audiology services; interpreting services; psychological services; physi- cal and occupational therapy; therapeutic recreation; and early identi- fication and assessment of disabilities in children. Read "Knowing Your Child's Rights" for an overview of what the IDEA requires regarding special education and related services.

Under the IDEA, special education instruction must be provided to students with disabilities in what is known as the "least restrictive envi- ronment," or LRE. IDEA's LRE provisions ensure that children with disabilities are educated with children who do not have disabilities, to the maximum extent appropriate. LRE requirements apply to students in public or private institutions or other care facilities.

There are several local organizations that help parents of children with disabilities better understand how the IDEA can help as their kids advance through the school system. Every state has at least one Parent Training and Information Center (PTI). PTIs provide parents with important information about special education so they can participate effectively in meeting the educational needs of their children. If your child is struggling with learning, visit the website of the National Center for Learning Disabilities. The Center website has a section of resources specifically for parents that includes a "Parent Guide to the IDEA." The Learning Disabilities Association of America (LDA) also has special education resources for parents. Find a LDA chapter near you. Finally, your state's department of education is an important point of entry for getting information about all the programs and services required under IDEA, and how you can help your child get the most out of their education.

Section 40.5

Free Appropriate Public Education (FAPE)

Text in this section is excerpted from "Free Appropriate Public
Education for Students With Disabilities: Requirements Under
Section 504, The Rehabilitation Act of 1973," U.S. Department of
Education (ED), August 2010. Reviewed February 2016.

Introduction

Section 504 of the Rehabilitation Act of 1973 protects the rights of individuals with disabilities in programs and activities that receive federal financial assistance, including federal funds. Section 504 provides that: "No otherwise qualified individual with a disability in the United States . . . shall, solely by reason of her or his disability, be excluded from the participation in, be denied the benefits of, or be subjected to discrimination under any program or activity receiving Federal financial assistance.

The U.S. Department of Education (ED) enforces Section 504 in programs and activities that receive funds from ED. Recipients of these funds include public school districts, institutions of higher education, and other state and local education agencies. ED has published a regulation implementing Section 504 (34 C.F.R. Part 104) and maintains an Office for Civil Rights (OCR), with 12 enforcement offices and a headquarters office in Washington, D.C., to enforce Section 504 and other civil rights laws that pertain to recipients of funds.

The Section 504 regulation requires a school district to provide a "free appropriate public education" (FAPE) to each qualified person with a disability who is in the school district's jurisdiction, regardless of the nature or severity of the person's disability.

This pamphlet answers the following questions about FAPE according to Section 504:

- Who is entitled to a free appropriate public education?

- How is an appropriate education defined?

- How is a free education defined?

Who Is Entitled to FAPE?

All qualified persons with disabilities within the jurisdiction of a school district are entitled to a free appropriate public education. The ED Section 504 regulation defines a person with a disability as "any person who: (i) has a physical or mental impairment which substantially limits one or more major life activities, (ii) has a record of such an impairment, or (iii) is regarded as having such an impairment."

For elementary and secondary education programs, a qualified person with a disability is a person with a disability who is:

- of an age during which it is mandatory under state law to provide such services to persons with disabilities;

- of an age during which persons without disabilities are provided such services; or

- entitled to receive a free appropriate public education under the Individuals with Disabilities Education Act (IDEA).

In general, all school-age children who are individuals with disabilities as defined by Section 504 and IDEA are entitled to FAPE.

How Is an Appropriate Education Defined?

An appropriate education may comprise education in regular classes, education in regular classes with the use of related aids and services, or special education and related services in separate classrooms for all or portions of the school day. Special education may include specially designed instruction in classrooms, at home, or in private or public institutions, and may be accompanied by related services such as speech therapy, occupational and physical therapy, psychological counseling, and medical diagnostic services necessary to the child's education.

An appropriate education will include:

- education services designed to meet the individual education needs of students with disabilities as adequately as the needs of nondisabled students are met;

- the education of each student with a disability with nondisabled students, to the maximum extent appropriate to the needs of the student with a disability;

- evaluation and placement procedures established to guard against misclassification or inappropriate placement of students, and a periodic reevaluation of students who have been provided special education or related services; and

- establishment of due process procedures that enable parents and guardians to:

- receive required notices;

- review their child's records; and

- challenge identification, evaluation and placement decisions.

Due process procedures must also provide for an impartial hearing with the opportunity for participation by parents and representation by counsel, and a review procedure.

Education Services Must Meet Individual Needs

To be appropriate, education programs for students with disabilities must be designed to meet their individual needs to the same

339

extent that the needs of nondisabled students are met. An appropriate education may include regular or special education and related aids and services to accommodate the unique needs of individuals with disabilities.

One way to ensure that programs meet individual needs is through the development of an individualized education program (IEP) for each student with a disability. IEPs are required for students participating in the special education programs of recipients of funding under the IDEA.

The quality of education services provided to students with disabilities must equal the quality of services provided to nondisabled students. Teachers of students with disabilities must be trained in the instruction of individuals with disabilities. Facilities must be comparable, and appropriate materials and equipment must be available.

Students with disabilities may not be excluded from participating in nonacademic services and extracurricular activities on the basis of disability. Persons with disabilities must be provided an opportunity to participate in nonacademic services that is equal to that provided to persons without disabilities. These services may include physical education and recreational athletics, transportation, health services, recreational activities, special interest groups or clubs sponsored by the school, and referrals to agencies that provide assistance to persons with disabilities and employment of students.

Students with Disabilities Must Be Educated with Nondisabled Students

Students with disabilities and students without disabilities must be placed in the same setting, to the maximum extent appropriate to the education needs of the students with disabilities. A recipient of ED funds must place a person with a disability in the regular education environment, unless it is demonstrated by the recipient that the student's needs cannot be met satisfactorily with the use of supplementary aids and services. Students with disabilities must participate with nondisabled students in both academic and nonacademic services, including meals, recess, and physical education, to the maximum extent appropriate to their individual needs.

As necessary, specific related aids and services must be provided for students with disabilities to ensure an appropriate education setting. Supplementary aids may include interpreters for students who are deaf, readers for students who are blind, and door-to-door transportation for students with mobility impairments.

340

A recipient of ED funds that places an individual with disabilities in another school is responsible for taking into account the proximity of the other school to the student's home. If a recipient operates a facility for persons with disabilities, the facility and associated activities must be comparable to other facilities, services, and activities of the recipient.

Evaluation and Placement Decisions Must Be Made in Accord with Appropriate Procedures

Failure to provide persons with disabilities with an appropriate education frequently occurs as a result of misclassification and inappropriate placement. It is illegal to base individual placement decisions on presumptions and stereotypes regarding persons with disabilities or on classes of such persons. For example, it would be a violation of the law for a recipient to adopt a policy that every student who is hearing impaired, regardless of the severity of the child's disability, must be placed in a state school for the deaf.

Section 504 requires the use of evaluation and placement procedures that ensure that children are not misclassified, unnecessarily labeled as having a disability, or incorrectly placed, based on inappropriate selection, administration, or interpretation of evaluation materials.

A school district must conduct or arrange for an individual evaluation at no cost to the parents before any action is taken with respect to the initial placement of a child who has a disability, or before any significant change in that placement.

Recipients of ED funds must establish standards and procedures for initial and continuing evaluations and placement decisions regarding persons who, because of a disability, need or are believed to need special education or related services.

These procedures must ensure that tests and other evaluation materials:

- have been validated for the specific purpose for which they are used, and are administered by trained personnel in conformance with the instructions provided by their producer;

- are tailored to assess specific areas of education need and are not designed merely to provide a single general intelligence quotient; and

- are selected and administered so as best to ensure that, when a test is administered to a student with impaired sensory, manual, or speaking skills, the test results accurately reflect the

341

student's aptitude or achievement level or whatever other factor the test purports to measure, rather than reflecting the student's impaired sensory, manual, or speaking skills (except where those skills are the factors that the test purports to measure).

Recipients must draw upon a variety of sources in the evaluation and placement process so that the possibility of error is minimized. All significant factors related to the learning process must be considered.

These sources and factors include, for example, aptitude and achievement tests, teacher recommendations, physical condition, social and cultural background, and adaptive behavior. "Adaptive behavior is the effectiveness with which the individual meets the standards of personal independence and social responsibility expected of his or her age and cultural group."

Information from all sources must be documented and considered by a group of knowledgeable persons, and procedures must ensure that the student is placed with nondisabled students to the greatest extent appropriate.

Periodic reevaluation is required. This may be conducted in accordance with the IDEA regulation, which requires reevaluation at three-year intervals (unless the parent and school district agree reevaluation is unnecessary) or more frequently if conditions warrant, or if the child's parent or teacher requests a reevaluation.

Recipients Must Have Due Process Procedures for the Review of Identification, Evaluation, and Placement Decisions

Public elementary and secondary schools must employ procedural safeguards regarding the identification, evaluation, or educational placement of persons who, because of disability, need or are believed to need special instruction or related services.

Parents must be told about these procedures. In addition, parents or guardians must be notified of any evaluation or placement actions, and must be allowed to examine the student's records. The due process procedures must allow the parents or guardians of students in elementary and secondary schools to challenge evaluation and placement procedures and decisions.

If parents or guardians disagree with the school's decisions, they must be afforded an impartial hearing, with an opportunity for their participation and for representation by counsel. A review procedure also must be available to parents or guardians who disagree with the hearing decision.

How Is a Free Education Defined?

Recipients operating federally funded programs must provide education and related services free of charge to students with disabilities and their parents or guardians. Provision of a free education is the provision of education and related services without cost to the person with a disability or his or her parents or guardians, except for fees equally imposed on nondisabled persons or their parents or guardians.

If a recipient is unable to provide a free appropriate public education itself, the recipient may place a person with a disability in, or refer such person to, a program other than the one it operates.

However, the recipient remains responsible for ensuring that the education offered is an appropriate education, as defined in the law, and for coverage of financial obligations associated with the placement.

The cost of the program may include tuition and other related services, such as room and board, psychological and medical services necessary for diagnostic and evaluative purposes, and adequate transportation. Funds available from any public or private source, including insurers, may be used by the recipient to meet the requirements of FAPE.

If a student is placed in a private school because a school district cannot provide an appropriate program, the financial obligations for this placement are the responsibility of the school district. However, if a school district makes available a free appropriate public education and the student's parents or guardian choose to place the child in a private school, the school district is not required to pay for the student's education in the private school. If a recipient school district places a student with a disability in a program that requires the student to be away from home, the recipient is responsible for the cost of room and board and nonmedical care.

To meet the requirements of FAPE, a recipient may place a student with a disability in, or refer such student to, a program not operated by the recipient. When this occurs, the recipient must ensure that adequate transportation is provided to and from the program at no greater personal or family cost than would be incurred if the student with a disability were placed in the recipient's program.

FAPE Provisions in the Individuals with Disabilities Education Act (IDEA)

Part B of IDEA requires participating states to ensure that a free appropriate public education (FAPE) is made available to eligible children with disabilities in mandatory age ranges residing in the state.

To be eligible, a child must be evaluated as having one or more of the disabilities listed in IDEA and determined to be in need of special education and related services. Evaluations must be conducted according to prescribed procedures.

The disabilities specified in IDEA include: mental retardation, hearing impairments including deafness, speech or language impairments, visual impairments including blindness, emotional disturbance, orthopedic impairments, autism, traumatic brain injury, other health impairments, specific learning disabilities, deaf-blindness, and multiple disabilities. Additionally, states and local education agencies (LEAs) may adopt the term "developmental delay" for children aged 3 through 9 (or a subset of that age range) who are experiencing a developmental delay as defined by the state and need special education and related services.

The requirements for FAPE under IDEA are more detailed than those under Section 504. In specific instances detailed in the Section 504 regulation (for example, with respect to reevaluation procedures and the provision of an appropriate education), meeting the requirements of IDEA is one means of meeting the requirements of the Section 504 regulation.

IDEA requirements apply to states receiving financial assistance under IDEA. States must ensure that their political subdivisions that are responsible for providing or paying for the education of children with disabilities meet IDEA requirements. All states receive IDEA funds. Section 504 applies to any program or activity receiving ED financial assistance.

Chapter 41

Classroom Management for Students with ASD

Managing Students with ASD

Managing a classroom for students with autism spectrum disorders (ASD) creates some challenges for teachers. Traditional classroom management techniques such as structure, routines, rules, and lesson plans may need to be adjusted to meet the students' needs and accommodate the additional staff members who will provide collaborative instruction and programming for the students. In addition, teachers may need to implement nontraditional techniques such as visual aids, behavior plans, and data collection systems in a classroom with students on the autism spectrum. Every child with ASD is unique, however, so classroom management should be handled on a case-by-case basis depending on the student's level of functioning and behavioral characteristics.

The following general strategies may be helpful in creating classroom management systems that maximize instruction and learning and minimize chaos and confusion:

Staff Collaboration

In the school setting, most students with ASD receive instruction and support from a team of staff members, including general education

"Classroom Management for Students with ASD," © 2016 Omnigraphics, Inc. Reviewed February 2016.

teachers, special education teachers, and paraprofessionals. Effective classroom management strategies can help coordinate the efforts of this team of educators and enable students with ASD to function better at school. Suggestions for improving staff collaboration include:

- preparing a written plan for classroom roles and responsibilities, such as taking attendance, preparing for snack time, or leading the art lesson.

- displaying a job chart that outlines individual and shared tasks;

- assigning each staff member to specific students, activities, or areas of the classroom to eliminate confusion;

- matching staff strengths and interests with classroom activities;

- establishing a schedule for breaks and lunch hours to ensure that enough staff members are available during key periods;

- holding a weekly debriefing session to discuss the needs and issues of students, review teaching and communication strategies, and adjust classroom schedules and responsibilities.

Structure and Schedules

Many children with ASD feel more comfortable and function more effectively in a structured, consistent classroom environment. Experts suggest establishing a daily routine that encourages independence. In the morning, for instance, the students' routine might include lining up, entering the classroom, greeting the teacher, hanging up their coats, unpacking their book bags, and taking their seats.

Students with ASD may also benefit from a customized daily schedule in visual form. This schedule would include such tasks and activities as independent work time, one-on-one instruction, fine motor skills development, sensory play, social skills instruction, and structured recreation activities. A personalized schedule can help reduce anxiety by letting students with ASD know what to expect.

Visual Strategies

There are many steps teachers can take in setting up the classroom environment to meet the needs of students with ASD. One recommended approach is to incorporate visual aids, which have been shown to help children with autism process information and learn more easily than oral or written instructions. Visual aids can be used to label areas of the classroom, post rules for appropriate behavior, or provide directions for activities. Pictures, symbols, and visual cues also play an important role in augmentative and alternative communication (AAC) techniques that can enhance learning for students with ASD.

Behavior Intervention Plans

Written behavior plans are another important element of classroom management for students with ASD. These plans should be developed in consultation with parents and shared with all members of the classroom staff so that everyone responds to targeted behavior in a consistent manner. Behavior plans should identify any inappropriate or challenging behaviors, designate preferred alternative behaviors, and list strategies for modifying the behaviors.

Accommodations for Sensory Issues

Many students with ASD experience problems with sensory processing. Each child's specific sensory issues should be identified and addressed as part of the classroom management system. Some possible accommodations to help children with sensory issues include:

- providing inflatable seat cushions or pillows to enable them to move around while remaining seated;
- offering opportunities for movement, such as jumping on a mini-trampoline or chewing gum;
- eliminating flickering fluorescent lights and distracting sources of noise;
- allowing them to skip loud and crowded school assemblies or take a break if they feel overwhelmed;
- allowing them to eat lunch in a quiet room with a friend or a teacher rather than in a busy cafeteria;

providing a quiet area for them to relax, listen to music, look out the window, or play with a toy for a few minutes to calm down and refocus.

Data Collection Systems

Finally, classroom management for students with ASD includes putting a system in place to measure and record the students' progress toward meeting the objectives in their Individualized Education Plans

(IEP). All members of the classroom staff should be familiar with this data collection system.

Reference

"Guidelines for Educating Students with Autism Spectrum Disorders." Virginia Department of Education, October 2010.

Chapter 42

Managing Challenging ASD Behavior

Most people with autism spectrum disorders (ASD) will display challenging behaviors at times. Common types of challenging behaviors that may occur with autism include physical or verbal aggression, disruption, noncompliance, tantrums, self-injury, destruction of property, obsessions or compulsions, repetitive rituals, sexual inappropriateness, and eloping (running away from home, school, or another safe place). Although autism does not cause challenging behaviors directly, the core symptoms of ASD—including difficulties with social interaction, verbal and nonverbal communication, sensory processing, and motor skills—can create feelings of confusion, frustration, anxiety, and lack of control that may result in challenging behaviors.

Researchers believe that some challenging behaviors with autism are biologically driven and may involve impulses or reflexes that are beyond the person's control. But some people with ASD may use challenging behavior as a form of communication to express their needs or concerns. The key to understanding challenging behavior is to determine its purpose or function. Some of the common functions of challenging behavior in people with ASD include escaping from a situation, avoiding a task, getting attention, obtaining an object, gaining control over an environment, responding to pain or discomfort, or attempting to calm down or self-regulate.

Although some behaviors may be biologically driven, much behavior is learned over time and shaped by experiences. As a result, parents, teachers, and medical professionals who work with people with ASD can often employ positive interventions to change challenging behavior into appropriate behavior. The response to challenging behavior can have a significant impact on how the person with ASD behaves upon encountering a similar situation in the future. Specialized approaches aimed at improving challenging behavior are often aimed at helping a person with ASD recognize their own environmental triggers, communicate their needs in a more acceptable manner, and develop self-regulation abilities.

Addressing Challenging Behaviors

It is vital to address challenging behaviors as soon as possible to prevent them from getting worse and to ensure a good quality of life for the individual with ASD and his or her family. Effective function-based behavior interventions should be positive, consistent, and continued even after the challenging behavior begins to abate. Reshaping challenging behaviors into appropriate adaptive behaviors requires commitment, because any subtle adjustments that caregivers make to accommodate the problem behaviors can accumulate over time and make the behaviors harder to change. Even if certain behaviors mostly seem annoying rather than truly problematic, they can still create tension at home, at school, and in the community if they are allowed to become more pronounced or frequent over time.

Challenging behaviors can make life more difficult for the person with ASD and his or her family. They can prevent the person from taking advantage of opportunities for growth and development, such as play dates, recreational activities, and job options. They can also affect the person's health and well-being by causing physical pain or injury and creating psychological stress, anxiety, or depression. They can impair social relationships with family members, friends, and classmates, and they can disrupt academic learning as well as long-term employability.

For parents, teachers, and caregivers of people with ASD, challenging behaviors can increase stress, worry, anxiety, and depression. They can also create fear of harm or physical danger, as well as lead to embarrassment, withdrawal, and social isolation. Challenging behaviors can also create financial hardships by forcing a parent to stop working, causing damage to property, or generating medical bills. For all of these reasons, it is vital to address challenging behaviors with positive interventions.

Building a Support Team

To determine the function of a challenging behavior and design an effective intervention, a team approach is needed. Ideally, the support team should include the person with autism, their parents or caregivers, a case manager from a school or state service agency, and a pediatrician or primary-care physician who has a relationship with the family. The doctor may wish to include additional specialists or therapists on the team—such as an audiologist, gastroenterologist, allergist, nutritionist, or immunologist—to focus on specific areas of concern. The support team should also include:

- A Board Certified Behavior Analyst (BCBA) with expertise in understanding, evaluating, and developing support strategies to address challenging behaviors. These providers use applied behavior analysis techniques to determine the environmental factors that precipitate the behavior and develop positive reinforcement strategies to reshape the behavior.

- A psychologist or psychiatrist to evaluate emotional and mental health concerns and provide training and supports for the person with ASD and their family.

- A speech-language pathologist to evaluate the communication abilities and deficits of the person with ASD and help them develop functional communication skills.

- A physical therapist or occupational therapist to evaluate motor skills, sensory processing differences, and other physical concerns and develop interventions and coping strategies to help an individual with ASD feel more comfortable in their surroundings.

Combining the different perspectives of these professionals can enable parents or caregivers to create a positive behavior intervention plan that addresses physical, mental, and learning concerns in order to help the person with ASD adapt more successfully.

351

Strategies for Positive Behavior Intervention

The essential elements of an effective behavior intervention plan include clarity, consistency, simplicity, and continuation even as the behavior improves. Research has shown that positive behavior supports, rather than punishment (which can actually increase aggression and strain the relationship with the caregiver), are most helpful in teaching appropriate behaviors and self-regulation skills. Since many skills take time to develop, changes in behavior may take time as well. In fact, challenging behavior may get worse or more frequent before it gets better. Experts recommend setting priorities and starting with the most dangerous behaviors first. They also suggest setting realistic goals and starting with small steps that grow larger over time.

Positive behavior supports are intended to increase desirable behaviors, instill a sense of what is expected, and build a sense of pride and personal responsibility in the person with ASD. Some tips include providing positive feedback, celebrating successes, and validating concerns. Experts also suggest providing clear expectations, ignoring the challenging behavior when it occurs, and rewarding desired behavior and instances of self-control. Finally, it may be helpful to allow the person with ASD to take breaks, offer them a safe place to calm down and refocus, and provide accommodations as needed.

Making changes to the environment can also help eliminate challenging behavior and promote desired behavior. If places, situations, or relationships seem to promote good behavior, it may be helpful to expand access to them. On the other hand, it is a good idea to avoid situations and places that seem to increase frustration and anxiety and trigger challenging behavior. Creating a more successful environment for people with ASD also involves providing structure and routines, using visual supports, eliminating distractions or upsetting stimuli, and providing an escape from crowded or noisy activities.

Managing Crisis Situation

In a crisis situation, when a person with ASD is behaving aggressively or destructively, it is usually not possible to reason with them or teach them appropriate alternative behaviors. Instead, the focus of parents and other caregivers needs to be on ensuring the safety of the person with ASD, as well as protecting other people and personal property. It may be helpful to develop a crisis management plan to help anticipate troubling situations, prevent them from escalating, and keep everyone involved safe.

Strategies for managing a behavioral crisis and staying safe include identifying triggers, developing tools for ensuring safety in various settings, establishing procedures for de-escalation, and collecting data to evaluate and revamp the plan. If the situation becomes dangerous for the individual with ASD or others, it may be helpful to know the location of the nearest emergency room or facility for hospitalization and treatment. If it becomes necessary to involve law enforcement, experts suggest preparing a card to hand out to police officers that provides information about autism and the person's specific behavior issues. Finally, for people with ASD who are over the age of eighteen, parents or caregivers should make sure that their crisis management plan includes a document that secures guardianship in case they need to make medical decisions for them.

Long Term Solutions

Although positive interventions can help individuals with autism learn the skills they need to succeed and thrive, sometimes challenging behaviors like aggression or self-injury exceed the resources and support families are able to provide. Parents who are exhausted, discouraged, or afraid may not be well equipped to follow a positive behavioral intervention plan. In that case, parents and other caregivers may need to consider alternative solutions, such as placing the person with ASD in a residential setting where they can receive the supports they need.

Reference

"Challenging Behaviors Tool Kit." Autism Speaks, 2016.

Chapter 43

Social Interaction Education for Students with ASD

Social interaction can be challenging for people with autism spectrum disorders (ASD). Programs designed to help children with autism develop social skills and learn to interact with other children are an increasingly common component of special education services. Studies have shown that students with ASD who participate in social interaction education programs with typically developing classmates experience significant improvements in language, appropriate conversation, social skills, and classroom behavior. These programs also offer benefits to typically developing children in terms of promoting acceptance and positive attitudes toward people with disabilities.

Designing an Effective Program

To increase the likelihood of successful outcomes, programs for facilitating social interaction between typically developing children and children with autism should be tailored to the individual students, settings, and circumstances involved. Since not all children are well suited for involvement in these programs, the participants must be selected carefully. The students with autism should have enough communication skills to follow simple directions and use two- to three-word phrases. The socially competent children should be open to involvement in the program, possess good role model qualities, and demonstrate an ability to interact positively with students with autism.

Prior to launching the social interaction program, the typically developing students should be educated about the characteristics and behaviors of children with autism. For instance, they might watch a child-friendly video that explains ways to help and support classmates with autism. Promoting an understanding of autism helps general education students approach interactions with greater confidence and a positive attitude. For the children with ASD, any aggressive or challenging behaviors should be brought under control prior to participation in the social interaction program. Typically developing children are unlikely to be willing to interact with children who hit them, scream at them, or exhibit other disruptive behaviors.

Although the general education students should be encouraged to be accepting, responsive, and patient toward their peers with autism, none of the children should be pressured to form intimate friendships. The foundations of such relationships—including mutual interests and compatibility—may not be present in associations between children with and without autism, and it is important for the expectations of the social interaction program to be realistic.

Some additional suggestions to help develop an effective social interaction education program include the following:

- Encourage social interactions in settings where they are most likely to occur naturally, such as an integrated classroom, playground, or lunchroom.

- Allow the students to interact during regular daily activities when classmates would ordinarily be talking with one another.

- Incorporate items and materials that have natural interactive qualities, like building toys or collaborative art projects.

- Include visual aids to serve as prompts. In a sharing activity, for instance, students could use a small sign with a picture and the phrase "May I have it?"

- Break down social interaction skills into component parts, and help the student with autism master each task before working on the entire skill.

- Prioritize skills that have greatest potential impact and can be used with a variety of people and situations.

- Review and practice skills even after the child with ASD has mastered them in order to avoid their forgetting and needing additional instruction.

- Generalize skills learned in a specific setting or under certain conditions so that they can be practiced and used with other people and in other environments.

- Emphasize the quality of social interactions over the frequency or duration. A long, rehearsed response is less meaningful than a short, spontaneous request or comment.

- Provide ongoing instruction, feedback, and supervision of the social interactions.

- Collect and analyze data on social interactions between students with and without autism in both structured and unstructured settings to decide whether the program is effective or may need modification.

References

1. "Considerations for Social Interaction with Autistic Students." TeacherVision, 2016.

2. "Social Training with Peers Helps Kids with Autism." Autism Speaks, April 8, 2015.

Chapter 44

Preparing for Postsecondary Education

More and more high school students with disabilities are planning to continue their education in postsecondary schools, including vocational and career schools, two- and four- year colleges, and universities. As a student with a disability, you need to be well informed about your rights and responsibilities as well as the responsibilities postsecondary schools have toward you. Being well informed will help ensure you have a full opportunity to enjoy the benefits of the postsecondary education experience without confusion or delay.

The information in this chapter, provided by the Office for Civil Rights (OCR) in the U. S. Department of Education, explains the rights and responsibilities of students with disabilities who are preparing to attend postsecondary schools. This chapter also explains the obligations of a postsecondary school to provide academic adjustments, including auxiliary aids and services, to ensure the school does not discriminate on the basis of disability.

OCR enforces Section 504 of the Rehabilitation Act of 1973 (Section 504) and Title II of the Americans with Disabilities Act of 1990 (Title II), which prohibit discrimination on the basis of disability. Practically every school district and postsecondary school in the United States is subject to one or both of these laws, which have similar requirements.

Text in this chapter is excerpted from "Students with Disabilities Preparing for Postsecondary Education: Know Your Rights and Responsibilities," U.S. Department of Education (ED), October 27, 2011. Reviewed February 2016.

Although Section 504 and Title II apply to both school districts and postsecondary schools, the responsibilities of postsecondary schools differ significantly from those of school districts.

Moreover, you will have responsibilities as a postsecondary student that you do not have as a high school student. OCR strongly encourages you to know your responsibilities and those of postsecondary schools under Section 504 and Title II. Doing so will improve your opportunity to succeed as you enter postsecondary education.

The following questions and answers provide more specific information to help you succeed.

As a Student with a Disability Leaving High School and Entering Postsecondary Education, Will I See Differences in My Rights and How They Are Addressed?

Yes. Section 504 and Title II protect elementary, secondary, and postsecondary students from discrimination. Nevertheless, several of the requirements that apply through high school are different from the requirements that apply beyond high school. For instance, Section 504 requires a school district to provide a free appropriate public education (FAPE) to each child with a disability in the district's jurisdiction. Whatever the disability, a school district must identify an individual's educational needs and provide any regular or special education and related aids and services necessary to meet those needs as well as it is meeting the needs of students without disabilities.

Unlike your high school, however, your postsecondary school is not required to provide FAPE. Rather, your postsecondary school is required to provide appropriate academic adjustments as necessary to ensure that it does not discriminate on the basis of disability. In addition, if your postsecondary school provides housing to nondisabled students, it must provide comparable, convenient, and accessible housing to students with disabilities at the same cost. Other important differences that you need to know, even before you arrive at your postsecondary school, are addressed in the remaining questions.

May a Postsecondary School Deny My Admission Because I Have a Disability?

No. If you meet the essential requirements for admission, a postsecondary school may not deny your admission simply because you have a disability.

Do I Have to Inform a Postsecondary School That I Have a Disability?

No. But if you want the school to provide an academic adjustment, you must identify yourself as having a disability. Likewise, you should let the school know about your disability if you want to ensure that you are assigned to accessible facilities. In any event, your disclosure of a disability is always voluntary.

What Academic Adjustments Must a Postsecondary School Provide?

The appropriate academic adjustment must be determined based on your disability and individual needs. Academic adjustments may include auxiliary aids and services, as well as modifications to academic requirements as necessary to ensure equal educational opportunity. Examples of adjustments are: arranging for priority registration; reducing a course load; substituting one course for another; providing note takers, recording devices, sign language interpreters, extended time for testing, and, if telephones are provided in dorm rooms, a TTY in your dorm room; and equipping school computers with screen-reading, voice recognition, or other adaptive software or hardware.

In providing an academic adjustment, your postsecondary school is not required to lower or substantially modify essential requirements. For example, although your school may be required to provide extended testing time, it is not required to change the substantive content of the test. In addition, your postsecondary school does not have to make adjustments that would fundamentally alter the nature of a service, program, or activity, or that would result in an undue financial or administrative burden. Finally, your postsecondary school does not have to provide personal attendants, individually prescribed devices, readers for personal use or study, or other devices or services of a personal nature, such as tutoring and typing.

If I Want an Academic Adjustment, What Must I Do?

You must inform the school that you have a disability and need an academic adjustment. Unlike your school district, your postsecondary school is not required to identify you as having a disability or to assess your needs.

Your postsecondary school may require you to follow reasonable procedures to request an academic adjustment. You are responsible for knowing and following those procedures. In their publications providing general information, postsecondary schools usually include information on the procedures and contacts for requesting an academic adjustment. Such publications include recruitment materials, catalogs, and student handbooks, and are often available on school websites. Many schools also have staff whose purpose is to assist students with disabilities. If you are unable to locate the procedures, ask a school official, such as an admissions officer or counselor.

When Should I Request an Academic Adjustment?

Although you may request an academic adjustment from your post-secondary school at any time, you should request it as early as possible. Some academic adjustments may take more time to provide than others. You should follow your school's procedures to ensure that the school has enough time to review your request and provide an appropriate academic adjustment.

Do I Have to Prove That I Have a Disability to Obtain an Academic Adjustment?

Generally, yes. Your school will probably require you to provide documentation showing that you have a current disability and need an academic adjustment.

What Documentation Should I Provide?

Schools may set reasonable standards for documentation. Some schools require more documentation than others. They may require you to provide documentation prepared by an appropriate professional, such as a medical doctor, psychologist, or other qualified diagnostician. The required documentation may include one or more of the following: a diagnosis of your current disability, as well as supporting information, such as the date of the diagnosis, how that diagnosis was reached, and the credentials of the diagnosing professional; information on how your disability affects a major life activity; and information on how the disability affects your academic performance. The documentation should provide enough information for you and your school to decide what is an appropriate academic adjustment.

An individualized education program (IEP) or Section 504 plan, if you have one, may help identify services that have been effective for you. This is generally not sufficient documentation, however, because of the differences between postsecondary education and high school education. What you need to meet the new demands of postsecondary education may be different from what worked for you in high school. Also, in some cases, the nature of a disability may change.

If the documentation that you have does not meet the postsecondary school's requirements, a school official should tell you in a timely manner what additional documentation you need to provide. You may need a new evaluation in order to provide the required documentation.

Who Has to Pay for a New Evaluation?

Neither your high school nor your postsecondary school is required to conduct or pay for a new evaluation to document your disability and need for an academic adjustment. You may, therefore, have to pay or find funding to pay an appropriate professional for an evaluation. If you are eligible for services through your state vocational rehabilitation agency, you may qualify for an evaluation at no cost to you.

Once the School Has Received the Necessary Documentation from Me, What Should I Expect?

To determine an appropriate academic adjustment, the school will review your request in light of the essential requirements for the relevant program. It is important to remember that the school is not required to lower or waive essential requirements. If you have requested a specific academic adjustment, the school may offer that academic adjustment, or it may offer an effective alternative. The school may also conduct its own evaluation of your disability and needs at its own expense.

You should expect your school to work with you in an interactive process to identify an appropriate academic adjustment. Unlike the experience you may have had in high school, however, do not expect your postsecondary school to invite your parents to participate in the process or to develop an IEP for you.

What If the Academic Adjustment We Identified Is Not Working?

Let the school know as soon as you become aware that the results are not what you expected. It may be too late to correct the problem if you wait until the course or activity is completed. You and your school should work together to resolve the problem.

May a Postsecondary School Charge Me for Providing an Academic Adjustment?

No. Nor may it charge students with disabilities more for participating in its programs or activities than it charges students who do not have disabilities.

What Can I Do If I Believe the School Is Discriminating against Me?

Practically every postsecondary school must have a person—frequently called the Section 504 Coordinator, ADA Coordinator, or Disability Services Coordinator—who coordinates the school's compliance with Section 504, Title II, or both laws. You may contact that person for information about how to address your concerns.

The school must also have grievance procedures. These procedures are not the same as the due process procedures with which you may be familiar from high school. But the postsecondary school's grievance procedures must include steps to ensure that you may raise your concerns fully and fairly, and must provide for the prompt and equitable resolution of complaints.

School publications, such as student handbooks and catalogs, usually describe the steps that you must take to start the grievance process. Often, schools have both formal and informal processes. If you decide to use a grievance process, you should be prepared to present all the reasons that support your request.

Chapter 45

Protection of Students Education under Section 504

Section 504 covers qualified students with disabilities who attend schools receiving Federal financial assistance. To be protected under Section 504, a student must be determined to: (1) have a physical or mental impairment that substantially limits one or more major life activities; or (2) have a record of such an impairment; or (3) be regarded as having such an impairment. Section 504 requires that school districts provide a free appropriate public education (FAPE) to qualified students in their jurisdictions who have a physical or mental impairment that substantially limits one or more major life activities.

What is a physical or mental impairment that substantially limits a major life activity?

The determination of whether a student has a physical or mental impairment that substantially limits a major life activity must be made on the basis of an individual inquiry. The Section 504 regulatory provision at 34 C.F.R. 104.3(j)(2)(i) defines a physical or mental impairment as any physiological disorder or condition, cosmetic disfigurement, or anatomical loss affecting one or more of the following body systems: neurological; musculoskeletal; special sense organs; respiratory, including speech organs; cardiovascular; reproductive;

Text in this chapter is excerpted from "Protecting Students with Disabilities," U.S. Department of Education (ED), October 16, 2015.

digestive; genito-urinary; hemic and lymphatic; skin; and endocrine; or any mental or psychological disorder, such as mental retardation, organic brain syndrome, emotional or mental illness, and specific learning disabilities. The regulatory provision does not set forth an exhaustive list of specific diseases and conditions that may constitute physical or mental impairments because of the difficulty of ensuring the comprehensiveness of such a list.

Major life activities, as defined in the Section 504 regulations at 34 C.F.R. 104.3(j)(2)(ii), include functions such as caring for one's self, performing manual tasks, walking, seeing, hearing, speaking, breathing, learning, and working. This list is not exhaustive. Other functions can be major life activities for purposes of Section 504. In the Amendments Act, Congress provided additional examples of general activities that are major life activities, including eating, sleeping, standing, lifting, bending, reading, concentrating, thinking, and communicating.

Congress also provided a non-exhaustive list of examples of "major bodily functions" that are major life activities, such as the functions of the immune system, normal cell growth, digestive, bowel, bladder, neurological, brain, respiratory, circulatory, endocrine, and reproductive functions. The Section 504 regulatory provision, though not as comprehensive as the Amendments Act, is still valid – the Section 504 regulatory provision's list of examples of major life activities is not exclusive, and an activity or function not specifically listed in the Section 504 regulatory provision can nonetheless be a major life activity.

Does the meaning of the phrase "qualified student with a disability" differ on the basis of a student's educational level, i.e., elementary and secondary versus postsecondary?

Yes. At the elementary and secondary educational level, a "qualified student with a disability" is a student with a disability who is: of an age at which students without disabilities are provided elementary and secondary educational services; of an age at which it is mandatory under state law to provide elementary and secondary educational services to students with disabilities; or a student to whom a state is required to provide a free appropriate public education under the Individuals with Disabilities Education Act (IDEA).

At the postsecondary educational level, a qualified student with a disability is a student with a disability who meets the academic and technical standards requisite for admission or participation in the institution's educational program or activity.

Does the nature of services to which a student is entitled under Section 504 differ by educational level?

Yes. Public elementary and secondary recipients are required to provide a free appropriate public education to qualified students with disabilities. Such an education consists of regular or special education and related aids and services designed to meet the individual educational needs of students with disabilities as adequately as the needs of students without disabilities are met.

At the postsecondary level, the recipient is required to provide students with appropriate academic adjustments and auxiliary aids and services that are necessary to afford an individual with a disability an equal opportunity to participate in a school's program. Recipients are not required to make adjustments or provide aids or services that would result in a fundamental alteration of a recipient's program or impose an undue burden.

Once a student is identified as eligible for services under Section 504, is that student always entitled to such services?

Yes, as long as the student remains eligible. The protections of Section 504 extend only to individuals who meet the regulatory definition of a person with a disability. If a recipient school district re-evaluates a student in accordance with the Section 504 regulatory provision at 34 C.F.R. 104.35 and determines that the student's mental or physical impairment no longer substantially limits his/her ability to learn or any other major life activity, the student is no longer eligible for services under Section 504.

Are current illegal users of drugs excluded from protection under Section 504?

Generally, yes. Section 504 excludes from the definition of a student with a disability, and from Section 504 protection, any student who is currently engaging in the illegal use of drugs when a covered entity acts on the basis of such use. (There are exceptions for persons in rehabilitation programs who are no longer engaging in the illegal use of drugs).

Are current users of alcohol excluded from protection under Section 504?

No. Section 504's definition of a student with a disability does not exclude users of alcohol. However, Section 504 allows schools to take disciplinary action against students with disabilities using drugs or alcohol to the same extent as students without disabilities.

Evaluation

At the elementary and secondary school level, determining whether a child is a qualified disabled student under Section 504 begins with the evaluation process. Section 504 requires the use of evaluation procedures that ensure that children are not misclassified, unnecessarily labeled as having a disability, or incorrectly placed, based on inappropriate selection, administration, or interpretation of evaluation materials.

What is an appropriate evaluation under Section 504?

Recipient school districts must establish standards and procedures for initial evaluations and periodic re-evaluations of students who need or are believed to need special education and/or related services because of disability. The Section 504 regulatory provision at 34 C.F.R. 104.35(b) requires school districts to individually evaluate a student before classifying the student as having a disability or providing the student with special education. Tests used for this purpose must be selected and administered so as best to ensure that the test results accurately reflect the student's aptitude or achievement or other factor being measured rather than reflect the student's disability, except where those are the factors being measured.

Section 504 also requires that tests and other evaluation materials include those tailored to evaluate the specific areas of educational need and not merely those designed to provide a single intelligence quotient. The tests and other evaluation materials must be validated for the specific purpose for which they are used and appropriately administered by trained personnel.

How much is enough information to document that a student has a disability?

At the elementary and secondary education level, the amount of information required is determined by the multi-disciplinary committee gathered to evaluate the student. The committee should include persons knowledgeable about the student, the meaning of the evaluation data, and the placement options. The committee members must determine if they have enough information to make a knowledgeable decision as to whether or not the student has a disability.

The Section 504 regulatory provision at 34 C.F.R. 104.35(c) requires that school districts draw from a variety of sources in the evaluation process so that the possibility of error is minimized. The information obtained from all such sources must be documented and all significant factors related to the student's learning process must be considered. These sources and factors may include aptitude and achievement tests, teacher recommendations, physical condition, social and cultural background, and adaptive behavior.

In evaluating a student suspected of having a disability, it is unacceptable to rely on presumptions and stereotypes regarding persons with disabilities or classes of such persons. Compliance with the IDEA regarding the group of persons present when an evaluation or placement decision is made is satisfactory under Section 504.

What process should a school district use to identify students eligible for services under Section 504? Is it the same process as that employed in identifying students eligible for services under the IDEA?

School districts may use the same process to evaluate the needs of students under Section 504 as they use to evaluate the needs of students under the IDEA. If school districts choose to adopt a separate process for evaluating the needs of students under Section 504, they must follow the requirements for evaluation specified in the Section 504 regulatory provision at 34 C.F.R. 104.35.

May school districts consider "mitigating measures" used by a student in determining whether the student has a disability under Section 504?

No. As of January 1, 2009, school districts, in determining whether a student has a physical or mental impairment that substantially limits that student in a major life activity, must not consider the ameliorating effects of any mitigating measures that student is using. This is a change from prior law. Before January 1, 2009, school districts had to consider a student's use of mitigating measures in determining whether that student had a physical or mental impairment that substantially limited that student in a major life activity. In the Amendments Act, however, Congress specified that the ameliorative effects of mitigating measures must not be considered in determining if a person is an individual with a disability.

Congress did not define the term "mitigating measures" but rather provided a non-exhaustive list of "mitigating measures." The mitigating measures are as follows: medication; medical supplies, equipment or appliances; low-vision devices (which do not include ordinary eyeglasses or contact lenses); prosthetics (including limbs and devices); hearing aids and cochlear implants or other implantable hearing devices; mobility devices; oxygen therapy equipment and supplies; use of assistive technology; reasonable accommodations or auxiliary aids or services; and learned behavioral or adaptive neurological modifications.

Congress created one exception to the mitigating measures analysis. The ameliorative effects of the mitigating measures of ordinary eyeglasses or contact lenses shall be considered in determining if an impairment substantially limits a major life activity. "Ordinary eyeglasses or contact lenses" are lenses that are intended to fully correct visual acuity or eliminate refractive error, whereas "low-vision devices" (listed above) are devices that magnify, enhance, or otherwise augment a visual image.

Does OCR endorse a single formula or scale that measures substantial limitation?

No. The determination of substantial limitation must be made on a case-by-case basis with respect to each individual student. The Section 504 regulatory provision at 34 C.F.R. 104.35 (c) requires that a group of knowledgeable persons draw upon information from a variety of sources in making this determination.

Are there any impairments which automatically mean that a student has a disability under Section 504?

No. An impairment in and of itself is not a disability. The impairment must substantially limit one or more major life activities in order to be considered a disability under Section 504.

Can a medical diagnosis suffice as an evaluation for the purpose of providing FAPE?

No. A physician's medical diagnosis may be considered among other sources in evaluating a student with an impairment or believed to have an impairment which substantially limits a major life activity. Other sources to be considered, along with the medical diagnosis, include aptitude and achievement tests, teacher recommendations, physical condition, social and cultural background, and adaptive behavior. The

Section 504 regulations require school districts to draw upon a variety of sources in interpreting evaluation data and making placement decisions.

Does a medical diagnosis of an illness automatically mean a student can receive services under Section 504?

No. A medical diagnosis of an illness does not automatically mean a student can receive services under Section 504. The illness must cause a substantial limitation on the student's ability to learn or another major life activity. For example, a student who has a physical or mental impairment would not be considered a student in need of services under Section 504 if the impairment does not in any way limit the student's ability to learn or other major life activity, or only results in some minor limitation in that regard.

How should a recipient school district handle an outside independent evaluation? Do all data brought to a multi-disciplinary committee need to be considered and given equal weight?

The results of an outside independent evaluation may be one of many sources to consider. Multi-disciplinary committees must draw from a variety of sources in the evaluation process so that the possibility of error is minimized. All significant factors related to the subject student's learning process must be considered. These sources and factors include aptitude and achievement tests, teacher recommendations, physical condition, social and cultural background, and adaptive behavior, among others. Information from all sources must be documented and considered by knowledgeable committee members. The weight of the information is determined by the committee given the student's individual circumstances.

What should a recipient school district do if a parent refuses to consent to an initial evaluation under the Individuals with Disabilities Education Act (IDEA), but demands a Section 504 plan for a student without further evaluation?

A school district must evaluate a student prior to providing services under Section 504. Section 504 requires informed parental permission for initial evaluations. If a parent refuses consent for an initial evaluation and a recipient school district suspects a student has a disability, the IDEA and Section 504 provide that school districts may use due process hearing procedures to seek to override the parents' denial of consent.

Who in the evaluation process makes the ultimate decision regarding a student's eligibility for services under Section 504?

The Section 504 regulatory provision at 34 C.F.R.104.35 (c) (3) requires that school districts ensure that the determination that a student is eligible for special education and/or related aids and services be made by a group of persons, including persons knowledgeable about the meaning of the evaluation data and knowledgeable about the placement options. If a parent disagrees with the determination, he or she may request a due process hearing.

Once a student is identified as eligible for services under Section 504, is there an annual or triennial review requirement? If so, what is the appropriate process to be used? Or is it appropriate to keep the same Section 504 plan in place indefinitely after a student has been identified?

Periodic re-evaluation is required. This may be conducted in accordance with the IDEA regulations, which require re-evaluation at three-year intervals (unless the parent and public agency agree that re-evaluation is unnecessary) or more frequently if conditions warrant, or if the child's parent or teacher requests a re-evaluation, but not more than once a year (unless the parent and public agency agree otherwise).

Is a Section 504 re-evaluation similar to an IDEA re-evaluation? How often should it be done?

Yes. Section 504 specifies that re-evaluations in accordance with the IDEA is one means of compliance with Section 504. The Section 504 regulations require that re-evaluations be conducted periodically. Section 504 also requires a school district to conduct a re-evaluation prior to a significant change of placement. OCR considers an exclusion from the educational program of more than 10 school days a significant change of placement. OCR would also consider transferring a student from one type of program to another or terminating or significantly reducing a related service a significant change in placement.

What is reasonable justification for referring a student for evaluation for services under Section 504?

School districts may always use regular education intervention strategies to assist students with difficulties in school. Section 504 requires recipient school districts to refer a student for an evaluation for possible special education or related aids and services or modification to regular education if the student, because of disability, needs or is believed to need such services.

A student is receiving services that the school district maintains are necessary under Section 504 in order to provide the student with an appropriate education. The student's parent no longer wants the student to receive those services. If the parent wishes to withdraw the student from a Section 504 plan, what can the school district do to ensure continuation of services?

The school district may initiate a Section 504 due process hearing to resolve the dispute if the district believes the student needs the services in order to receive an appropriate education.

A student has a disability referenced in the IDEA, but does not require special education services. Is such a student eligible for services under Section 504?

The student may be eligible for services under Section 504. The school district must determine whether the student has an impairment which substantially limits his or her ability to learn or another major life activity and, if so, make an individualized determination of the child's educational needs for regular or special education or related aids or services. For example, such a student may receive adjustments in the regular classroom.

How should a recipient school district view a temporary impairment?

A temporary impairment does not constitute a disability for purposes of Section 504 unless its severity is such that it results in a substantial limitation of one or more major life activities for an extended period of time. The issue of whether a temporary impairment is substantial enough to be a disability must be resolved on a case-by-case basis, taking into consideration both the duration (or expected duration) of the impairment and the extent to which it actually limits a major life activity of the affected individual.

In the Amendments Act, Congress clarified that an individual is not "regarded as" an individual with a disability if the impairment is transitory and minor. A transitory impairment is an impairment with an actual or expected duration of 6 months or less.

Is an impairment that is episodic or in remission a disability under Section 504?

Yes, under certain circumstances. In the Amendments Act, Congress clarified that an impairment that is episodic or in remission is a disability if it would substantially limit a major life activity when active. A student with such an impairment is entitled to a free appropriate public education under Section 504.

Part Seven

Living with Autism Spectrum Disorder and Transitioning to Adulthood

Chapter 46

Living Arrangements

After your child is diagnosed with autism spectrum disorder (ASD), you may feel unprepared or unable to provide your child with the necessary care and education. Know that there are many treatment options, social services and programs, and other resources that can help.

Understanding Teens with ASD

The teen years can be a time of stress and confusion for any growing child, including teenagers with autism spectrum disorder (ASD).

During the teenage years, adolescents become more aware of other people and their relationships with them. While most teenagers are concerned with acne, popularity, grades, and dates, teens with ASD may become painfully aware that they are different from their peers. For some, this awareness may encourage them to learn new behaviors and try to improve their social skills. For others, hurt feelings and problems connecting with others may lead to depression, anxiety, or other mental disorders. One way that some teens with ASD may express the tension and confusion that can occur during adolescence is through increased autistic or aggressive behavior. Teens with ASD

Text in this chapter is excerpted from "Autism Spectrum Disorder," National Institute of Mental Health (NIMH), October 27, 2011. Reviewed February 2016; and text from "Living with ASD," Centers for Disease Control and Prevention (CDC), February 26, 2015.

will also need support to help them understand the physical changes and sexual maturation they experience during adolescence.

If your teen seems to have trouble coping, talk with his or her doctor about possible co-occurring mental disorders and what you can do. Behavioral therapies and medications often help.

Preparing for Your Child's Transition to Adulthood

The public schools' responsibility for providing services ends when a child with ASD reaches the age of 22. At that time, some families may struggle to find jobs to match their adult child's needs. If your family cannot continue caring for an adult child at home, you may need to look for other living arrangements. For more information, see the section, "Living arrangements for adults with ASD."

Long before your child finishes school, you should search for the best programs and facilities for young adults with ASD. If you know other parents of adults with ASD, ask them about the services available in your community. Local support and advocacy groups may be able to help you find programs and services that your child is eligible to receive as an adult.

Another important part of this transition is teaching youth with ASD to self-advocate. This means that they start to take on more responsibility for their education, employment, health care, and living arrangements. Adults with ASD or other disabilities must self-advocate for their rights under the Americans with Disabilities Act at work, in higher education, in the community, and elsewhere.

Living Arrangements for Adults with ASD

There are many options for adults living with ASD. Helping your adult child choose the right one will largely depend on what is available in your state and local community, as well as your child's skills and symptoms. Below are some examples of living arrangements you may want to consider:

- **Independent living**. Some adults with ASD are able to live on their own. Others can live in their own home or apartment if they get help dealing with major issues, such as managing personal finances, obtaining necessary health care, and interacting with government or social service agencies. Family members, professional agencies, or other types of providers can offer this assistance.

- **Living at home**. Government funds are available for families who choose to have their adult child with ASD live at home. These programs include Supplemental Security Income, Social Security Disability Insurance, and Medicaid waivers. Information about these programs and others is available from the Social Security Administration (SSA). Make an appointment with your local SSA office to find out which programs would be right for your adult child.

- **Other home alternatives**. Some families open their homes to provide long-term care to adults with disabilities who are not related to them. If the home teaches self-care and housekeeping skills and arranges leisure activities, it is called a "skill-development" home.

- **Supervised group living**. People with disabilities often live in group homes or apartments staffed by professionals who help with basic needs. These needs often include meal preparation, housekeeping, and personal care. People who are more independent may be able to live in a home or apartment where staff only visit a few times a week. Such residents generally prepare their own meals, go to work, and conduct other daily activities on their own.

- **Long-term care facilities**. This alternative is available for those with ASD who need intensive, constant supervision.

Ensuring Support at Home

Family Issues

Living with a person with an ASD affects the entire family—parents, siblings, and in some families, grandparents, aunts, uncles, and cousins. Meeting the complex needs of a person with an ASD can put families under a great deal of stress—emotional, financial, and sometimes even physical. Respite care can give parents and other family caregivers a needed break and help maintain family well-being.

Healthy Living

To stay healthy, people with disabilities need the same basic health care as everyone else. They need to eat well, exercise, get enough rest, drink plenty of water, and have complete access to health care, including regular physical and dental check-ups. It is important to

379

find health care providers who are comfortable with persons who have an ASD.

Sometimes when people with disabilities have a behavioral change or behavioral issue, it may be because they have a medical problem they cannot describe. For instance, head banging could be related to a disability, or it could be due to a headache or toothache. For this reason, it is important to find out if there is a physical problem before making changes in a person's treatment or therapy.

Safety

Safety is important for everyone. We all need to be safe in order to live full and productive lives. People with disabilities can be at higher risk for injuries and abuse. It is important for parents and other family members to teach their loved one how to stay safe and what to do if they feel threatened or have been hurt in any way. It can sometimes be helpful to give a person with a disability a bracelet or other item that has his or her name, address, phone number, and disability on it in case he or she gets lost.

Transitions

For some people with disabilities and their parents, change can be difficult. Planning ahead of time may make transitions easier for everyone.

The transition from high school to adulthood can be especially challenging. There are many important, life-changing decisions to make, such as whether to go to college or a vocational school or whether to enter the workforce, and if so, how and where. It is important to begin thinking about this transition in childhood, so that educational transition plans are put in place—preferably by age 14, but no later than age 16—to make sure the individual has the skills he or she needs to begin the next phase of life. The transition of health care from a pediatrician to a doctor who treats adults is another area that needs a plan.

Chapter 47

Pets for Easing Social Anxiety in Kids with Autism

When animals are present, children with autism spectrum disorders (ASDs) have lower readings on a device that detects anxiety and other forms of social arousal when interacting with their peers.

According to a study funded in part by the National Institutes of Health (NIH), companion animals—like dogs, cats or the guinea pigs in the study—may prove to be a helpful addition to treatment programs designed to help children with ASDs improve their social skills and interactions with other people.

The study, published online in Developmental Psychobiology, was conducted by Marguerite O'Haire, Ph.D., from the Center for the Human-Animal Bond in the College of Veterinary Medicine of Purdue University in West Lafayette, Indiana, and colleagues in the School of Psychology at the University of Queensland in Brisbane, Australia.

"Previous studies suggest that in the presence of companion animals, children with autism spectrum disorders function better socially," said James Griffin, Ph.D., of the Child Development and Behavior Branch at NIH's Eunice Kennedy Shriver National Institute of Child Health and Human Development (NICHD). "This study provides physiological

---

Text in this chapter is excerpted from "Animals' Presence May Ease Social Anxiety in Kids with Autism," National Institutes of Health (NIH), May 20, 2015.

evidence that the proximity of animals eases the stress that children with autism may experience in social situations."

This study is among several funded under a public-private partnership established in 2008 between NICHD and the WALTHAM Centre for Pet Nutrition, a division of Mars Inc., to establish a human-animal interaction research program to support studies relevant to child development, health, and the therapeutic use of animals.

"By providing support for these research studies, we hope to generate more definitive answers about how human-animal interaction affects health," he said.

ASDs affect the structure and function of the brain and nervous system. People with these conditions have difficulty communicating and interacting with other people. They also have restricted and repetitive interests and behaviors.

For the current study, Dr. O'Haire and her colleagues measured skin conductance, the ease at which an unnoticeable electric charge passes through a patch of skin, in children with ASDs and in typically developing children. Researchers divided the 114 children, ages 5 to 12 years old, into 38 groups of three. Each group included one child with ASD and two of their typically developing peers.

Each child wore a wrist band fitted with a device that measures skin conductance. When people are feeling excited, fearful, or anxious, the electric charge travels faster through the skin, providing an objective way for researchers to gauge social anxiety and other forms of psychological arousal.

For the first few minutes, the children read a book silently, giving researchers a baseline measure of skin conductance while carrying out a non-stressful, familiar task. Next, each child was asked to read aloud from the book in the presence of the two peers in their group, a task designed to measure their level of apprehension during social situations.

The researchers then brought toys in the room and allowed the children 10 minutes of free play time. These situations may be stressful for children with ASDs, who may have difficulty relating socially to their typically developing peers.

The researchers brought two guinea pigs into the room and allowed the children to have 10 minutes of supervised play with the animals. The researchers chose guinea pigs because of their small size and docile nature—much easier to manage in a classroom than larger animals.

The researchers found that, compared to the typically developing children, the children with autism had higher skin conductance levels when reading silently, reading aloud, and in the group toy session. These higher levels are consistent with reports from parents and teachers, and from other studies, that children with ASDs are more likely to be anxious in social situations than typically developing children.

When the session with the guinea pigs began, however, skin conductance levels among the children with ASDs dropped significantly. The researchers speculate that because companion animals offer unqualified acceptance, their presence makes the children feel more secure.

Whereas human counterparts inherently pass social judgment, animals are often perceived as sources of unconditional, positive support, the researchers wrote.

For reasons the researchers cannot explain, skin conductance levels in the typically developing children rose during the session with the guinea pigs. The researchers believe that these higher readings may indicate excitement at seeing the animals, rather than any nervousness or apprehension.

Dr. O'Haire added that earlier studies have shown that children with ASDs were less likely to withdraw from social situations when companion animals are present. These studies, along with the current findings, indicate that animals might "play a part in interventions seeking to help children with autism develop their social skills," she said. She cautioned, however, that the findings do not mean that parents of children with ASDs should rush to buy an animal for their children. Further research is needed to determine how animals might be used in programs aimed at developing social skills.

"Our study was conducted in a supervised setting, by researchers experienced in working with kids with autism spectrum disorders who understand the needs and requirements of the animals," Dr. O'Haire said. She added that careful supervision was provided during the study, to ensure the welfare of the children as well as the animals.

Chapter 48

Safety and Children with Disabilities

Wandering (Elopement)

Wandering, also called elopement, is an important safety issue that affects some people with disabilities, their families, and the community. There are steps that parents, teachers, healthcare providers, and others can take to help keep children safe.

Wandering is when someone leaves a safe area or a responsible caregiver. This typically includes situations where the person may be injured or harmed as a result. This goes beyond the brief time that a typical toddler might run off from a caregiver. Some children and youth with disabilities, such as those with an autism spectrum disorder (ASD) or an intellectual disability (ID), have challenges understanding safety issues and communicating with others. For example, such a child might run off from home to play in the pond down the street-and be unable to respond to his name or say where he lives. This can happen quickly, even under constant supervision. The child's parents are left searching desperately for him or her.

Based on a survey of parents, about half of children and youth with an ASD were reported to wander. Of those children, 1 in 4 were missing

Text in this chapter is excerpted from "Safety and Children with Disabilities," Centers for Disease Control and Prevention (CDC), July 13, 2015; and text from "Keeping Children with Disabilities Safe," Centers for Disease Control and Prevention (CDC), March 25, 2015.

long enough to cause concern and were most commonly in danger of drowning or traffic injury. Children wandered most often from their own home or another home, stores, and classrooms or schools. The primary reasons for wandering included:

- Enjoyment of running or exploring

- To get to a place he or she enjoys (like a pond)

- To get out of a situation that causes stress (for example, being asked to do something at school or getting away from a loud noise)

- To go see something interesting (for example, running to the road to see a road sign)

The Interagency Autism Coordinating Committee (IACC) has called attention to wandering as a serious safety issue. Although many examples of dangerous wandering have focused on children with ASD, we know that challenges with communication, social interaction, attention, and learning can put many children and youth with developmental disabilities at risk for becoming lost or injured due to wandering.

What Can We Do to Keep Children Safe Who Might Wander?

Parents, Teachers, and Other Caregivers

Plan

- Watch the child's behaviors

- Have an emergency plan to respond

- Keep information about the child up-to-date (picture, description)

- Secure your home (fences, door locks)

- Keep identification on the child (ID bracelet or information card)

Prevent

- Notice signs that the child may wander off before it happens (for example, child makes a certain sound or looks towards the door)

- Be alert about the child's location

- Provide a safe location

- Inform neighbors and school workers
- Alert first responders

Teach Safety Skills

- Responding to safety commands ("stop")
- Stating name and phone number (or showing ID)
- Swimming, crossing the street

First Responders

First responders are vital for maintaining the health and safety of members of our communities. They are likely to be called upon in the event of a missing child or youth. It is important for first responders to be prepared by knowing which children in the community might wander, having family contact information, and having a plan to respond. Tools and training materials are available through the AWAARE organization and through the National Center for Missing and Exploited Children.

Healthcare Providers and Other Professionals

Healthcare and other professionals need to be aware of wandering as a safety issue. Their role includes discussing safety issues and helping caregivers come up with prevention and response plans.

In October 2011, an ICD-9-CM code was created to help document wandering and to prompt important discussions about safety among healthcare providers, caregivers, and the person with a disability to the full extent possible. The ICD-9-CM Code V40.31 Wandering in diseases classified elsewhere is not linked to a specific diagnosis, nor is it part of the diagnostic codes used for autism or intellectual disabilities. Wandering should be coded if documented in the medical record by the provider (i.e., physician).

CDC's Work

CDC works to keep people safe and healthy and this includes addressing the special needs that people with disabilities may have. CDC has partnered with others to understand how common wandering or elopement is among children with ASD and other developmental disabilities. CDC has served on the Interagency Autism Coordinating Committee (IACC) Safety Subcommittee, assisted in data collection on wandering, and worked with partners to raise awareness of wandering as an important safety issue.

Keeping Children with Disabilities Safe

We all want to keep our children safe and secure and help them to be happy and healthy. Preventing injuries and harm is not very different for children with disabilities compared to children without disabilities. However, finding the right information and learning about the kinds of risks children might face at different ages is often not easy for parents of children with disabilities. Each child is different – and the general recommendations that are available to keep children safe should be tailored to fit your child's skills and abilities.

There are steps that parents and caregivers can take to keep children with disabilities safe.

To keep all children safe, parents and caregivers need to:

• Know and learn about what things are unique concerns or a danger for their child.

• Plan ways to protect their child and share the plan with others.

• Remember that their child's needs for protection will change over time.

What Can We Do?

Parents or caregivers can talk to their child's doctor or healthcare professional about how to keep him or her safe. Your child's teacher or child care provider might also have some good ideas. Once you have ideas about keeping your child safe, make a safety plan and share it with your child and other adults who might be able to help if needed.

Here are some things to think about when making a safety plan for your child:

Moving Around and Handling Things

Does your child have challenges with moving around and handling things around them? Sometimes children are faced with unsafe situations, especially in new places. Children who have limited ability to move, see, hear, or make decisions, and children who do not feel or understand pain might not realize that something is unsafe, or might have trouble getting away.

Take a look around the place where your child will be to make sure every area your child can reach is safe for your child. Check your child's clothing and toys – are they suitable for his or her abilities, not just age and size? For example, clothing and toys that are meant for older children might have strings that are not safe for a child who cannot easily untangle themselves, or toys might have small parts that are not safe for children who are still mouthing toys.

Safety Equipment

Do you have the right kind of safety equipment? Safety equipment is often developed for age and size, and less for ability.

For example, a major cause of child death is motor vehicle crashes. Keeping your child safe in the car is important. When choosing the right car seat, you might need to consider whether your child has difficulties sitting up or sitting still in the seat, in addition to your child's age, height, and weight. If you have a child with disabilities, talk to your healthcare professional about the best type of car seat or booster seat and the proper seat position for your child. You can also ask a certified child passenger safety technician who is trained in special needs.

Other examples of special safety equipment include:

- Life jackets may need to be specially fitted for your child.

- Smoke alarms that signal with a light and vibration may be better in a home where there is a child who cannot hear.

- Hand rails and safety bars can be put into homes to help a child who has difficulty moving around or a child who is at risk for falling.

Speak to your healthcare professional about the right equipment for your child and have this equipment ready and available before you may need it.

Talking and Understanding

- **Does your child have problems with talking or understanding?** Children who have problems communicating might have limited ability to learn about safety and danger.

For example, children who cannot hear might miss spoken instructions. Children who have trouble understanding or remembering might not learn about safety as easily as other children. Children who have a hard time communicating might not be able to ask questions about safety. Adults might think that children with disabilities are aware of dangers when they actually are not.

389

Parents and caregivers may need to find different ways to teach their children about safety, such as:

- Showing them what to do

- Using pretend play to rehearse

- Practicing on a regular basis

Parents and caregivers may need to find different ways to let their children communicate that they are in danger. For example, teaching your child to use a whistle, bell, or alarm can alert others to danger. Tell adults who take care of your child about the ways to communicate with your child if there is any danger.

It's also useful to contact your local fire department and explain any special circumstances you have, so that they don't have to rely on the child or others to explain their special needs in case of an emergency. Read more about preparing for emergencies.

Making Decisions

Does your child have problems with making decisions? Children might have limited ability to make decisions either because of developmental delays or limits in their thinking skills, or in their ability to stop themselves from doing things that they want, but should not do.

For example, children with attention-deficit/hyperactivity disorder (ADHD) or fetal alcohol spectrum disorders (FASDs) might be very impulsive and fail to think about the results of their actions. People often put more dangerous things higher up, so that little children cannot reach them. Your older child might be able to reach something that he or she is not ready to handle safely. Check your child's environment, particularly new places.

Some children might also have problems distinguishing when situations and people are safe or dangerous. They might not know what to do. Parents and caregivers can give children specific instructions on how to behave in certain situations that might become dangerous.

Moving and Exploring

Does your child have enough chances to move and explore? Children with disabilities often need some extra protection. But just like all children, they also need to move and explore so that they can develop healthy bodies and minds.

Some parents of children with special needs worry about their children needing extra protection. It is not possible to protect children from every bump and bruise. Exploring can help children learn what's safe and what might be difficult or dangerous. Being fit and healthy can help children stay safe, and an active lifestyle is important for long-term health.

Children with disabilities might find it hard to take part in sports and active play – for example, equipment may need to be adjusted, coaches may need extra information and support to help a child with a disability, or a communication problem may make it more difficult for some children to play as part of a team.

Talk to your child's teachers, potential coaches, care providers, or health professional about ways to find the right balance between being safe and being active.

Other Concerns

Do you have other concerns? Every child is different. This is not a complete list of questions and concerns, these are just examples. Your questions and concerns may be different. Speak with your healthcare provider, teacher, or child care provider to learn more about keeping your child safe.

Chapter 49

Toilet Training for Children with ASD

Toilet Training for Children with ASD

Many parents are unsure about when to start toilet teaching or "potty training." Not all kids are ready at the same age, so it's important to watch your child for signs of readiness, such as stopping an activity for a few seconds or clutching his or her diaper.

Most children begin to show these signs between 18 and 24 months, although some may be ready earlier or later than that. And boys often start later and take longer to learn to use the potty than girls.

Instead of using age as a readiness indicator, look for other signs that your child may be ready to start heading for the potty, such as the ability to:

- follow simple instructions

- understand words about the toileting process

- control the muscles responsible for elimination

- verbally express a need to go

- keep a diaper dry for 2 hours or more

- get to the potty, sit on it, and then get off the potty

Text in this chapter is excerpted from "Toilet Teaching Your Child," © 1995–2016. The Nemours Foundation/KidsHealth®. Reprinted with permission.

- pull down diapers, disposable training pants, or underpants
- show an interest in using the potty or wearing underpants

About Timing

There are some stressful or difficult times when you may want to put off starting the toilet-teaching process—when traveling, around the birth of a sibling, changing from the crib to the bed, moving to a new house, or when your child is sick (especially if diarrhea is a factor). It may be better to postpone it until your child's environment is stable and secure.

Also, while some experts recommend starting the process during summer because kids wear less clothing, but it is not a good idea to wait if your child is ready.

How Long Does It Take?

Of course, teaching a toddler to use the potty isn't an overnight experience. The process often takes between 3 and 6 months, although it may take more or less time for some children.

And although some little ones can learn to both make it through the night without wetting or soiling themselves (or the bed) and use the potty around the same time, it may take an additional month to even years to master staying dry at night.

Potty Types

The two basic potty options are:

- a standalone, toddler-size potty chair with a bowl that can be emptied into the toilet

- a toddler-size seat that can be placed on top of your toilet seat that will let your child feel more secure and not fear falling in

If you choose the modified toilet seat, consider getting a stepping stool so that your child can reach the seat comfortably and feel stable and supported while having a bowel movement.

It's usually best for boys to first learn to use the toilet sitting down before learning to pee standing up. For boys who feel awkward—or scared—about standing on a stool to pee in the toilet, a potty chair may be a better option.

394

Buy a training potty or seat for every bathroom in your house. You may even want to keep a potty in the trunk of your car for emergencies. When traveling long distances, be sure to take a potty seat with you and stop every 1 to 2 hours. Otherwise, it can take more time than your child may have to find a discreet location or restroom.

About Training Pants

Experts sometimes disagree about whether to use disposable training pants. Some think that they're just bigger diapers and might make kids think it's OK to use them like diapers, thus slowing the toilet-teaching process.

Others feel that training pants are a helpful step between diapers and underwear. Because kids' nighttime bladder and bowel control often lags behind their daytime control, some parents like using training pants at night. Others prefer that their child use training pants when they're out and about. Once the training pants remain dry for a few days, kids can make the switch to wearing underwear.

Ask your doctor if your child would benefit from using disposable training pants as a transitional step.

Common Problems

It's common for a previously toilet-taught child to have some trouble using the potty during times of stress. For example, a 2- or 3-year-old dealing with a new sibling may regress (return to a previous level of development).

But if your child was previously potty trained and is having problems, talk with your doctor just to be on the safe side and to rule out things like an infection.

If your child is 3 years or older and is not yet potty trained, talk to the doctor, who can help determine the problem and offer advice to make the process easier.

Tips for Toilet Teaching

Even before your child is ready to try the potty, you can prepare your little one by teaching about the process:

- Use words to express the act of using the toilet ("pee," "poop," and "potty").

- Ask your child to let you know when a diaper is wet or soiled.

- Identify behaviors ("Are you going poop?") so that your child can learn to recognize peeing and pooping.

- Get a potty chair your child can practice sitting on. At first, your child can sit on it clothed. Then, he or she can sit on the chair with a diaper. And when ready, your child can go bare-bottomed.

If you've decided that your child is ready to start learning how to use the potty, these tips may help:

- Set aside some time to devote to the potty-training process.

- **Don't** make your child sit on the toilet against his or her will.

- Show your child how you sit on the toilet and explain what you're doing (because your child learns by watching you). You also can have your child sit on the potty seat and watch while you (or a sibling) use the toilet.

- Establish a routine. For example, you may want to begin toilet teaching by having your child sit on the potty after waking with a dry diaper, or 45 minutes to an hour after drinking lots of fluid. You may be able to catch your child peeing. Only put your child on the potty for a few minutes a couple of times a day, and let your child get up if he or she wants to.

- Try catching your child in the act of pooping. Children often give clear cues that they need to use the bathroom—their faces turn red, and they may grunt or squat. And many kids are regular as to the time of day they tend to have a bowel movement.

- Have your child sit on the potty within 15 to 30 minutes after meals to take advantage of the body's natural tendency to have a bowel movement after eating (this is called the gastro-colic reflex).

- Remove a bowel movement (poop) from your child's diaper, put it in the toilet, and tell your child that poop goes in the potty.

- Make sure your child's wardrobe is adaptable to potty training. In other words, avoid overalls and shirts that snap in the crotch. Simple clothes are a must at this stage and kids who are potty training need to be able to undress themselves.

- Some parents like to let their child have some time during the day without a diaper. If he or she urinates without wearing a diaper, your child may be more likely to feel what's happening and express discomfort. (But if you opt to keep your child's bottom bare for a little while, you'll probably need to keep the potty close by, protect your rugs and carpet, and be willing to clean up.)

- When your son is ready to start peeing standing up, have "target practice." Show him how to stand so that he can aim his urine stream into the toilet. Some parents use things like cereal pieces as a sort of bull's-eye for their little guys to try aiming at.

- Offer your child small rewards, such as stickers or time reading with Mommy, every time your child goes in the potty. Keep a chart to track of successes. Once your little one appears to be mastering the use of the toilet, let him or her pick out a few new pairs of big-kid underwear to wear.

- Make sure all of your child's caregivers—including babysitters, grandparents, and childcare workers—follow the same routine and use the same names for body parts and bathroom acts. Let them know how you're handling the issue and ask that they use the same approaches so your child won't become confused.

Above all, be sure to praise all attempts to use the toilet, even if nothing happens. And remember that accidents will happen. It's important not to punish potty-training children or show disappointment when they wet or soil themselves or the bed. Instead, tell your child that it was an accident and offer your support. Reassure your child that he or she is well on the way to using the potty like a big kid.

And if you're torn about when to start the toilet-teaching process altogether, let your child be your guide. Don't feel pressured by others (your parents, in-laws, friends, siblings, coworkers, etc.) to begin. Many parents of past generations started potty training much sooner than many parents do today. And it all depends on the child. Kids will let parents know when they're ready.

Chapter 50

Disciplining Your Child with Special Needs

Introduction

From the moment you heard the diagnosis, you knew life would be more challenging for your child than for most. So when you ask him to do something and it's not done, you let it go. Does he really need you to point out his limitations? Or maybe you fear that what you'd like him to do, or not do, is impossible for him to achieve.

But here's the truth: If you feel that your son or daughter doesn't deserve discipline, it's like telling your child, "I don't believe you can learn." And if you don't believe it, how will your child?

What experts call "behavior management" is not about punishing or demoralizing your child. Instead, it's a way to set boundaries and communicate expectations in a nurturing, loving way. Discipline—correcting kids' actions, showing them what's right and wrong, what's acceptable and what's not—is one of the most important ways that **all** parents can show their kids that they love and care about them.

Here are some strategies to help parents discipline a child who has special needs.

Text in this chapter is excerpted from "Disciplining Your Child with Special Needs," © 1995–2016. The Nemours Foundation/KidsHealth®. Reprinted with permission.

Be Consistent

The benefits of discipline are the same whether kids have special needs or not. In fact, kids who have trouble learning respond very well to discipline and structure. But for this to work, parents have to make discipline a priority and be consistent.

Correcting kids is about establishing standards—whether that's setting a morning routine or dinnertime manners—and then teaching them how to meet those expectations. All kids, regardless of their needs and abilities, crave this consistency. When they can predict what will happen next in their day, they feel confident and safe.

Yes, they will test these boundaries—all kids do. But it's up to you to affirm that these standards are important and let your child know that you believe he or she can meet them.

Learn about Your Child's Condition

To understand your child's behavior, you have to understand the things that affect it—including his or her condition. So no matter what challenge your child faces, try to learn as much about the unique medical, behavioral, and psychological factors that affect his or her development.

Read up on the condition and ask the doctor about anything you don't understand. Also talk to members of your child's care team and other parents (especially those with kids who have similar issues) to help determine if your child's challenging behavior is typical or related to his or her individual challenges. For example, can another parent relate to the trouble you have getting your 5-year-old dressed each morning? Sharing experiences will give you a way to measure your expectations and learn which behaviors are related to your child's diagnosis and which are purely developmental. You also might pick up some helpful tips about how to handle the behavior you are noticing.

If you have trouble finding parents of kids with similar challenges, consider joining an online support or advocacy group for families of kids with special needs. Once you know what is typical behavior for your child's age and health challenges, you can set realistic behavioral expectations.

Defining Expectations

Establishing rules and discipline are a challenge for any parent. So keep your behavior plan simple and work on one challenge at a time. And as your child meets one behavioral goal, he or she can strive for the next one.

Use Rewards and Consequences

Work within a system that includes **rewards** (positive reinforcement) for good behavior and **natural consequences** for bad behavior. Natural consequences are punishments that are directly related to the behavior. For example, if your child is throwing food, you would take away the plate.

But not every kid responds to natural consequences, so you might have to match the consequence to your child's values. For instance, a child with **autism** who likes to be alone might consider a traditional "time out" rewarding—instead, take away a favorite toy or video game for a period of time.

After correcting your child for doing something wrong, offer a **substitute behavior**. So if your child is talking too loudly or hitting you to get your attention, work on replacing that with an appropriate behavior such as saying or signaling "help me" or getting your attention in appropriate ways, such as tapping your shoulder. **Active ignoring** is a good consequence for misbehavior meant to get your attention. This means not rewarding bad behavior with your attention (even if it's negative attention, like scolding or yelling).

Use Clear and Simple Messages

Communicate your expectations to your child in a simple way. For kids with special needs, this may require more than just telling them. You may need to use pictures, role playing, or gestures to be sure your child knows what he or she is working toward.

Keep verbal and visual language simple, clear, and consistent. Explain as simply as possible what behaviors you want to see. Consistency is key, so make sure that grandparents, babysitters, siblings, and teachers are all on board with your messages.

Offer Praise

Encourage accomplishment by reminding your child about what he or she can earn for meeting the goals you've set, whether it's getting stickers, screen time, or listening to a favorite song. And be sure to praise and reward your child for effort as well as success. So a child who refuses to poop in the toilet may be rewarded for using a potty near the toilet.

Another strategy: practice "time-in"—when you catch your child doing something right, praise him or her for it. In certain cases, time-in can be more effective than punishment, because kids naturally want to please their parents. By getting credit for doing something right, they'll likely want to do it again.

If your efforts don't result in changes after a week or two, pick a different strategy or reward to see if it works any better. If you're still not successful, consider asking a social worker or other developmental professional for help. He or she can help you reevaluate your behavior plan, identify triggers, develop a rewards system, or come up with consequences for behaviors you want to eliminate.

Establish a Routine

Children with certain conditions, like autism and ADHD (attention deficit hyperactivity disorder), respond particularly well to discipline that's based on knowing exactly what will happen next. So try to stick to the same routine every day. For example: If your child tends to melt down in the afternoon after school, set a schedule for free time. Maybe he or she needs to have a snack first and then do homework before playtime.

Charts can be helpful. If your child is non-verbal or pre-verbal, draw pictures or use stickers to indicate what comes next. Set a schedule that's realistic and encourage input from your child where appropriate.

Believe in Your Child

If, after taking his first few steps, your little one kept falling down, would you get him some crutches or a wheelchair? No. So don't do the same with a child with special needs. Maybe your child can't put on his or her shoes the first time, or 10th time, but keeps trying. Encourage that!

When you believe your child can do something, you empower him or her to reach that goal. The same is true for behavior. For example, if your child is too aggressive when playing with other kids, don't stop the play altogether. Instead, work with your child to limit the physicality of the play. You may want to plan for non-physical activities during play dates, like arts and crafts projects. Use discipline where necessary in the form of time-outs, enforced turn-taking, and rules like "no touching"—and provide rewards when your wishes are met.

Whatever you do, don't give up on your child when the going gets tough. Bad behavior that's ignored in the early years can become unbearable, even dangerous, in the teen years and adulthood. Be patient and take the time to work with your child to help reach his or her best potential. Your vote of confidence is sometimes all your child needs to succeed.

Have Confidence in Your Abilities

Discipline is an exhausting undertaking. There will be good days when you're amazed by your child's progress, bad days when it seems like all your hard work was forgotten, and plateaus where it seems like further progress is impossible. But remember this: Behavior management is a challenge for all parents, even those of kids who are typically developing. So don't give up!

If you set an expectation in line with your child's abilities, and you believe he or she can accomplish it, odds are it will happen. In the meantime, use whatever online, personal, and professional resources you have to help reach your goals.

Chapter 51

Practical Oral Care for People with ASD

Providing oral care to people with autism requires adaptation of the skills you use every day. In fact, most people with mild or moderate forms of autism can be treated successfully in the general practice setting. This chapter will help you make a difference in the lives of people who need professional oral care.

Autism is a complex developmental disability that impairs communication and social, behavioral, and intellectual functioning. Some people with the disorder appear distant, aloof, or detached from other people or from their surroundings. Others do not react appropriately to common verbal and social cues, such as a parent's tone of voice or smile. Obsessive routines, repetitive behaviors, unpredictable body movements, and self-injurious behavior may all be symptoms that complicate dental care.

Autism varies widely in symptoms and severity, and some people have coexisting conditions such as intellectual disability or epilepsy. They can be among the most challenging of patients, but following the suggestions in this chapter can help make their dental treatment successful.

Text in this chapter is excerpted from "Practical Oral Care for People with Autism," National Institute of Dental and Craniofacial Research (NIDCR), November 3, 2014.

Damaging Oral Habits

These are common and include bruxism; tongue thrusting; self-injurious behavior such as picking at the gingiva or biting the lips; and pica—eating objects and substances such as gravel, cigarette butts, or pens. If a mouth guard can be tolerated, prescribe one for patients who have problems with self-injurious behavior or bruxism.

Dental Caries

Dental caries risk increases in patients who have a preference for soft, sticky, or sweet foods; damaging oral habits; and difficulty brushing and flossing.

- Recommend preventive measures such as fluorides and sealants.

- Caution patients or their caregivers about medicines that reduce saliva or contain sugar. Suggest that patients drink water often, take sugar-free medicines when available, and rinse with water after taking any medicine.

- Advise caregivers to offer alternatives to cariogenic foods and beverages as incentives or rewards.

- Encourage independence in daily oral hygiene. Ask patients to show you how they brush, and follow up with specific recommendations. Perform hands-on demonstrations to show patients the best way to clean their teeth. If appropriate, show patients and caregivers how a modified toothbrush or floss holder might make oral hygiene easier.

- Some patients cannot brush and floss independently. Talk to caregivers about daily oral hygiene and do not assume that they know the basics. Use your experiences with each patient to demonstrate oral hygiene techniques and sitting or standing positions for the caregiver. Emphasize that a consistent approach to oral hygiene is important--caregivers should try to use the same location, timing, and positioning.

Periodonatal Disease

Periodonatal diseases occurs in people with autism in much the same way it does in persons without developmental disabilities.

- Some patients benefit from the daily use of an antimicrobial agent such as chlorhexidine.

- Stress the importance of conscientious oral hygiene and frequent prophylaxis.

Tooth Eruption

It may be delayed due to phenytoin-induced gingival hyperplasia. Phenytoin is commonly prescribed for people with autism.

Trauma and Injury to the mouth from falls or accidents occur in people with seizure disorders. Suggest a tooth saving kit for group homes. Emphasize to caregivers that traumas require immediate professional attention and explain the procedures to follow if a permanent tooth is knocked out. Also, instruct caregivers to locate any missing pieces of a fractured tooth, and explain that radiographs of the patient's chest may be necessary to determine whether any fragments have been aspirated.

Chapter 52

Transition to Adulthood for Individuals with ASD

Autism spectrum disorders (ASDs) are a group of developmental disabilities that range from mild to severe and are characterized by social impairment, difficulty communicating, and repetitive motions or other unusual behaviors. These characteristics are usually noticeable before the age of 3 and remain as a lifelong chronic condition with both medical and psychological implications. ASDs include autistic disorder, Asperger's disorder, pervasive developmental disorder–not otherwise specified (PDD-NOS), Rett syndrome, and childhood disintegrative disorder.

Based on 2008 data from the 14 sites in its Autism and Developmental Disabilities Monitoring Network, the Centers for Disease Control estimates 1 in 88 8-year-old children have ASDs. Prevalence in these sites had increased 23 percent from two years earlier and 78 percent since 2002. Although there is disagreement about whether the true prevalence has increased (since guidelines for diagnosis have changed, more services are available, and awareness of ASD has increased), the CDC numbers are based on evaluation records, not parental reports.

Text in this chapter is excerpted from "The Feasibility of Using Electronic Health Data for Research on Small Populations. Population #3: Adolescents with Autism Spectrum Disorders," U.S. Department of Health and Human Services (HHS), September 1, 2013.

Measuring ASD prevalence continues to be a challenge due to the complexity of the disorder, the lack of consistent and reliable diagnostic standards, and changes in the definition of such conditions. ASD prevalence is about five times higher in boys than in girls (ratio of 4.5 boys to 1 girl). Prevalence is also significantly higher among non-Hispanic white children than among black and Hispanic children. Intellectual ability is highly variable, with 38 percent reported as intellectually disabled, 24 percent as borderline, and 38 percent with average or above average intellectual ability.

There are controversies about what should be included in the category of autism spectrum disorders. The NIH classifies Rett syndrome as an ASD, but some argue that it is more similar to non-autistic spectrum disorders such as fragile X syndrome or Down syndrome. Unlike other ASDs, Rett syndrome is also almost always in girls. There is also debate over whether Asperger's disorder is a separate disorder or simply a less severe form of autism.

The next revision of the American Psychiatric Association's Diagnostic and Statistical Manual (DSM) will drop individual classifications for autistic disorder, Asperger's disorder, childhood disintegrative disorder and PDD-NOS, grouping all of them under "autism spectrum disorder"—a term that is already widely used. APA has said this change will help "more accurately and consistently diagnose children with autism." Rett syndrome will be dropped from the DSM altogether. There is concern among the Asperger's and Rett communities that these changes will result in a loss of identity among individuals with these specific disorders and that it may affect health insurance coverage and school funding for special education.

The exact causes of ASDs remain unknown, but research suggests genetics and environment both play important roles. Researchers are studying factors such as family medical conditions, parental age and other demographic factors, exposure to toxins, and complications during birth or pregnancy. CDC and IOM studies have found no link to childhood immunizations.

Transition to Adulthood

Most research on ASDs focuses on the identification, assessment, and treatment of children. Few studies examine their transition into the adult world. The health care transition between adolescence and adulthood requires planning in order to maximize lifelong functioning and well-being. This process would ideally include ensuring uninterrupted, developmentally appropriate health care services as the person moves from adolescence to adulthood. For those with ASDs, there are a number of special considerations for this transitional period. The transition period from pediatric to adult care and from child to adult special services will have lifelong implications for their education, employment, social activities, and health. Because their conditions range in severity, a wide range of individualized adult services and supports is needed for this population.

Two key aspects of transition planning for teens with ASDs are helping them take increased responsibility for their health care, and plan for the transfer of care from a pediatric to an adult provider. Unfortunately, providers who care for adults often lack training and experience in dealing with this transitioning population. For those whose disability is impaired enough to interfere with the ability to make financial or medical decisions, parents can file for a petition to maintain guardianship. Most individuals diagnosed with autism during childhood remain dependent into adulthood on their parents or caregivers for support in education, accommodation, and occupational situations.

Teens with ASDs who are transitioning to adulthood need help in understanding their disability, opportunities to talk about topics such as safety, substance abuse and sexuality, education about how to take medications and make routine health care appointments, and continual insurance coverage. An adult provider also needs to be identified, and the adolescent's medical records transferred. None of this is simple.

Unfortunately, health care transition planning is not common for youth with ASDs. One national survey found only 14 percent had a discussion with their pediatrician about transitioning to an adult provider, and fewer than 25 percent had discussed retaining health insurance. Being from a racial or ethnic minority, having low income, being from a non-English speaking family, and not having a medical home reduces the odds that youth with ASDs will receive comprehensive transition services. Even within medical homes, both parents and pediatricians have reported dissatisfaction with the time and resources dedicated to this transition.

Chapter 53

Finding Appropriate and Affordable Housing

Where Can I Get Help Finding a Place to Live?

The Department of Housing and Urban Development (HUD), as well as many housing organizations in your state, can help you with your search for an affordable, accessible home. Below are a few search tools and organizations that can help you get started.

- HUD's Low Rent Apartment Search can help you find low-rent apartments near you. You can search by city, town or zip code to find apartments of any size that are accessible to people with disabilities or senior citizens. You can also contact the HUD office in your state or a HUD Approved Housing Counseling Agency for help finding a place to live. These offices provide advice on buying a home, programs that can help you pay your rent and answer other housing-related questions you may have.

- Use HUD's Resource Locator mobile application (app) on your smartphone or electronic tablet to find available HUD housing in your area, including affordable housing for people with disabilities and seniors.

- Socialserve.com has information about affordable and accessible housing in most states. You can search for housing based on where

Text in this chapter is excerpted from "Disability.gov's Guide to Housing," Disability.gov, December 22, 2013.

you want to live, how much you can afford to pay, and accessibility features such as wheelchair ramps, accessible parking, widened doorways and low kitchen counters for wheelchair users.

- State Housing Finance Agencies (HFA) help meet the affordable housing needs of the residents in their states, including people with disabilities and low-income families. Many of these offices also have online tools you can use to search for an affordable apartment or house.

- The U.S. Department of Agriculture (USDA) provides funding for rural multi-family apartment complexes for seniors and families throughout the country.

- The National Low Income Housing Coalition (NLIHC) works with state housing and homelessness advocacy organizations to make sure that people with low incomes have affordable, safe housing. Many of these state and local organizations can help you with your search for affordable housing.

- Habitat for Humanity volunteers build and repair safe, affordable houses throughout the world.

Are There Any Programs That Can Help Me Pay My Rent?

- Housing Choice Vouchers (formerly called "Section 8" vouchers) help very low-income families, the elderly and people with disabilities pay for decent, safe housing. Housing may include single-family homes, townhouses and apartments, and is not limited to just units in subsidized housing projects. The individual who is approved for a housing voucher is responsible for finding a housing unit where the owner agrees to rent under the program. To apply, contact your local Public Housing Agency or HUD office. Be aware that the demand for this type of housing assistance is high, so there are often waiting lists of individuals in need of subsidized housing.

- HUD's Public Housing Program provides housing for eligible low-income families, the elderly and persons with disabilities. Public housing comes in all sizes and types, from single family houses to high-rise apartments.

- State Housing Finance Agencies provide information about rental assistance programs in each state, as well as resources to help you buy a home, learn about your housing rights and find accessible housing for people with disabilities.

- HUD's Housing Counseling Program works through organizations in cities and towns across the country to help people with their housing needs. Counselors can help you search for affordable housing and learn about rental assistance programs. They can also provide advice and referrals on foreclosure and credit issues.

- HUD's Housing Opportunities for Persons with AIDS Program (HOPWA) is the only federal program dedicated to address the housing needs of persons living with HIV/AIDS and their families. HOPWA works through local nonprofit organizations and housing agencies to provide housing and support to individuals and families. HOPWA programs provide short- and long-term rental assistance, run community residences and provide supportive housing facilities.

- In addition, some Community Action Agencies, and organizations such as Catholic Charities and Lutheran Services in America, provide housing and rental assistance.

Where Can I Get Help Paying for Home Repairs or Modifications to Make My Home Accessible?

Home modifications may involve converting or adapting your environment so you can live independently. Examples of home modifications include replacing regular door handles with ones that open by using a push button; adding handrails on both sides of a staircase and outside steps; installing ramps for so you can come and go from your home by wheelchair or scooter; building a walk-in shower; and lowering kitchen counters.

These types of home modifications enable people with disabilities and older adults to "age in place" and live independently. An occupational or physical therapist may be able to suggest other ways to adapt your home for safety and accessibility.

Here are a few resources and organizations that will help you get information about making your home accessible:

- Rebuilding Together is a nonprofit organization that provides home repair and modification services for low-income families, people with disabilities, seniors and Veterans and military families. Also helps families whose homes have been damaged by natural disasters.

- The National Resource Center on Supportive Housing and Home Modification promotes aging in place for seniors and people who are aging with a disability. The Center gives families and individuals the knowledge they need to plan for their housing, health and supportive service needs. Check your state's listings for agencies and organizations near you that can help with home modifications.

- Your local Independent Living Center (ILC) may be able to make some suggestions about how to pay for home modifications such as adding a wheelchair ramp or widening the doorway to your bathroom. ILCs also provide advocacy and support services for people with disabilities, including assistance with housing, health care and independent living skills.

- Easy Access Housing for Easier Living is a brochure from Easter Seals that has tips on how to adapt your home to accommodate a person with a disability. Your local Easter Seals chapter can provide you with information about possible financing options to pay for modifications to make your home accessible.

- Your local Aging and Disability Resource Center (ADRC) may be able to refer you to an organization or company that provides home modifications services. ADRCs offer information on long-term supports and services for older adults and people with disabilities.

- The Department of Veterans Affairs (VA) makes grants available to service members and veterans with certain permanent and total service-connected disabilities to help them buy or build an adapted home, or modify an existing home to accommodate a disability. The two grant programs are the Specially Adapted Housing (SAH) grant and the Special Housing Adaptation (SHA) grant.

- According to Eldercare.gov, many minor home modifications and repairs cost between $150 and $2,000. Some home remodeling contractors offer reduced rates and charge sliding-scale fees based on a person's income and ability to pay. Some Area Agencies on Aging (AAA) have home modification programs or can refer you to other organizations that can help pay for home repairs and modifications.

- The USDA's Single Family Housing Repair program provides loans to very low-income homeowners to repair, improve or modernize their homes and grants to elderly very low-income homeowners to remove health and safety hazards.

- Some state housing finance agencies have loan programs that help people with disabilities (or who have a family member living in the household with disabilities) who are buying a home that needs accessibility modifications. Many states have home modification programs that are part of their state Assistive Technology programs. These programs provide low-interest loans to buy assistive technology or to help pay for home modifications and adaptations to make your home safe and accessible.

- The United Spinal Association offers a guide on home modifications that includes information about resources that can help people with spinal cord injuries pay for home modifications.

Where Can I Get Information about Assisted Living Facilities?

According to the Assisted Living Federation of America (ALFA), assisted living is a long-term care option that combines housing, support services and health care. Assisted living is usually for individuals who need assistance with everyday activities such as cooking, taking medications, or help with bathing, getting dressed and transportation. Some assisted living residents may have memory disorders such as Alzheimer's, or may need help related to mobility, incontinence or other challenges.

Here are some search tools and organizations that can help you find assisted living facilities near you:

- Read Disability.gov's "What Do I Need to Consider When Choosing an Assisted Living Facility of Nursing Home?" to find resources to guide you to the right assisted living option for you or your loved one.

- Use ALFA's Senior Living Community Search to find senior living options in your area.

- Your Area Agency on Aging (AAA) can refer you to assisted living facilities in your state, as well as information about other long-term care services and supports and information for caregivers.

- Every state has a Department of Aging (your state's agency may be called something slightly different) that protects the rights and quality of life of older persons. These agencies can provide you with information about programs for seniors relating to housing, health education and in-home services. Many of these state offices have lists of certified assisted living communities, as well as information on how to pay for the monthly cost of assisted living.

- The Eldercare Locator connects you to services for older adults and their families.

- A Guide for Making Housing Decisions – Housing Options for Older Adults provides information on housing options for older adults, including types of assisted living facilities, home modifications and legal and financial issues involved in long-term care.

- Long-term care ombudsmen are advocates for residents of nursing homes, board and care homes and assisted living facilities. They are trained to resolve problems and can assist you with complaints. Ombudsmen also provide information about how to find a facility and how to get quality care.

- Read "Common Nursing Home Problems and How to Resolve Them" to learn how to address issues in nursing home and assisted living facilities, including improper use of physical restraints and failure to provide needed services. Includes information about the rights of nursing home residents.

What Is Supportive Housing and What Types of Services Does It Provide?

Supportive housing helps people with disabilities and others who may be at risk for becoming homeless. This type of housing provides more than just a roof over a person's head. Supportive housing usually offers a range of services, including mental health counseling and vocational rehabilitation in order to create a stable living environment for residents.

The Section 811 Supportive Housing for Persons with Disabilities program is a U.S. Department of Housing and Urban Development (HUD) program that helps people with disabilities who have low incomes to live independently in the community by providing affordable housing along with needed services and supports.

Here are some other organizations that can refer you to supportive housing programs:

- Your local Independent Living Center

- Your local Public Housing Agency

- A local affiliate of a nonprofit organization such as Easter Seals or United Cerebral Palsy (UCP). In addition, many chapters of The Arc, which advocates for people with intellectual and developmental disabilities, have supportive housing programs.

What Are My Housing Rights as a Person with a Disability?

Under the Fair Housing Act, it is against the law to discriminate against people when renting or selling homes, or in mortgage lending, based on race, color, national origin, religion, sex, familial status or disability. People with disabilities who use assistance animals are also protected by both the Fair Housing Act and the Americans with Disabilities Act (ADA).

If you have been trying to buy or rent a home or apartment, and you believe your civil rights have been violated, you can file a housing discrimination complaint online.

Chapter 54

Autism and Employment

Chapter Contents

Section 54.1

Employment Training for Adolescents with Autism Spectrum Disorder

Text in this section is excerpted from "Protecting Students With Disabilities," U.S. Department of Education (ED), October 16, 2015.

Placement

Once a student is identified as being eligible for regular or special education and related aids or services, a decision must be made regarding the type of services the student needs.

If a student is eligible for services under both the IDEA and Section 504, must a school district develop both an individualized education program (IEP) under the IDEA and a Section 504 plan under Section 504?

No. If a student is eligible under IDEA, he or she must have an IEP. Under the Section 504 regulations, one way to meet Section 504 requirements for a free appropriate public education is to implement an IEP.

Must a school district develop a Section 504 plan for a student who either "has a record of disability" or is "regarded as disabled"?

No. In public elementary and secondary schools, unless a student actually has an impairment that substantially limits a major life activity, the mere fact that a student has a "record of" or is "regarded as" disabled is insufficient, in itself, to trigger those Section 504 protections that require the provision of a free appropriate public education (FAPE). This is consistent with the Amendments Act, in which Congress clarified that an individual who meets the definition of disability solely by virtue of being "regarded as" disabled is not entitled to reasonable accommodations or the reasonable modification of policies, practices or procedures. The phrases "has a record of disability" and "is regarded as disabled" are meant to reach the situation in which a student either does not currently have or never had a disability, but is treated by others as such.

In the Amendments Act, Congress clarified that an individual is not "regarded as" an individual with a disability if the impairment is transitory and minor. A transitory impairment is an impairment with an actual or expected duration of 6 months or less.

What is the receiving school district's responsibility under Section 504 toward a student with a Section 504 plan who transfers from another district?

If a student with a disability transfers to a district from another school district with a Section 504 plan, the receiving district should review the plan and supporting documentation. If a group of persons at the receiving school district, including persons knowledgeable about the meaning of the evaluation data and knowledgeable about the placement options determines that the plan is appropriate, the district is required to implement the plan. If the district determines that the plan is inappropriate, the district is to evaluate the student consistent with the Section 504 procedures at 34 C.F.R. 104.35 and determine which educational program is appropriate for the student. There is no Section 504 bar to the receiving school district honoring the previous IEP during the interim period.

What are the responsibilities of regular education teachers with respect to implementation of Section 504 plans? What are the consequences if the district fails to implement the plans?

Regular education teachers must implement the provisions of Section 504 plans when those plans govern the teachers' treatment of students for whom they are responsible. If the teachers fail to implement the plans, such failure can cause the school district to be in noncompliance with Section 504.

What is the difference between a regular education intervention plan and a Section 504 plan?

A regular education intervention plan is appropriate for a student who does not have a disability or is not suspected of having a disability but may be facing challenges in school. School districts vary in how they address performance problems of regular education students. Some districts employ teams at individual schools, commonly referred to as "building teams." These teams are designed to provide regular education classroom teachers with instructional support and strategies for helping students in need of assistance. These teams are typically composed of regular and special education teachers who provide ideas to classroom teachers on methods for helping students experiencing academic or behavioral problems.

The team usually records its ideas in a written regular education intervention plan. The team meets with an affected student's classroom teacher(s) and recommends strategies to address the student's problems within the regular education environment. The team then follows the responsible teacher(s) to determine whether the student's performance or behavior has improved. In addition to building teams, districts may utilize other regular education intervention methods, including before-school and after-school programs, tutoring programs, and mentoring programs.

Procedural Safeguards

Public elementary and secondary schools must employ procedural safeguards regarding the identification, evaluation, or educational placement of persons who, because of disability, need or are believed to need special instruction or related services.

Must a recipient school district obtain parental consent prior to conducting an initial evaluation?

Yes. OCR has interpreted Section 504 to require districts to obtain parental permission for initial evaluations. If a district suspects a student needs or is believed to need special instruction or related services and parental consent is withheld, the IDEA and Section 504 provide that districts may use due process hearing procedures to seek to override the parents' denial of consent for an initial evaluation.

If so, in what form is consent required?

Section 504 is silent on the form of parental consent required. OCR has accepted written consent as compliance. IDEA as well as many state laws also require written consent prior to initiating an evaluation.

What can a recipient school district do if a parent withholds consent for a student to secure services under Section 504 after a student is determined eligible for services?

Section 504 neither prohibits nor requires a school district to initiate a due process hearing to override a parental refusal to consent with respect to the initial provision of special education and related services. Nonetheless, school districts should consider that IDEA no longer permits school districts to initiate a due process hearing to override a parental refusal to consent to the initial provision of services.

What procedural safeguards are required under Section 504?

Recipient school districts are required to establish and implement procedural safeguards that include notice, an opportunity for parents to review relevant records, an impartial hearing with opportunity for participation by the student's parents or guardian, representation by counsel and a review procedure.

What is a recipient school district's responsibility under Section 504 to provide information to parents and students about its evaluation and placement process?

Section 504 requires districts to provide notice to parents explaining any evaluation and placement decisions affecting their children and explaining the parents' right to review educational records and appeal any decision regarding evaluation and placement through an impartial hearing.

Is there a mediation requirement under Section 504?

No.

Section 54.2

Disability Employment

Text in this section is excerpted from "Disability Employment," U.S. Office of Personnel Management (OPM), February 2015.

Job Seekers

The Federal Government is actively recruiting and hiring persons with disabilities. The government offers a variety of exciting jobs, competitive salaries, excellent benefits, and opportunities for career advancement.

Hiring people with disabilities into Federal jobs is fast and easy. People with disabilities can be appointed to Federal jobs non-competitively through a process called Schedule A. Learn how to be considered for Federal jobs under the noncompetitive process. People with disabilities may also apply for jobs through the traditional or competitive process.

Getting a Job

Learn the difference between the competitive and non-competitive hiring processes, how to use the Schedule A Authority, and how to conduct a job search in the Federal government.

Find a Selective Placement Program Coordinator

Most Federal agencies have a Selective Placement Program Coordinator, a Special Emphasis Program Manager (SEPM) for Employment of Adults with Disabilities, or equivalent, who helps to recruit, hire and accommodate people with disabilities at that agency.

Reasonable Accommodations

The Federal Government may provide you reasonable accommodation in appropriate cases. Requests are considered on a case-by-case basis.

Federal Agencies

As the Nation's largest employer, the Federal Government has a special responsibility to lead by example in including people with disabilities in the workforce. This website contains important information for federal agencies to use in recruiting, hiring, and retaining individuals with disabilities and targeted disabilities.

Background

On July 26, 2010, President Obama issued Executive Order 13548, which provides that the Federal Government, as the Nation's largest employer, must become a model for the employment of individuals with disabilities. The order directs Executive departments and agencies (agencies) to improve their efforts to employ Federal workers with disabilities and targeted disabilities through increased recruitment, hiring, and retention of these individuals. This is not only the right thing to do, but it is also good for the Government, as it increases the potential pool of highly qualified people from which the Federal Government draws its talent. Importantly, the Executive Order adopts the goal set forth in Executive Order 13163 of hiring 100,000 people with disabilities into the Federal Government over 5 years, including individuals with targeted disabilities.

The Executive Order also instructed the Director of the Office of Personnel Management (OPM), in consultation with the Secretary of Labor, the Chair of the Equal Employment Opportunity Commission (EEOC), and the Director of the Office of Management and Budget (OMB), to design model recruitment and hiring strategies for agencies to facilitate their employment of people with disabilities.

In addition to the Executive Order, federal agencies are obligated under the Rehabilitation Act of 1973, as amended to affirmatively employ people with disabilities. The specific requirements of this obligation are spelled out in the Equal Employment Opportunity Commission Management Directive (MD) 715.

Recruiting

This section contains recruiting information and resources for selective placement program coordinators, human resources professionals, managers and hiring officials.

Hiring

There are two types of hiring processes. In the non-competitive hiring process, agencies use a special authority (Schedule A) to hire

427

persons with disabilities without requiring them to compete for the job. In the competitive process, applicants compete with each other through a structured process.

Retention

Retention is essential to making the investment of identifying and hiring people pay off. Learn helpful practices for retaining people with disabilities.

Providing Accommodation

In order to meet their accommodation obligations, agencies should think creatively about ways to make their workplace more accessible and create an environment where their employees who have disabilities can thrive. Here are some suggestions that relate specifically to reasonable accommodation issues.

Section 54.3

Self-Employment for People with Disabilities

Text in this section is excerpted from "Self-Employment for People with Disabilities," Office of Disability Employment Policy (ODEP), December 15, 2013.

Self-Employment

Many Americans are the descendants of people who came to the United States from across the globe to realize opportunity and exercise freedom. Steeped in the spirit of independence, the earliest Americans were self-employed, primarily in agriculture. However, as the nation's economic base shifted from farming to manufacturing and then on to the "Information ! Age," the nature of employment in America did as well, with wage employment replacing self-employment as the primary means of livelihood.

Yet, America continues to be associated the world over with the spirit of self-determination that embodies its roots as an entrepreneurial, self-reliant society. Furthermore, in economic downturns, job loss and lack of employment opportunities may produce additional incentive to pursue self-employment for people in a variety of situations and circumstances.

People with disabilities demonstrate the same passion, independence and self-direction as all Americans, and given certain characteristics—including being on average older and less educated—it is not surprising that the rate of self-employment for people with disabilities in the labor force in 2011 was about 50 percent higher than the corresponding rate for people without disabilities. In 2011, among employed individuals, a higher proportion of those with disabilities were unincorporated self-employed (11.8 percent) than individuals without disabilities (6.6 percent)

Self-Employment among People with Disabilities

Self-employment allows people to customize their work experiences specifically to their needs and to design a work environment that optimizes flexibility and accommodation. Several public programs support employment preparation and work incentives to achieve self-sufficiency. Although limited, available statistics indicate that there has been little engagement by public programs to help people with disabilities explore self- employment as a viable work option. Prior to START-UP, several federal programs acknowledged self- employment as an outcome for people both with and without disabilities, but with few exceptions, it is fair to say that not many programs specifically *promoted* self-employment.

The WIA, which authorizes DOL's American Job Centers (AJCs) (formerly known as One-Stop Career Centers), makes numerous references to self-employment. In fact, self-employment, entrepreneurship and small businesses are mentioned in WIA, as amended, in several titles and sections: definitions; migrant and seasonal farm workers programs; demonstration, pilot, multi-service research, and multi-state projects; employment statistics; people with significant disabilities; VR services for individuals and groups; research; special projects and demonstrations; and provider and individual training. Furthermore, self-employment is an allowed exit outcome for individuals receiving services authorized by WIA.

In 2010, the Employment and Training Administration (ETA) issued guidance on self-employment to state and local workforce agencies and rapid response coordinators. But the proportion of AJC exiters who entered self-employment is unknown. AJCs report outcomes as employment of any type, with no distinction between self-employment and wage employment.

In 2011, ETA reported that 4.3 percent of all 2010 WIA exiters disclosed disabilities, and 3 percent who exited for employment reported disabilities. ETA reported that less than 1 percent of WIA exiters in 2010 received entrepreneurial training, suggesting that a very small percentage of all exiters (with and without disclosed disabilities) prepared for self-employment.

The Social Security Administration (SSA) sponsors work incentive programs to encourage employment of people with disabilities who receive Social Security Disability Insurance (SSDI) and Supplemental Security Income (SSI) due to disability. SS!'s Plan to Achieve Self-Support (PASS) and Ticket to Work incentive programs include self-employment as an outcome for people with disabilities, but available data suggest self-employment is an infrequent outcome for program exiters.

ETA sponsored a study that matched AJC clients in four states (Colorado, Iowa, Maryland, and Oregon) with SSI and SSDI records to find out what proportion received SSA disability benefits (information not routinely recorded by AJCs). In Program Years 2002–2007, in all four states, only 2-4 percent of AJC users were SSA beneficiaries when they registered for services; slightly higher percentages (3 -6 percent) had once been SSA beneficiaries. Despite these low percentages, AJCs served a substantial percentage of all SSA beneficiaries actively seeking employment (26 percent in Iowa and Colorado). These percentages are similar to, or much greater than, the percentage of SSA beneficiaries receiving employment services from vocational rehabilitation (VR) agencies in the same states.

People with disabilities may prepare for employment through their state VR programs, funded by the Rehabilitation Services Administration (RSA) in the Department of Education. RSA collects data on self-employment outcomes for people with disabilities who receive VR services. The Rehabilitation Act of 1973, Sections 7(11) (C) and 103(a) (13), supports state VR agencies in offering a self-employment outcome as follows:

(C) Satisfying any other vocational outcome the Secretary may determine to be appropriate (including satisfying the vocational outcome of self-employment, telecommuting or business ownership), in a manner consistent with the Act.

(13) Technical assistance and other consultation services to conduct market analyses, develop business plans, and otherwise provide

resources, to the extent such resources are authorized to be provided through the statewide workforce investment system, to eligible individuals who are pursuing self-employment or telecommuting or establishing a small business operation as an employment outcome.

Despite this authority, an analysis of RSA case closure statistics for VR clients indicated that self-employment remains a small percentage of overall VR status 26 closures in employment, ranging from 1.97 percent in 2003 to 1.66 percent in 2007 and 1.99 percent in 2009, although there has been a small increase to 2.40 percent in 2012.

VR agencies with the highest percentage of self-employment outcomes were in states generally considered to have more disbursed populations and generally more rural communities.

Average hourly and weekly earnings for individuals closed in self-employment were consistently higher than the average wages for all Status 26 (successfully employed) closures. The average hourly wage for persons closed in self-employment in FY 2012 was $14.46, compared to $11.33 for all Status 26 closures. Average weekly wage in self-employment in FY 2012 was $445, compared to $365 for all Status 26 closures.

The mean average case service expenditure by VR agencies for persons closed in self-employment in FY 2012 was approximately $7,910. In comparison, the average expenditure for all Status 26 closures in FY 2012 was approximately $5,436.

The mean average time period from the point that the Individual Plan for Employment was initiated to closure in self-employment in FY 2012 was 663 days. The comparative time period for all Status 26 closures in employment was 630 days.

VR State agency involvement in facilitating self-employment outcomes does vary substantially from state to state, particularly for persons with a primary intellectual disability. There are states, such as Florida and Ohio, whose VR agencies are involved in initiatives to implement policies and practices that expand participation in self-employment. These agencies are implementing a step-by-step vocational rehabilitation process that provides a variety of resources to the individual with a disability potentially interested in self-employment. This process focuses on individual support needs and emphasizes the development of a business design team to assist and support the self-employment initiative. It also focuses on the ongoing supports needed for the development of a viable business plan and the successful implementation and maintenance of the self-employment venture.

Section 54.4

ASD and Job Accommodations

"Employees with ASD," Job Accommodation Network, a service of
U.S. DOL's Office of Disability Employment Policy, July 17, 2013.

The ADA does not contain a list of medical conditions that constitute disabilities. Instead, the ADA has a general definition of disability
that each person must meet on a case by case basis. A person has a
disability if he/she has a physical or mental impairment that substantially limits one or more major life activities, a record of such an
impairment, or is regarded as having an impairment.

However, according to the Equal Employment Opportunity Commission (EEOC), the individualized assessment of virtually all people
with ASD will result in a determination of disability under the ADA;
given its inherent nature, ASD will almost always be found to substantially limit the major life activity of brain function.

Accommodating Employees with ASD

Questions to Consider

1. What limitations does the employee with ASD experience?

2. How do these limitations affect the employee's job
   performance?

3. What specific job tasks are problematic as a result of these
   limitations?

4. What accommodations are available to reduce or eliminate
   these problems? Are all possible resources being used to determine accommodations?

5. Can the employee with Autism Spectrum Disorder provide
   information on possible accommodation solutions?

6. Once accommodations are in place, would it be useful to meet
   with the employee with Autism Spectrum Disorder to evaluate

the effectiveness of the accommodations and to determine whether additional accommodations are needed?

7. Do supervisory personnel and employees need training regarding Autism Spectrum Disorder?

Accommodation Ideas

Speaking/Communicating: Individuals with ASD may have difficulty communicating with co-workers or supervisors.

- Provide advance notice of topics to be discussed in meetings to help facilitate communication
- Provide advance notice of date of meeting when employee is required to speak to reduce or eliminate anxiety
- Allow employee to provide written response in lieu of verbal response
- Allow employee to have a friend or coworker attend meeting to reduce or eliminate the feeling of intimidation
- Allow employee to bring an advocate to performance reviews and disciplinary meetings

Atypical Body Movements: Individuals with ASD may exhibit atypical body movements such as fidgeting. Atypical body movements are sometimes called
stimulatory behavior, or "stimming." These body movements often help calm the person or assist in concentrating on tasks, but can also disturb coworkers at times.

- Provide structured breaks to create an outlet for physical activity
- Allow employee to use items such as hand-held squeeze balls and similar objects to provide sensory input or calming effect
- Allow the employee to work from home
- Schedule periodic rest breaks away from the workstation
- Review conduct policy with employee
- Provide private workspace where employee will have room to move about and not disturb others by movements such as fidgeting

Time Management: Individuals with ASD may experience difficulty managing time. This limitation can affect their ability to complete tasks within a specified timeframe. It may also be difficult to prepare for, or to begin, work activities.

- Divide large assignments into several small tasks

- Set a timer to make an alarm after assigning ample time to complete a task

- Provide a checklist of assignments

- Supply an electronic or handheld organizer and train how to use effectively

- Use a wall calendar to emphasize due dates

Maintaining Concentration: Individuals with ASD may experience decreased concentration and may not be able to tolerate distractions such as office traffic, employee chatter, and common office noises such as fax tones and photocopying.

- To reduce auditory distractions:

  - Purchase a noise canceling headset

  - Hang sound absorption panels

  - Provide a white noise machine

  - Relocate employee's office space away from audible distractions

  - Redesign employee's office space to minimize audible distractions

- To reduce visual distractions:

  - Install space enclosures (cubicle walls)

  - Reduce clutter in the employee's work environment

  - Redesign employee's office space to minimize visual distractions

  - Relocate employee's office space away from visual distractions

- To reduce tactile distractions:

  - Instruct other employees to approach the individual in a way that is not startling, such as approaching from behind, touching the employee, or other tactile interactions, if the employee is bothered by those interactions.

Organization and Prioritization: Individuals with ASD may have difficulty getting or staying organized, or have difficulty prioritizing tasks at work. The employee may need assistance with skills required to prepare and execute complex behavior like planning, goal setting, and task completion.

- Develop color-code system for files, projects, or activities
- Use weekly chart to identify daily work activities
- Use the services of a professional organizer
- Use a job coach to teach/reinforce organization skills
- Assign a mentor to help employee
- Allow supervisor to prioritize tasks
- Assign new project only when previous project is complete
- Provide a "cheat sheet" of high-priority activities, projects, people, etc.

Memory: Individuals with ASD may experience memory deficits that can affect their ability to complete tasks, remember job duties, or recall daily actions or activities. They also may have difficulty recognizing faces.

- Provide written instructions
- Allow additional training time for new tasks
- Offer training refreshers
- Prompt employee with verbal cues
- Use a flowchart to describe the steps involved in a complicated task (such as powering up a system, closing down the facility, logging into a computer, etc.)
- Provide pictorial cues
- Use post-it notes as reminders of important dates or tasks
- Safely and securely maintain paper lists of crucial information such as passwords
- Allow employee to use voice activated recorder to record verbal instructions
- Provide employee directory with pictures or use name tags and door/cubicle name markers to help employee remember coworkers' faces and names

435

- Encourage employee to ask (or e-mail) work-related questions

Multi-tasking: Individuals with ASD may experience difficulty performing many tasks at one time. This difficulty could occur regardless of the similarity of tasks, the ease or complexity of the tasks, or the frequency of performing the tasks.

- Create a flow-chart of tasks that must be performed at the same time

- Separate tasks so that each one can be completed one at a time

- Label or color-code each task in sequential or preferential order

- Provide individualized/specialized training to help employee learn techniques for multi-tasking (e.g., typing on computer while talking on phone)

- Identify tasks that must be performed simultaneously and tasks that can be performed individually

- Provide specific feedback to help employee target areas of improvement

- Remove or reduce distractions from work area

- Supply proper working equipment to complete multiple tasks at one time, such as workstation and chair, lighting, and office supplies

- Explain performance standards such as completion time or accuracy rates

Issues of Change:

- Recognize that a change in the office environment, job tasks, or of supervisors may be difficult for a person with autism

- Maintain open channels of communication between the employee and the new and old supervisor in order to ensure an effective transition

- Provide weekly or monthly meetings with the employee to discuss workplace issues and productions levels

Stress Management: Individuals with ASD may have difficulty managing stress in the workplace. Situations that create stress can vary from person to person, but could likely involve heavy workloads, unrealistic time frames, shortened deadlines, or conflict among coworkers.

- Provide praise and positive reinforcement
- Refer to EAP
- Allow employee to make telephone calls for support
- Provide sensitivity training for workforce
- Allow the presence and use of a support animal
- Modify work schedule

Social Skills: People with ASD may have difficulty exhibiting typical social skills on the job. This might manifest itself as interrupting others when working or talking, difficulty listening, not making eye contact when communicating, or difficulty interpreting typical body language or nonverbal innuendo. This can affect the person's ability to adhere to conduct standards, work effectively with supervisors, or interact with coworkers or customers.

- Social skills on the job:
  - Provide a job coach to help understand different social cues
  - Provide concrete examples of accepted behaviors and consequences for all employees
  - Recognize and reward acceptable behavior to reinforce
  - Review conduct policy with employee to reduce incidents of unacceptable behavior
  - Use training videos to demonstrate appropriate social skills in workplace
  - Encourage all employees to model appropriate social skills
  - Use role-play scenarios to demonstrate appropriate social skills in workplace
- Working effectively with supervisors:
  - Provide detailed day-to-day guidance and feedback
  - Offer positive reinforcement
  - Identify areas of improvement for employee in a fair and consistent manner
  - Provide clear expectations and the consequences of not meeting expectations

- Give assignments verbally, in writing, or both, depending on what would be most beneficial to the employee (e.g., use of visual charts)
- Assist employee in assigning priority to assignments
- Assign projects in a systematic and predictable manner
- Establish long term and short term goals for employee
- Adjust supervisory method by modifying the manner in which conversations take place, meetings are conducted, or discipline is addressed

- Interacting with coworkers:
  - Provide sensitivity training to promote disability awareness
  - Allow employee to work from home when feasible
  - Help employee "learn the ropes" by providing a mentor
  - Make employee attendance at social functions optional
  - Allow employee to transfer to another work group, shift, or department
  - Encourage employees to minimize personal conversation or move personal conversation away from work areas
  - Provide telework, or work-at-home, as an accommodation
  - Allow alternative forms of communication between coworkers, such as e-mail, instant messaging, or text messaging

Sensory Issues: Individuals with ASD may have difficulty with sensory processing and can experience over sensitivity to touch, sights, sounds, and smells in the workplace.

- Fragrance sensitivity:
  - Maintain good indoor air quality
  - Discontinue the use of fragranced products
  - Use only unscented cleaning products
  - Provide scent-free meeting rooms and restrooms
  - Modify workstation location
  - Modify the work schedule
  - Allow for fresh air breaks

- Provide an air purification system
- Modify or create a fragrance-free workplace policy
- Allow telework
- Fluorescent light sensitivity:
  - Move employee to a private area to allow for personal adjustment to appropriate lighting
  - Change lighting completely
  - Allow telework
- Noise sensitivity:
  - Move employee to a more private area or away from high traffic areas
  - Move employee away from office machinery, equipment, and other background noises
  - Provide an environmental sound machine to help mask distracting sounds
  - Provide noise canceling headsets
  - Provide sound absorption panels
  - Encourage coworkers to keep non-work related conversation to a minimum
  - Allow telework

Company Structure, Conduct Policy, and Discipline: Individuals with ASD may not be familiar with or understand abstract concepts like corporate structure, hierarchies of responsibility, reporting requirements, and other structural elements of the workplace.

- Explain corporate structure to employee, using visual charts and clear descriptions of positions and reporting structure. Do not assume that employee will understand structure from a simple chart of job titles
- Review conduct policy with employee
- Adjust method of supervision to better prepare employee for feedback, disciplinary action, and other communication about job performance
- Provide concrete examples to explain expected conduct

- Provide concrete examples to explain consequences of violating company policy

- Use services of the Employee Assistance Program (EAP) if available

Situations and Solutions:

An employee with ASD works for a large marketing firm. Though knowledgeable in her field, she had difficulty participating in work activities with her team. JAN suggested job restructuring, which allowed her to work independently while providing information to her team electronically. This gave the employee the social distance she needed to be comfortable, yet also provided the team with information needed to move forward with marketing campaigns.

A new hire at a fast-food restaurant has ASD. He completed his new job tasks quickly and efficiently, but then remained idle until someone told him the next task to perform. The manager complained that the employee "just stands around" and "looks bored." JAN suggested the use of a job coach to help learn the job and how to stay occupied during down time. JAN also suggested using a training DVD to help build workplace social skills.

An applicant with ASD applied for a research position with a chemical company. He has a verbal communication deficit, though can communicate through handwriting and by e-mail. The employer wanted to provide accommodations during the first stage interview, which involved answering questions from a three-person search committee. JAN suggested providing the questions in advance and allowing the applicant to furnish written responses during the interview.

A professor with ASD had difficulty keeping daily office hours and experienced anxiety because the timing of students' consultations was unpredictable. JAN suggested modifying the schedule as an accommodation, for example the professor could reduce the number of days he has office hours, but have more office hours on those days. JAN also suggested adjusting the method by which students obtain appointments, asking students to schedule at least one day in advance and when possible, allow the professor to conduct consultations electronically, by phone, or by instant messenger. In addition, JAN suggested documenting each student consultation to ease the professor's anxiety about the meeting and to refresh his memory about previous meetings with the student.

Chapter 55

Affordable Care Act and Autism and Related Conditions

What Is the Affordable Care Act?

The ACA is a historic health care reform law to improve health care coverage and access while putting in place new protections for people who already have health insurance. Under the law, health insurance coverage will become affordable and accessible for millions of people, a factor that will help reduce health disparities. By 2019, it is estimated that 32 million individuals will obtain health insurance coverage as a result of the ACA.

The ACA affects everyone in the United States, so it is important to understand what the law means for community members that you will interact with during your education and outreach activities. This Resource Kit is designed to help you understand what the law is and how it will benefit individuals and families in your target communities.

This chapter includes excerpts from "The Affordable Care Act Resource Kit," Office of Minority Health (OMH), February 18, 2014; and text from "The Affordable Care Act and Autism and Related Conditions," U.S. Department of Health and Human Services (HHS), April 9, 2015.

Why Is the Affordable Care Act Important?

Prior to the ACA, Insurance companies could turn away the 129 million Americans with pre-existing conditions. Premiums had more than doubled over the last decade. Tens of millions were underinsured, many had coverage but were afraid of losing it, and 50 million individuals had no insurance at all. Racial and ethnic minorities continued to lag behind in many health indicators, including prevalence of chronic illness and access to quality care.

Rising health insurance costs previously meant that fewer people could afford or access health care. From 2003-2010, the average health insurance premium for a worker with a family was approximately $14,000 per year. The high cost of health insurance forced many individuals and families to choose between paying for coverage or other basic needs.

In addition to the problem of rising health care costs, many people did not have the security that health insurance is suppose to provide. Prior to the Affordable Care Act, individuals could be denied coverage because of a pre-existing condition; health insurance companies could raise costs if people were sick, making coverage unaffordable for many small businesses and individuals; and insurance companies could place lifetime limits on benefits.

The Affordable Care Act offers solutions to the problems outlined above. Essentially, the ACA ends many insurance company abuses, makes health insurance more affordable, strengthens the Medicare program, and provides better options for getting health coverage. Together, the law takes a big step forward towards eliminating health disparities.

Improvements in coverage have already been documented:

- 3.1 million young adults have gained insurance through their parents' plans

- 6.1 million people with Medicare through 2012 received $5.7 billion in prescription drug discounts

- An estimated 34 million people with Medicare received a free preventive service in 2012

- 71 million privately insured people gained improved coverage for preventive services

- 105 million individuals have had lifetime limits removed from their insurance

What Are the Major Themes of the Affordable Care Act?

The Affordable Care Act:

1. **Strengthens Insurance Coverage** by generally ending discrimination based on preexisting conditions or gender and doing away with lifetime limits on essential health benefits.

2. **Makes Health Care More Affordable** by offering eligible individuals new tax credits to lower premiums, reduced cost-sharing, and better access to Medicaid and the Children's Health Insurance Program (CHIP).

3. **Strengthens the Medicare Program** by eliminating cost-sharing for most preventive services, adding an Annual Wellness Visit, and lowering beneficiaries' prescription drug costs when they hit the prescription drug coverage gap known as the "donut hole."

4. **Expands Access to Coverage and Care** for uninsured and underinsured individuals, including people with low or no incomes, people who live in medically underserved areas, people in rural communities, and youth.

The Affordable Care Act and Autism and Related Conditions

The Affordable Care Act contains important provisions for individuals with autism and related conditions and their families:

- Most health insurance plans are no longer allowed to deny, limit, exclude or charge more for coverage to anyone based on a pre-existing condition, including autism and related conditions.

- All Marketplace health plans and most other private insurance plans must cover preventive services for children without charging a copayment or coinsurance. This includes autism screening for children at 18 and 24 months.

- Health plans cannot put a lifetime dollar limit on most benefits you receive. The law also does away with annual dollar limits a health plan can place on most of your benefits. Prior to the Affordable Care Act, many plans set a dollar limit on what they would spend for covered benefits during the time individuals were enrolled in the plan, leaving individuals on the autism

443

spectrum and their families to pay the cost of all care exceeding that limit.

- Young adults can remain covered under their parents' insurance up to the age of 26. For a young adult with autism or related conditions and their family, that means more flexibility, more options, and greater piece of mind.

- Individuals on the autism spectrum and families of children on the autism spectrum now have expanded access to affordable insurance options through the new Health Insurance Market-place and expansion in Medicaid.

- New health plans sold in the individual and small group mar-kets, including the Marketplace, must cover "essential health benefits," including hospitalizations, preventive services, and prescription drugs, to help ensure you have the coverage you need to stay healthy. Health insurers will also have annual out-of-pocket limits to protect families' incomes against the high cost of health care services.

Part Eight

Additional Help and Information

Chapter 56

Glossary of ASD-Related Acronyms and Terms

ASD-Related Acronyms

ABA: applied behavior analysis

ADA: Americans with Disabilities Act

ADD: attention deficit disorder

ADHD: attention deficit hyperactivity disorder

ADI: Autism Diagnostic Interview—a diagnostic tool developed in London by the Medical Research Council

ADOS: Autism Diagnostic Observation Schedule

AS: Asperger syndrome

ASA: Autism Society of America

ASD: autism spectrum disorders

CARS: Childhood Autism Rating Scale

CHAT: Checklist for Autism in Toddlers—a diagnostic tool

DD: developmental disabilities

This glossary contains terms excerpted from documents produced by several sources deemed reliable.

EEG: electroencephalogram

FC: facilitated communication

GARS: Gilliam Autism Rating Scale

HFA: high-functioning autism

IDEA: Individuals with Disabilities Education Act

IEP: individualized education plan

LRE: least restrictive environment

NOS: not otherwise specified

OCD: obsessive-compulsive disorder

OT: Occupational therapist

PDD: pervasive developmental disorder

PDDNOS: pervasive developmental disorder not otherwise specified

PECS: picture exchange communication system

PRT: pivotal response training

PT: physical therapy

SI: sensory integration

SIB: self-injurious behavior

SIT: sensory integration therapy

TEACCH: Treatment and Education of Autistic and Related Communication Handicapped Children

ASD-Related Terms

absence epilepsy: Epilepsy in which the person has repeated absence seizures.

absence seizures: Seizures seen in absence epilepsy, in which the person experiences a momentary loss in consciousness.

Affordable Care Act: The comprehensive health care reform law enacted in March 2010 is known as the Affordable Care Act.

angelman syndrome: Microdeletion of 15q-13, of maternal origin, resulting in mental retardation, ataxia, paroxysms of laughter, seizures, characteristic facies, and minimal speech.

asperger disorder: A pervasive developmental disorder characterized by severe and enduring impairment in social skills and restrictive and repetitive behaviors and interests, leading to impaired social and occupational functioning but without significant delays in language development.

assistive devices: Technical tools and devices such as alphabet boards, text telephones, or text-to-speech conversion software used to aid individuals who have communication disorders perform actions, tasks, and activities.

atonic seizures: Seizures which cause a sudden loss of muscle tone, also called drop attacks.

audiologist: Health care professional who is trained to evaluate hearing loss and related disorders, including balance (vestibular) disorders and tinnitus, and to rehabilitate individuals with hearing loss and related disorders. An audiologist uses a variety of tests and procedures to assess hearing and balance function and to fit and dispense hearing aids and other assistive devices for hearing.

auras: Unusual sensations or movements that warn of an impending, more severe seizure.

autism spectrum disorders (ASD): ASD demonstrate deficits in 1) social interaction, 2) verbal and nonverbal communication, and 3) repetitive behaviors or interests. In addition, they will often have unusual responses to sensory experiences, such as certain sounds or the way objects look. Each of these symptoms runs the gamut from mild to severe. There are five pervasive developmental disorders referred to as ASD.

autistic disorder (also called classic autism): This is what most people think of when hearing the word autism. People with autistic disorder usually have significant language delays, social and communication challenges, and unusual behaviors and interests. Many people with autistic disorder also have intellectual disability.

automatisms: Automatic involuntary or mechanical actions.

449

bundling: Bundling is a payment structure in which different health care providers who are treating you for the same or related conditions are paid an overall sum for taking care of your condition, rather than being paid for each individual treatment, test, or procedure.

Center for Medicare and Medicaid Innovation (Innovation Center): The Innovation Center's mission is to help transform Medicare, Medicaid, and the Children's Health Insurance Program (CHIP) by reducing costs while preserving or enhancing quality of care.

central auditory processing disorder: Inability to differentiate, recognize, or understand sounds; hearing and intelligence are normal.

childhood disintegrative disorder (CDD): Loss of such skills as vocabulary are more dramatic in CDD than they are in classical autism. The diagnosis requires extensive and pronounced losses involving motor language, and social skills. CDD is also accompanied by loss of bowel and bladder control and oftentimes seizures and a very low intelligence quotient (IQ).

clonic seizures: Seizures that cause repeated jerking movements of muscles on both sides of the body.

cognition: Thinking skills that include perception, memory, awareness, reasoning, judgment, intellect, and imagination.

community first choice option: The Community First Choice Option lets states provide home and community-based attendant services to Medicaid enrollees with disabilities, under their State Plan.

Community-based Care Transitions Program: A major component of the Partnership for Patients is the Community-based Care Transitions Program (CCTP), a program created by Section 3026 of the Affordable Care Act.

compulsion: Uncontrollable thoughts or impulses to perform an act, often repetitively, as an unconscious mechanism to avoid unacceptable ideas and desires which, by themselves, arouse anxiety; the anxiety becomes fully manifest if performance of the compulsive act is prevented; may be associated with obsessive thoughts.

Consumer Assistance Program Grants: The Consumer Assistance Program grants will ensure that consumers get accurate information about their new rights and benefits under the Affordable Care Act by providing nearly $30 million in new resources to help states and territories.

convulsions: Sudden severe contractions of the muscles that may be caused by seizures.

corpus callosotomy: Surgery that severs the corpus callosum, or network of neural connections between the right and left hemispheres.

cost-sharing: The share of costs covered by your insurance that you pay out of your own pocket. This term generally includes deductible, coinsurance and copayments, or similar charges, but it doesn't include premiums, balance-billing amounts for non-network providers, or the cost of non-covered services.

de novo: New, for the first time.

déjà vu: A sense that something has happened before.

developmental disability: Loss of function brought on by prenatal and postnatal events in which the predominant disturbance is in the acquisition of cognitive, language, motor, or social skills; for example, mental retardation, autistic disorder, learning disorder, and attention deficit hyperactivity disorder.

the donut hole: Most plans with Medicare prescription drug coverage (Part D) have a coverage gap (called a "donut hole"). This means that after you and your drug plan have spent a certain amount of money for covered drugs, you have to pay most costs out-of-pocket for your prescriptions up to a yearly limit.

dravet syndrome: A type of intractable epilepsy that begins in infancy.

drop attacks: Seizures that cause sudden falls; another term for atonic seizures.

echolalia: Involuntary parrot-like repetition of a word or sentence just spoken by another person.

encephalitis: Inflammation of the brain caused by a virus. Encephalitis can result in permanent brain damage or death.

epilepsy syndromes: Disorders with a specific set of symptoms that include epilepsy.

etiology: The cause of.

febrile seizures: Seizures in infants and children that are associated with a high fever.

focal seizures: Seizures that occur in just one part of the brain.

fragile X syndrome: This disorder is the most common inherited form of mental retardation. It was so named because one part of the X chromosome has a defective piece that appears pinched and fragile when under a microscope.

frontal lobe epilepsy: A type of epilepsy that originates in the frontal lobe of the brain. It usually involves a cluster of short seizures with a sudden onset and termination.

generalized seizures: Seizures that result from abnormal neuronal activity in many parts of the brain.

genetic counselor: A health professional who provides information and support to individuals and families who have a genetic disease or who are at risk for such a disease.

grand mal seizures: An older term for tonic-clonic seizures.

health disparities: A health disparity is a particular type of health difference that is closely linked with social, economic, and/or environmental disadvantage.

Health Insurance Marketplaces: Health Insurance Marketplaces are designed to make buying health coverage easier and more affordable.

hemispherectomy: Surgery involving the removal or disabling of one hemisphere of the brain.

hemispheres: The right and left halves of the brain.

hemispherotomy: Removing half of the brain's outer layer (cortex).

Hospital Value Based Purchasing Program (VBP): The Affordable Care Act includes a number of policies to help physicians, hospitals, and other caregivers improve the safety and quality of patient care and make health care more affordable.

hypothalamic hamartoma: A rare form of childhood epilepsy that is associated with malformations of the hypothalamus at the base of the brain.

immunization: The process by which a person or animal becomes protected against a disease. This term is often used interchangeably with vaccination or inoculation.

infantile spasms: Clusters of seizures that usually begin before the age of 6 months. During these seizures the infant may bend and cry out.

intractable: Hard to treat; about 30 to 40 percent of people with epilepsy will continue to experience seizures even with the best available treatment.

jaundice: Yellowing of the skin and eyes. This condition is often a symptom of hepatitis infection.

juvenile myoclonic epilepsy: A type of epilepsy characterized by sudden muscle (myoclonic) jerks that usually begins in childhood or adolescence.

ketogenic diet: A strict diet rich in fats and low in carbohydrates that causes the body to break down fats instead of carbohydrates to survive.

lafora disease: A severe, progressive form of epilepsy that begins in childhood and has been linked to a gene that helps to break down carbohydrates.

landau-kleffner syndrome: Childhood disorder of unknown origin which often extends into adulthood and can be identified by gradual or sudden loss of the ability to understand and use spoken language.

language: System for communicating ideas and feelings using sounds, gestures, signs, or marks.

language disorders: Any of a number of problems with verbal communication and the ability to use or understand a symbol system for communication.

learning disabilities: Childhood disorders characterized by difficulty with certain skills such as reading or writing in individuals with normal intelligence.

lennox-gastaut syndrome: A type of epilepsy that begins in childhood and usually causes several different kinds of seizures, including absence seizures.

lesion: Damaged or dysfunctional part of the brain or other parts of the body.

lesionectomy: Surgical removal of a specific brain lesion.

lobectomy: Surgical removal of a lobe of the brain.

Medicaid: Each state operates a Medicaid program that provides health coverage for some lower-income people, families and children, the elderly, and people with disabilities.

Medicaid expansion: Under the ACA, more people than ever before will qualify for Medicaid. Each state will determine whether to expand Medicaid to cover low-income adults.

Medicare: Medicare is health insurance for people age 65 or older, people under 65 with certain disabilities, and people of all ages with End-Stage Renal Disease.

Medicare Part D: Medicare Part D offers prescription drug coverage to everyone with Medicare. This coverage is referred to as Medicare Part D.

monotherapy: Treatment with only one antiepileptic drug.

multiple subpial transection: A type of operation in which surgeons make a series of cuts in the brain that are designed to prevent seizures from spreading into other parts of the brain while leaving the person's normal abilities intact.

myoclonic seizures: Seizures that cause sudden jerks or twitches, especially in the upper body, arms, or legs.

neocortical epilepsy: Epilepsy that originates in the brain's cortex, or outer layer. Seizures can be either focal or generalized, and may cause strange sensations, hallucinations, or emotional changes.

nonconvulsive: Any type of seizure that does not include violent muscle contractions.

nonepileptic seizures: Any phenomena that look like seizures but do not result from abnormal brain activity.

nonverbal: Denoting communication without words, for example, by signs, symbols, facial expressions, gestures, posture.

obsession: A recurrent and persistent idea, thought, or impulse to carry out an act that is ego-dystonic, that is experienced as senseless or repugnant, and that the individual cannot voluntarily suppress.

pervasive developmental disorder (PDD): A group of mental disorders of infancy, childhood, or adolescence characterized by distortions in the acquisition of the multiple basic psychologic functions necessary for the elaboration of social skills, language skills, and imagination; also characterized by restricted or stereotypical activities and interests.

pervasive developmental disorder not otherwise specified (PDDNOS): People who meet some of the criteria for autistic disorder or Asperger syndrome, but not all, may be diagnosed with PDDNOS. People with PDDNOS usually have fewer and milder symptoms than those with autistic disorder. The symptoms might cause only social and communication challenges.

placebo: A substance or treatment that has no effect on human beings.

post-ictal: Post-seizure.

Pre-existing Condition Insurance Plan (PCIP): PCIP was created by the Affordable Care Act to help uninsured people with a pre-existing condition get high quality care at affordable prices.

prevalence: The number of people in a population that have a condition relative to all of the people in the population.

Prevention and Public Health Fund: The Affordable Care Act establishes a fund to invest in promoting wellness, preventing disease, and protecting against public health emergencies.

prodrome: A feeling that a seizure is imminent, which may last hours or days prior to the seizure.

progressive myoclonus epilepsy: A type of epilepsy that has been linked to an abnormality in the gene that codes for a protein called cystatin B.

Rasmussen's encephalitis: A progressive type of epilepsy in which half of the brain shows continual inflammation.

responsive stimulation: A form of treatment that uses an implanted device to detect a forthcoming seizure and administer intervention such as electrical stimulation or a fast-acting drug to prevent the seizure from occurring.

Rett syndrome: A pervasive developmental disorder characterized by the development of several specific deficits after an apparently normal prenatal and perinatal period, including deceleration in head growth, loss of purposeful hand skills with deterioration into stereotypical hand movements, impairment in expressive and receptive language, and significant psychomotor retardation.

screening: Examination of a group of usually asymptomatic individuals to detect those with a high probability of having a given disease, typically by means of an inexpensive diagnostic test. Also, in the mental health professions, initial patient evaluation that includes medical and psychiatric history, mental status evaluation, and diagnostic formulation to determine the patients suitability for a particular treatment modality.

seizure focus: An area of the brain where seizures originate.

seizure threshold: A term that refers to a person's susceptibility to seizures.

seizure triggers: Phenomena that trigger seizures in some people.

sign language: Method of communication for people who are deaf or hard of hearing in which hand movements, gestures, and facial expressions convey grammatical structure and meaning.

The Small Business Health Options Program (SHOP): The SHOP marketplace makes it possible for small businesses to provide qualified health plans to their employees.

specific language impairment (SLI): Difficulty with language or the organized-symbol system used for communication in the absence of problems such as mental retardation, hearing loss, or emotional disorders.

speech disorder: Any defect or abnormality that prevents an individual from communicating by means of spoken words. Speech disorders may develop from nerve injury to the brain, muscular paralysis, structural defects, hysteria, or mental retardation.

speech-language pathologist: Health professional trained to evaluate and treat people who have voice, speech, language, or swallowing disorders (including hearing impairment) that affect their ability to communicate.

status epilepticus: A potentially life-threatening condition in which a seizure is abnormally prolonged.

stuttering: Frequent repetition of words or parts of words that disrupts the smooth flow of speech.

sudden unexpected death in epilepsy (SUDEP): Death that occurs suddenly for no discernible reason. Epilepsy increases the risk of unexplained death about two-fold.

temporal lobe epilepsy: The most common epilepsy syndrome with focal seizures.

temporal lobe resection: A type of surgery for temporal lobe epilepsy in which all or part of the affected temporal lobe of the brain is removed.

tonic seizures: Seizures that cause stiffening of muscles of the body, generally those in the back, legs, and arms.

tonic-clonic seizures: Seizures that cause a mixture of symptoms, including loss of consciousness, stiffening of the body, and repeated jerks of the arms and legs.

Tourette syndrome: Neurological disorder characterized by recurring movements and sounds (called tics).

tuberous sclerosis: Tuberous sclerosis is a rare genetic disorder that causes benign tumors to grow in the brain as well as in other vital organs. It has a consistently strong association with ASD.

vagus nerve stimulator: A surgically implanted device that sends short bursts of electrical energy to the brain via the vagus nerve and helps some individuals reduce their seizure activity.

Chapter 57

Directory of Additional ASD Resources

Government Organizations

Agency for Healthcare Research and Quality (AHRQ)
5600 Fishers Ln.
7th Fl.
Rockville, MD 20857
Phone: 301-427-1104
Website: www.ahrq.gov

Brain Resources and Information Network (BRAIN)
P.O Box 5801
Bethesda, MD 20824
Fax: 301-402-2186
Toll-Free: 800-352-9424
Website: www.ninds.nih.gov/
find_people/government_
agencies/volorg738.htm
E-mail: braininfo@ninds.nih.gov

Centers for Autism and Developmental Disabilities Research and Epidemiology National Center on Birth Defects and Developmental Disabilities
1600 Clifton Rd.
Atlanta, GA 30329-4027
Toll-Free: 800-232-4636
TTY: 888-232-6348
Website: www.cdc.gov/ncbddd/
autism/caddre.html

Centers for Disease Control and Prevention (CDC)
1600 Clifton Rd.
Atlanta, GA 30329-4027
Toll-Free: 800-232-4636
TTY: 888-232-6348
Website: www.cdc.gov

Resources in this chapter were compiled from several sources deemed reliable; all contact information was verified and updated in February 2016.

CDC Act Early
1600 Clifton Rd.
Atlanta, GA 30329-4027
Toll-Free: 800-232-4636
TTY: 888-232-6348
Website: www.cdc.gov/ncbddd/
actearly/index.html

CDC Autism Information Center
1600 Clifton Rd.
Atlanta, GA 30329-4027
Toll-Free: 800-232-4636
TTY: 888-232-6348
Website: www.cdc.gov/ncbddd/
autism/index.html

Disability.gov
Office of Disability Employment Policy (ODEP)
U.S. Department of Labor
Website: www.disability.gov

ED Pubs
P.O. Box 22207
Alexandria, VA 22304
Fax: 703-605-6794
Toll-Free: 877-433-7827
TTY: 877-576-7734
Website: www.edpubs.gov/
EDPubsMenu/ContactUs.aspx
E-mail: edpubs@edpubs.ed.gov

Epilepsy Foundation
Genetic and Rare Diseases Information Center (GARD)
P.O. Box 8126
Gaithersburg, MD 20898-8126
Phone: 301-251-4925
Fax: 301-251-4911
Toll-Free: 888-205-2311
TTY: 888-205-3223
Website: rarediseases.info.nih.
gov/gard

Lister Hill National Center for Biomedical Communications
8600 Rockville Pike
Bethesda, MD 20894
Phone: 301-496-4441
Fax: 301-402-0118
Toll-Free: 888-346-3656
Website: lhncbc.nlm.nih.gov

National Dissemination Center for Children with Disabilities
1825 Connecticut Ave. N.W.
Ste. 700
Washington, DC 20009
Phone: 202-884-8200
Toll-Free: 800-695-0285
Website: www.parentcenterhub.
org/nichcy-gone
E-mail: nichcy@aed.org

*National Institute of
Child Health and Human
Development (NICHD)*
31 Center Dr.
Bldg. 31, Rm. 2A32
Bethesda, MD 20892-2425
Fax: 866-760-5947
Toll-Free: 800-370-2943
TTY: 888-320-6942
Website: www.nichd.nih.gov/
Pages/index.aspx
E-mail:
NICHDInformationResource
Center@mail.nih.gov

*National Institute of
Environmental Health
Sciences (NIEHS)*
P.O. Box 12233
MD K3-16
Research Triangle Park, NC
27709-2233
Phone: 919-541-3345
Fax: 301-480-2978
Website: www.niehs.nih.gov
E-mail: webcenter@niehs.nih.gov

*National Institute of Mental
Health (NIMH)*
6001 Executive Blvd.
Rm. 6200, MSC 9663
Bethesda, MD 20892-9663
Fax: 301-443-4279
Toll-Free: 866-615-6464
Toll-Free TTY: 866-415-8051
TTY: 301-443-8431
Website: www.nimh.nih.gov/
index.shtml
E-mail: nimhinfo@nih.gov

*National Institute of
Neurological Disorders and
Stroke (NINDS)*
P.O. Box 5801
Bethesda, MD 20824
Phone: 301-496-5751
Toll-Free: 800-352-9424
Website: www.ninds.nih.gov

*National Institute on
Deafness and Other
Communication Disorders
(NIDCD)*

Information Clearinghouse
31 Center Dr.
MSC 2320
Bethesda, MD 20892-2320
Phone: 301-496-7243
Fax: 301-402-0018
Website: www.nidcd.nih.gov/
Pages/default.aspx
E-mail: nidcdinfo@nidcd.nih.gov

*National Dissemination
Center for Children with
Disabilities (NICHCY)*
1825 Connecticut Ave. N.W.
Ste. 700
Washington, DC 20009
Fax: 202-884-8441
Toll-Free: 800-695-0285
Website: www.parentcenterhub.
org/nichcy-gone
E-mail: nichcy@aed.org

National Database for Autism Research (NDAR)
6001 Executive Blvd.
Rm. 7162, MSC 9640
Bethesda, MD 20892-9645
Phone: 301-443-3265
Website: ndar.nih.gov

Office for Civil Rights U.S. Department of Education (DOE)
400 Maryland Ave. S.W.
Washington, DC 20202
Toll-Free: 800-872-5327
TTY: 800-877-8339
Website: www2.ed.gov/about/
offices/list/ocr/aboutocr.html

U.S. Department of Education
400 Maryland Ave. S.W.
Washington, DC 20202
Toll-Free: 800-872-5327
TTY: 800-877-8339
Website: www.ed.gov

U.S. Department of Health & Human Services
200 Independence Ave. S.W.
Washington, DC 20201
Toll-Free: 877-696-6775
Website: www.hhs.gov

U.S. Department of Labor
200 Constitution Ave. N.W.
Washington, DC 20210
Toll-Free: 866-487-2365
Website: www.dol.gov

U.S. Food and Drug Administration
10903 New Hampshire Ave.
Silver Spring, MD 20993
Toll-Free: 888-463-6332
Website: www.fda.gov

U.S. National Library of Medicine
8600 Rockville Pike
Bethesda, MD 20894
Phone: 301-594-5983
Fax: 301-402-1384
Toll-Free: 888-346-3656
Toll-Free TDD: 800-735-2258
Website: www.nlm.nih.gov

U.S. Office of Personnel Management
1900 E. St. N.W.
Washington, DC 20415-1000
Phone: 202-606-2402
Toll-Free: 800-877-8339
Website: www.opm.gov

Private Organizations

American Speech- Language-Hearing Association (ASHA)
2200 Research Blvd.
Rockville, MD 20850-3289
Phone: 301-296-5700
Fax: 301-296-8580
TTY: 301-296-5650
Website: www.asha.org

Asperger Syndrome Education Network (ASPEN)
9 Aspen Cir.
Edison, NJ 08820
Phone: 732-321-0880
Website: www.aspennj.org/
index.asp

Association for Behavioral Analysis International (ABAI)
550 W. Centre Ave.
Portage, MI 49024
Phone: 269-492-9310
Website: www.abainternational.org/welcome.aspx

Association for Science in Autism Treatment
Website: www.asatonline.org

AutismCares Family Financial Support
1 E. 33rd St.
4th Fl.
New York, NY 10016
Phone: 212-252-8584
Fax: 212-252-8676
Website: www.autismspeaks.org/AS-cares
E-mail: update@autismspeaks.org

Autism National Committee (AUTCOM)
Website: www.autcom.org

Autism Network International
P.O. Box 35448
Syracuse, NY 13235-5448
Website: www.autreat.com

Autism Research Institute (ARI)
Website: www.autism.com/index.asp

Autism Science Foundation
106 W. 32nd St.
Ste. 182
New York, NY 10001
Phone: 914-810-9100
Website: www.autismsciencefoundation.org
E-mail: contactus@autismsciencefoundation.org

Autism Society of America
4340 East-West Hwy
Ste. 350
Bethesda, MD 20814
Toll-Free: 800-328-8476
Website: www.autism-society.org

Autism Speaks
1 E. 33rd St.
4th Fl.
New York, NY 10016
Phone: 212-252-8584
Fax: 212-252-8676
Website: www.autismspeaks.org/index2.php

Autism Support Network
P.O. Box 1525
Fairfield, CT 06824
Phone: 203-404-4929
Fax: 203-404-4969
Website: www.autismsupportnetwork.com
E-mail: info@AutismSupportNetwork.com

Autism Today
1425 Broadway
Ste. 444
Seattle, WA 98122
Phone: 780-416-4448
Fax: 780-416-4330
Toll-Free: 866-928-8476
Website: www.autismtoday.com
E-mail: support@autismtoday.com

AWAARE Collaboration
Working to prevent
wandering incidents and
death
Website: awaare.
nationalautismassociation.org

Birth Defect Research for
Children, Inc.
976 Lake Baldwin Ln.
Ste. 104
Orlando, FL 32814
Phone: 407-895-0802
Website: www.ninds.nih.gov/
find_people/voluntary_orgs/
volorg42.htm
E-mail: betty@birthdefects.org

Center for Autism and
Related Disorders Inc.
(CARD)
21600 Oxnard St.
Ste. 1800
Woodland Hills, CA 91367
Phone: 818-345-2345
Fax: 818-758-8015
Toll-Free: 855-345-2273
Website: www.centerforautism.com

Children's Craniofacial
Association
13140 Coit Rd.
Ste. 517
Dallas, TX 75240
Phone: 214-570-9099
Fax: 214-570-8811
Toll-Free: 800-535-3643
Website: www.ccakids.com
E-mail: contactCCA@ccakids.com

Easter Seals
233 S. Wacker Dr.
Ste. 2400
Chicago, IL 60606
Toll-Free: 800-221-6827
Website: www.easterseals.com

Families and Advocates
Partnership for Education
(FAPE)
PACER Center
8161 Normandale Blvd.
Minneapolis, MN 55437
Phone: 952-838-9000
Website: www.fape.org
E-mail: pacer@pacer.org

Family Center on Technology
and Disability (FCTD)
Academy for Educational
Development (AED)
1825 Connecticut Ave. N.W.
Washington, DC 20009
Website: www.ctdinstitute.org
E-mail: ctd@fhi360.org

First Signs, Inc.
P.O. Box 358
Merrimac, MA 01860
Phone: 978-346-4380
Website: www.firstsigns.org
E-mail: FirstSigns1@gmail.com

Heeling Autism
Guiding Eyes for the Blind
611 Granite Springs Rd.
Yorktown Heights, NY 10598
Phone: 914-245-4024
Fax: 914-245-1609
Toll-Free: 800-942-0149
Website: www.guidingeyes.
org/prospective-students/
children-with-autism

Indiana Resource Center for
Autism (IRCA)
Indiana Institute on
Disability and Community
1905 N. Range Rd.
Bloomington, IN 47408
Phone: 812-855-6508
Fax: 812-855-9630
Toll-Free: 800-825-4733
TTY: 812-855-9396
Website: www.iidc.indiana.edu/
index.php?pageId=32

Interactive Autism Network
611 Granite Springs Rd.
Yorktown Heights, NY 10598
Phone: 914-245-4024
Fax: 914-245-1609
Toll-Free: 800-942-0149
Website: www.ianresearch.org

International Rett Syndrome
Foundation
4600 Devitt Dr.
Cincinnati, OH 45246
Toll-Free: 800-818-7388
Website: www.rettsyndrome.org
E-mail: admin@rettsyndrome.
org

March of Dimes
1275 Mamaroneck Ave.
White Plains, NY 10605
Website: www.marchofdimes.org

Moebius Syndrome
Foundation
P.O. Box 147
Pilot Grove, MO 65276
Phone: 660-834-3406
Toll-Free: 844-663-2487
Website: www.
moebiussyndrome.org
E-mail: info@moebiussyndrome.
org

National Center for Medical
Home Implementation
c/o American Academy of
Pediatrics
141 N.W. Point Blvd.
Elk Grove Village, IL 60007
Phone: 847-434-4000
Website: medicalhomeinfo.aap.
org/Pages/default.aspx

National Center on Accessible Instructional Materials at Cast, Inc.
40 Harvard Mills Sq.
Ste. 3
Wakefield, MA 01880-3233
Phone: 781-245-2212
Website: aem.cast.org/error/404-new-website.html
E-mail: aem@cast.org

National Organization for Rare Disorders (NORD)
55 Kenosia Ave.
Danbury, CT 06810
Phone: 203-744-0100
Fax: 203-798-2291
Toll-Free: 800-999-6673
Website: www.rarediseases.org

Online Asperger Syndrome Information and Support (OASIS)
@ MAAP Services for Autism, Asperger Syndrome, and PDD
Website: www.aspergersyndrome.org

Operation Autism Resource Guide for Military Families
2000 N. 14th St.
Ste. 240
Arlington, VA 22201
Phone: 866-366-9710
Website: www.operationautismonline.org

Organization for Autism Research (OAR)
Website: www.researchautism.org/resources/reading/index.asp

PEDSTest.com, LLC
Tools for Developmental-Behavioral Screening
1013 Austin Ct.
Nolensville, TN 37135
Phone: 615-776-4121
Fax: 615-776-4119
Toll-Free: 877-296-9972
Website: www.pedstest.com/default.aspx
E-mail: evpress@pedstest.com

Rehabilitation Engineering and Assistive Technology Society of North America (RESNA)
1700 N. Moore St.
Ste. 1540
Arlington, VA 22209
Phone: 703-24-6686
Fax: 703-524-6630
Website: www.resna.org
E-mail: membership@resna.org

Rett Syndrome Research Trust
67 Under Cliff Rd.
Trumbull, CT 06611
Phone: 203-445-0041
Website: www.reverserett.org
E-mail: info@rsrt.org

Tourette Association of America
42-40 Bell Blvd.
Ste. 205
Bayside, NY 11361
Phone: 718-224-2999
Website: tourette.org/
E-mail: support@tourette.org

Tourette Syndrome Association
42-40 Bell Blvd.
Ste. 205
Bayside, NY 11361
Phone: 718-224-2999
Website: www.tourette.org
E-mail: support@tourette.org

University of South Florida CARD-USF MHC2113A
4202 E. Fowler Ave.
Tampa, FL 33620
Phone: 813-974-2011
Website: card-usf.fmhi.usf.edu

Index

Index

Page numbers followed by 'n' indicate a footnote. Page numbers in *italics* indicate a table or illustration.

471

Epilepsy Foundation Genetic and
Rare Diseases Information Center
(GARD), contact 460
epilepsy
autism 4
described 185
pregnancy 191
symptoms 40
epilepsy syndromes, defined 451
etiology, defined 451
exercise, seizure control 191
exome sequencing, genetic
abnormalities 151
eye response, autism biomarker 83

F

facial expressions, social skills 75
facial recognition, oxytocin 48
facilitated communication, treatment
251
Families and Advocates Partnership
for Education (FAPE)
contact 464
overview 338–44
Family Center on Technology and
Disability (FCTD), contact 464
family issues, support at home 379
family studies, Tourette
syndrome 217
FAPE *see* Families and Advocates
Partnership for Education
FCTD *see* Family Center on
Technology and Disability
"The Feasibility of Using Electronic
Health Data for Research on
Small Populations. Population #3:
Adolescents with Autism Spectrum
Disorders" (HHS) 409n
febrile seizures, defined 451
First Signs, Inc., contact 465
"Five Major Mental Disorders Share
Genetic Roots" (NIMH) 49n
flame retardants, autism 42
flu vaccine, thimerosal 57
fluency disorders, speech-language
therapy 269
focal seizures, defined 451
Follow the Leader, described 123

Food and Drug Administration (FDA)
publications
fraud scams 295n
misleading claims for autism
295n
fragile X syndrome
defined 452
overview 198–200
risk factors 309
Rett syndrome 410
"Fragile X syndrome" (NLM) 198n
free appropriate public education
(FAPE)
overview 337–44
postsecondary education 360
school-based therapies 278
Section 504 365
"Free Appropriate Public Education
for Students With Disabilities:
Requirements Under Section 504,
The Rehabilitation Act of 1973" (ED)
337n
friendships
autism 356
social skills 75
frontal lobe epilepsy, defined 452
functional behavior, described 148
functional diagnoses, clinical
diagnosis 151

G

GARS *see* Gilliam Autism Rating
Scale
gene expression, oxytocin receptor
Prader-Willi syndrome 210
prenatal origin 314
Tourette syndrome 217
generalization, intervention 247
generalized seizures, defined 452
"Gene Disruptions Associated with
Autism Risk" (NIH) 51n
genes
Angelman syndrome 197
Asperger syndrome 14
autism 5
autism biomarkers 313
brain growth 46
chromosomes 3 50

481

NDAR *see* National Database for
Autism Research
The Nemours Foundation
Asperger syndrome 257n
auditory processing disorder
178n
individualized education
program 330n
occupational therapy 264n
special needs to children 399n
autism 80n
speech-language therapy 267n
toilet training 393n
neocortical epilepsy, defined 454
neurodevelopment disorders, Asperger
syndrome 11
neurofibromatosis, brain tumors 188
neurologists, diagnose 89
neuronal migration, mutation 188
NICHCY *see* National Dissemination
Center for Children with
Disabilities
NICHD *see* National Institute of Child
Health and Human Development
NIDCD *see* National Institute on
Deafness and Other Communication
Disorders
NIEHS *see* National Institute of
Environmental Health Sciences
"NIH-Supported NeuroBioBank Joins
Autism BrainNet in Brain Donation
Initiative" (NIMH) 311n
"NIH Joins Public-Private
Partnership to Fund Research on
Autism Biomarkers" (NIMH) 311n
NIH *see* National Institutes of
Health
NIMH *see* National Institute of
Mental Health
NINDS *see* National Institute of
Neurological Disorders and Stroke
"NINDS Landau-Kleffner Syndrome
Information Page" (NINDS) 200n
"NINDS Pervasive Developmental
Disorders Information Page"
(NINDS) 9n
nonconvulsive, defined 454
nonepileptic seizures, defined 454
nonverbal, defined 454

NORD *see* National Organization for
Rare Disorders

O

OAR *see* Organization for Autism
Research
OASIS *see* Online Asperger syndrome
Information and Support
obesity
developmental disabilities 233
maternal diabetes 41
metabolic symptoms 208
obesity and adolescents, tabulated
233
obsession, defined 454
obsessive compulsive disorder (OCD),
Asperger syndrome 11
occupational therapists, described 265
occupational therapy (OT)
described 283
kidney tumors 230
overview 264–6
"Occupational Therapy" The Nemours
Foundation 264n
occupational therapy practitioners,
described 266
Office for Civil Rights U.S.
Department of Education (DOE),
contact 462
Office of Disability Employment Policy
(ODEP)
publication
self-employment 428n
Office of Personnel Management
(OPM)
publication
disability employment 426n
Omnigraphics, Inc.
publications
ASD behavior 349n
ASD interventions 239n
ASD social interaction 355n
autistic intelligence 163n
classroom management 345n
types of ASD assessment 101n
Online Asperger syndrome
Information and Support (OASIS),
contact 466